William Ellis

The Martyr Church

A Narrative of the Introduction, Progress, and Triumph of Christianity in

Madagascar

William Ellis

The Martyr Church
A Narrative of the Introduction, Progress, and Triumph of Christianity in Madagascar

ISBN/EAN: 9783337209780

Printed in Europe, USA, Canada, Australia, Japan

Cover: Foto ©ninafisch / pixelio.de

More available books at **www.hansebooks.com**

THE MARTYR CHURCH:

A NARRATIVE OF THE

INTRODUCTION, PROGRESS, AND TRIUMPH

OF

CHRISTIANITY IN MADAGASCAR.

WITH NOTICES OF

PERSONAL INTERCOURSE AND TRAVEL IN THAT ISLAND.

BY

REV. WILLIAM ELLIS,
AUTHOR OF
"*Polynesian Researches,*" "*Three Visits to Madagascar,*" &c., &c.

NEW EDITION.

LONDON:
JOHN SNOW AND CO.,
2, IVY LANE, PATERNOSTER ROW.

PREFACE.

THE present volume is offered to the Christian public, more especially to the friends of missions, in the hope that it may gratify a desire, which it is believed is at the present time very generally felt, for a more complete account than has been hitherto given of the Martyr Church of Madagascar, including the progress of Christianity in that country, from its introduction to its recent and marvellous extension among the people.

My former volumes on Madagascar * contained such information as I had been able to gather respecting the country, its productions and its inhabitants, as well as some account of the progress of the gospel.

The present work is confined chiefly to an account of the growth of Christianity among the inhabitants

---

* "Three Visits to Madagascar," and "Madagascar Revisited," published by Mr. Murray; to whom the author and publishers feel grateful for his courtesy in allowing some of the illustrations prepared for the above works to be used in illustrating the present volume.

of the capital and the central provinces, its reception by the sovereign, many of the government officers, civilians, and general population, as well as its extension to more distant races. The narrative is brought down to the present time.

The succinct account given of the state of the people at the time when they were first visited by the English, will enable the reader to understand, more clearly than would otherwise be possible, the remarkable change which the influence of Christianity has wrought amongst all classes.

It is hoped that the evidence of the divine origin and undiminished efficacy of the gospel, as manifested in Madagascar, may be welcome to many as a confirmation of the faith and hope which we cherish respecting the ultimate and universal triumphs of the cross; at the same time it will encourage every faithful missionary of Christ throughout the world. Madagascar stands forth at the present time, before enemies and friends, a witness for God, demonstrating to all that what the gospel of salvation by Jesus Christ accomplished in the days of the apostles it is accomplishing before all the world in the present day.

W. ELLIS.

Hoddesdon, Dec., 1869.

CONTENTS.

CHAPTER I.

Brief notice of the country and people—Radama and his army at Tamatave—Abolition of the slave trade—Destructive character of Radama's wars—Incipient civilization among the Hovas—Resources of the country—General condition of the people—Disastrous effects of slavery on bond and free—Sanguinary character of the Malagasy laws—Administration of justice—the tangena or poison ordeal—Mental faculties of the people—Defective morals of the community—Malagasy tombs—Robbery of the dead—Licentiousness of the people—Idolatries of Madagascar—Worship and sacrifices—The god of the tangena or poison—The sikidy or divination—Hardening influence of idolatry on the heart—Its mercenary character 1

CHAPTER II.

Arrival of the first missionaries on the coast of Madagascar—Fearful ravages of illness and death—Renewal of the mission at the capital under the auspices of Radama—The English language taught in the first schools—Radama's letter to the Missionary Society—Alarm of parents respecting their children—The native language reduced to writing—Arrival of missionary artisans—The native language taught in the schools—Commencement of public Christian worship on the Lord's day—Wide extension of education—Increasing attendance at the Sunday services—Singing introduced into Christian worship—Arrival of the first printing press—Review of the first ten years of the mission—Death of Radama—Assassination of his successor and friends—Ranavalona placed on the throne—The character and reign of Radama...... 36

CHAPTER III.

Destruction of Radama's family—Drafting of scholars into the army—Appeal of the queen to the idols at her coronation—The New Testament and other books printed—Attention of the people to religious teaching—Baptism and partaking of the Lord's Supper by the first converts—Disapproval of Christian fellowship by the government—Formation of the first churches of Madagascar—Officers, soldiers, and scholars in the government schools, forbidden to receive baptism or unite with the church—Christian officer accused of witchcraft, and subjected to drink the ordeal of poison—Masters forbidden to allow their slaves to read—Conversion and death of a young slave—Refusal of Christian soldiers to acknowledge the idols—30,000 readers, the result of ten years' educational labour—Idols rejected—Description of a Malagasy idol—Evidences of the power of the gospel among the people—Efficiency of native agency—Disastrous end of a teacher of a new religion 59

CHAPTER IV.

Christian refusal to offer heathen sacrifice—False accusation of preaching sedition—A national assembly summoned—Christian worship declared unlawful—Missionaries forbidden to teach Christianity—Christians required to accuse themselves—Books to be given up—Stedfastness of the Christians—Their noble confession before the judges—Midnight meetings for prayer—Translation of the Scriptures—Compilation of dictionaries—Translation of "Pilgrim's Progress"—Last missionaries leave the country—Accusation against Rafaravavy and her companions.................... 87

CHAPTER V.

Arrest of Rafaravavy—Confession of Paul before the judges—A Christian's feelings on the way to execution—Fearful conflagration in the city—Postponement of Rafaravavy's execution—Arrest, examination, and execution of the second martyr—Torture of his wife—Flight of Rafaravavy and her companions—Perils and suffering—Honesty of Christian slaves—Flight of the Christians to Tamatave—Safe embarkation—Their song of praise to God—Welcomes in London and among the churches in England—Their return to Mauritius—Capture, torture, and execution of the praying people in the capital—Friendship among the Christians—Condition of the fugitives in Madagascar 114

CHAPTER VI.

Attempt of the Christians to reach the coast—Their capture on the road—Remarkable escape of two prisoners—Execution of the rest—Influence of public executions on the people—Extreme affection of the Christian captives, and cheerful death of Christians at Vonizongo—Savage execution of Raharo and his friends—Death of Rev. David Johns—The Prince Royal's friendship to the Christians—His efforts in their favour—Kindness of Prince Ramonja—Severe persecution in 1849—Noble confession of the Christians—The faithful Ranivo—The burning of the nobles—The hurling over the precipice of the Christians—Vast number punished 143

CHAPTER VII.

Severity of Prince Ramonja's punishment—Convict labour of Christian officers—Kindness of the princes to the Christians—Numbers of the Christians—Voyage of Messrs. Cameron and Ellis to Madagascar—Opening the ports to foreign commerce—Second visit to Madagascar—Protracted intercourse with Christians from the capital—Visit to Mahavelona—Correspondence with Christians at the capital—Andriambelo—Midnight meetings with the Christians—Want of the Scriptures—Third visit to Madagascar—Arrival at the capital—Reception by the government—Statement of the object of visit—Interviews with the prince and Ramonja 174

CHAPTER VIII.

Favourable effect of message of friendship from England—Visits to remarkable places—Interview with the commander-in-chief—The queen's hospitality—Deeply affecting recitals of sufferings of the Christians—Hopes inspired by the results of persecution in other countries—Conferences and prayer with the leaders of the Christians—Social life among the disciples—The prevalence of prayer—Times and places of united worship—Christians from Vonizongo—Conversation with the young—Visit of Mr. Lambert to the capital, and his statements to the Christians—Places

Chapter VIII.—(continued).

where the martyrs suffered—Farewell visit from the prince and princess—Last night with the Christians—Departure from Madagascar and return to England—Review of the progress and state of Christianity in the country—Return of Mr. Lambert to the capital—The last persecution—Numbers implicated—Barbarity of the executions—Illness and death of the queen—Notice of her character and reign 198

CHAPTER IX.

The end of the persecutions—Radama II. proclaimed king—Proclamation of religious liberty—The exiles and Christians in fetters recalled—The claims of the idols disregarded—The use of the tangena and sorcery abolished—The king's orders for the administration of justice—His treatment of the conquered races—His want of better counsellors—Increase of intemperance in the country—Return of French traders and priests—Voyage to Mauritius—First movement towards the erection of memorial churches—Letter to the king on the subject—Arrival in Madagascar—Journey to the capital—Interview with the king and queen—Visits from the widows and children of the martyrs—Prince Ramonja and the Prime Minister—Visit to Ambohipotsy and Ampamarinana—First Sunday in the capital—Deliverance from dread of slavery 223

CHAPTER X.

Teaching English—The king not a Christian—Early commencement of Sabbath services—Conversations with the Christians—Influences favouring the reception of the gospel—Family religion—Parental attention to the young—The mother's good influence—Statistics of the progressive increase of the Christians during the successive persecutions—Astonishing results—Influence of character—Arrival of foreign embassies—Visits to the places where the martyrs suffered—Present to the English embassy—Notice of a converted warrior priest—Introduction of the gospel to Betsileo—Description of the idols—Satisfactory conversation with the Bishop of Mauritius respecting Church of England missionaries—Views of the Society for the Propagation of the Gospel respecting Madagascar—Principles on which Scriptures were distributed among the people 256

CHAPTER XI.

Welcome of the missionaries from England—United communion—Liberality of the English embassy—The sacred city of Ambohimanga—Sabbath services in the city—Death of Malagasy chieftains—Organization of native churches—Titles given for sites of memorial churches—First church at Ankadibevava—Uneasiness in the capital—Pretended supernatural messages to the king—The dancing sickness—Warnings of danger—Remonstrance of the nobles—Revolution—Death of the king—Reflections on his character—Accession of Rasoherina—Germs of constitutional government—Religious liberty continued—The first missionary prayer meeting—Visits of Christians from the north—Extensive and beneficial influence of the medical department of the mission 286

CHAPTER XII.

Coronation of Rasoherina—Rumours respecting Radama—First public recognition of the Christians—Religious services at Ambohimanga during the queen's visit—Christian procession to the palace on Christmas day—Review of the events of the year—Opening of the central school—Visit to Vonizongo—Employment of native preachers—The Christians at Betsileo—Instance of the power of the gospel—Chapel at Ambohitantely—Historical statistics of Ilafy—Visit to the Martyrs' Home—Chapels opened in the capital—Return of a captured slave to her home—Christians at Imerinamandrosa—Scene of the martyrs' suffering 315

CHAPTER XIII.

Bereavements of the Mission—New churches and increased attendance—Introduction of public Christian marriage—Visit to Lazaina—Notice of Ranivo's family—Treaty with England—Queen Victoria's message and Queen Rasoherina's reply—Journey to the west—Reinforcement of the mission—Departure of Mr. Ellis—Prosperous close of the year—Opening of the first memorial church—Its influence on the people—Welcome arrival of missionaries from the Friends—The queen's visit to the coast—Zealous efforts of the Christians among the heathen—Return of the queen to the capital—Results of the preaching of the gospel—Remarkable increase of the Christians at the close of the year............... 343

CHAPTER XIV.

Illness of the queen—Failure of the conspiracy to change the dynasty—Death of the queen—Proclamation of her successor—Trial and punishment of the conspirators—Ranavalona's refusal to acknowledge the priests, idols, and diviners—Edicts respecting the Sabbath—Christian worship within the precincts of the palace—General religious awakening among the people—Missionary visit to Fianarantsoa—Buildings of stone and bricks authorized in the capital—Multitudes assembled at the coronation—The crown and the Bible—Speech of the queen—Declaration of religious liberty—Influence of the coronation—Opening of the second memorial church—Presence of the queen and court—Review of the year—Baptism of the queen and prime minister—Religious services within the palace—The queen and prime minister partake of the Lord's Supper—Training of a native ministry—Mr. Sewell's testimony—Spread of the gospel in Betsileo—Foundation-stone of the Chapel Royal—Fifty years of missionary labour in Madagascar—Their glorious results—Inadequacy of present missionary agencies—Appeal for help 369

LIST OF ILLUSTRATIONS.

Native Pastor and Deacons at Ambatonakanga ... ... *Frontispiece*

	PAGE		PAGE
Punishment of Slaves	20	Consolation to a Christian in Fetters	220
Malagasy Tombs	24	Interior of Malagasy Kitchen	287
Tomb of a Noble	26	Ambohimanga, from the North-west	295
Ambodinandohalo	66		
Malagasy Idol	80	Rev. R. Toy, and Class of Native Preachers	310
Native Smiths and Iron Smelting	104		
The Tsitisalaingia and other Spears	120	Isarotrafohy, the Martyrs' Home	334
Place of the First Martyrdom	122	View in Antananarivo ...	338
		Village of Lazaina	350
The Traveller's Tree	133	Bridge over the Andromba...	352
Hova Officers, &c.	177	Martyr Memorial Church at Ambohipotsy	384
The Lace-leaf Plant	192		

THE
MARTYR CHURCH OF MADAGASCAR.

CHAPTER I.

Brief notice of the country and people—Radama and his army at Tamatave—Abolition of the slave trade—Destructive character of Radama's wars—Incipient civilization among the Hovas—Resources of the country—General condition of the people—Disastrous effects of slavery on bond and free—Sanguinary character of the Malagasy laws—Administration of justice—The tangena or poison ordeal—Mental faculties of the people—Defective morals of the community—Malagasy tombs—Robbery of the dead—Licentiousness of the people—Idolatries of Madagascar—Worship and sacrifices—The god of the tangena or poison—The sikidy or divination—Hardening influence of idolatry on the heart—Its mercenary character.

TOWARDS the close of the thirteenth century, Marco Paolo, the celebrated Venetian traveller, made known to Europe the existence of a large African island, which he called Magaster, but which is now known as Madagascar. This is not the native name of the island. The inhabitants themselves, according to their former insular ideas of the world, called their country *Izao ambany lanitra*, "This beneath the sky;" or *Ny anivony ny riaka*, "The (all) in the centre of the sea;" and inscribed this latter designation on the tomb of Radama, the first sovereign whose authority extended over the greater part of the country. This splendid island, one of the largest in the world, which is separated from the eastern coast of Southern Africa by the Mosambique Channel, is 900 miles long and 300 broad, and has been estimated to contain more than 2,000,000 of acres of land.

The central regions of Madagascar are at least 6,000 feet above the sea, while some of the single mountains rise to double that elevation. The lower ranges of the country are fertile, richly wooded, and well watered, the mountain streams occasionally forming extensive lakes, and the pent-up waters near the coast frequently spreading out into marshy swamps, which render the surrounding country at certain seasons of the year highly insalubrious to natives of other parts, as well as to foreigners. Iron is abundant, and other metals exist in the country. Valuable gums are found in the forests, which also yield serviceable timber. The geographical position, extent, climate, and other natural advantages of the country, seem admirably suited to stimulate the enterprise of its inhabitants to render it, by their intelligence and industry, the cherished home of a civilized and prosperous people.

According to the census of a former government, calculated from a return of the number of houses in the country, the population of Madagascar was stated to be four and a half millions. This could only be an approximate estimate, and was, according to subsequent observation and inquiry, probably nearly a million larger than the existing number of the people. Native traditions describe the country as formerly inhabited by a single homogeneous people, called Vazimba. The present population evidently comprises several races. Chief among these are the Malayo-Polynesian from the east, the East African, the Arabs, and the Moors from the north. The Hovas, who have evidently a Polynesian origin, occupy the elevated and central parts of the island. This race, though themselves formerly tributary to the more numerous Sakalavas of Menabe in the south-west, have, since their alliance with the English, subjugated the other races, established their military posts in every province, and now receive acknowledgment and homage, if not tribute, as the rulers over the entire country.

Until within the present century the natives of Europe had regarded the Malagasy as untamed savages, and valued their country chiefly as a vast preserve, or hunting-ground for slaves. Shipwrecked mariners had, at different times, been cast upon the shores of Madagascar, and though some of these had found shelter and aid, others had been murdered, or kept as slaves by the chiefs on the coast. The only Europeans who, prior to this period, had penetrated the interior of the country, had been connected with the traffic in slaves; and the inhabitants, naturally supposing that the revolting vices and rapine of the slave-hunters characterized all white men, beheld the arrival of the latter with alarm and terror, some regarding them as cannibals.

The earliest embassy of friendship to the central regions of Madagascar was sent by the English in 1816 to the first Radama, ruler of the Hovas, and then in the twenty-fourth year of his age. This young prince, the most enlightened ruler ever known in Madagascar, joyfully welcomed the peaceful and friendly envoy, and treated him with assiduous and gentle kindness when prostrate beneath the dreaded Malagasy fever, under which a number of his companions died. Radama finally ratified his treaty of amity and good-will with the English by the solemn and binding oath of blood.

Dissatisfied, during the following year, with the two chiefs of tribes on the eastern coast, one of whom had insultingly called him "a beardless boy," Radama, with his usual prompt decision and action, marched down to the coast with 20,000 men to call these chiefs to account, and proclaim himself king of Madagascar. He was encamped near Tamatave when the *Phaeton*, having on board his brothers with the British agent, and presents from the Governor of Mauritius, entered the harbour. On landing, the party from the frigate were received by Radama's body-guard of 200 men, by whom they were escorted about half a mile from the coast, when, coming suddenly to a small bank, the whole Hova army appeared before them. Radama was seated in a kind of palanquin borne by slaves, the scantily clothed troops formed a circle around, squatting on their heels, and holding their muskets or spears upright before them. The men rose up as the strangers came in sight, and the king, having advanced and welcomed them, made a signal to the troops, who, firing a salute, enveloped them in a cloud of smoke. Radama then led his visitors into a house, and, offering them wine, expressed his thanks for the attention paid to his brothers whom he had sent to Mauritius for education, and for the presents, which included three horses sent for his own use.

On Captain Stanfell expressing a wish to see a portion of his army march past, the king gave the order, and a large number of the men immediately commenced running past, shouting at the top of their voices, "Tsara be Radama!" (Greatly good Radama), which was, probably, their battle cry. After the captain had returned to his ship, several young officers, marching between the royal bodyguard, accompanied the king to his camp, which occupied an open space in the midst of an extensive forest. The tents were formed of branches of trees, and roofed with the broad leaves of the Traveller's and other trees; or spears were fixed in the ground, and covered with rofia cloth, or with the lambas (large scarfs) of the officers. The men took their meals on the ground, using broad leaves for plates. The rice and other food in the place being in a few days consumed, the Hovas returned to the capital. On the march the king was carried in his palanquin, at the head of his forces, attended by his guard, and a number of singing-women, who also fanned him with bunches of feathers fastened to the ends of long elastic wands. These women, who, with heads and feet uncovered, were clothed in gaily coloured dresses, wore strings of beads, or silver chains of native manufacture, some of them massive and heavy, on their necks, wrists, and ankles.*

Notwithstanding Radama's desire to render his government just and humane, the miseries of the people at this period were often painfully visible. As the British agent, with the charge of the horses, followed the army to Imerina, he found in the nearest village to the port only a single house standing; fifty dwellings were reduced to ashes, and the rest had been torn down to make rafts for the troops crossing the river. Other villages presented only heaps of ashes, and dead bodies frequently lay unburied in the open roads or paths through the forest. These incidents, connected with the earliest intercourse between the English and the Hovas, are noticed somewhat in detail on account of the results which followed that intercourse, and as showing the condition of the people at the time when, as the natives express it, "England was the first to hold out the hand of friendship to Madagascar."

The first great fruit of this friendship was the

* The above notices of this interview are derived from an interesting letter from the late Professor Henslow's younger brother, who was an officer on board the *Phaeton* at the time, and accompanied the captain on shore.

abolition of the slave trade, which was accomplished by a formal treaty between England and Madagascar, duly signed by the representatives of Radama, and of the Governor of Mauritius, at Tamatave, in 1817, four months after the English and the Hovas had met for the first time at that port.

There is no reason to suppose that the traffic in slaves in Madagascar was less productive of misery and death there than in other countries; but it is estimated that not fewer than 3,000 or 4,000 were annually shipped from Tamatave and other ports on the eastern coast. They were formed into gangs of from 50 to 200, with iron handcuffs on their wrists, and thus bound together in companies with cords, were driven like cattle to the ports, whence they were conveyed to Réunion or Mauritius, America or the West Indies. From these miseries the treaty with England delivered the Malagasy. They belong to the past, but one affecting memorial of the sorrows thus produced still survives on the summit of a hill over which the traveller passes, on one of the mountain roads leading from the coast to the capital. Here the unhappy captives first came in sight of that dreaded sea across which they were to pass, never to return; while from the same spot, looking back, they often saw for the last time the summits of the mountains on the borders of Ankova, their own beloved home. This spot is called the "weeping-place of the Hovas."

Motives of humanity influenced the English in these efforts to put an end to the slave trade, and many important benefits were secured by the treaty which destroyed it; but other consequences followed, some of them as afflicting, and for a time as destructive of human life, as that traffic had been. The king had a royalty of a dollar on each slave taken from his dominions, and in order to compensate him for this loss other advantages were promised by the English. These included the education in England of a number of native youths, the receiving of others on board our ships to learn seamanship, together with aid to enable the king to arm and train his soldiers after the European plan. Thus aided, he deemed himself superior to any other native ruler, and impelled by his thirst for conquest, enrolled the able-bodied free men of his dominions in his army, invaded the territories, and commenced hostilities against the independent rulers of the several races in the island. Some of these wars lasted for years, and all ended in the defeat of the chieftains, and the nominal subjection of the whole island to Radama.

The king was not addicted to needless slaughter in his wars, but whatever clemency he himself might show to the vanquished, his lieutenants, or those on whom devolved the chastisement of any who still aspired after freedom, or hesitated to acknowledge his supremacy, were rarely influenced by humane considerations. Most of them appear to have been impelled by lust of power and of plunder, and by a sort of fiendish satisfaction in the wanton destruction of human life.

Not unfrequently the men who had been vanquished,

or decoyed by specious promises to surrender, were disarmed and cruelly murdered, their towns or villages burned, their cattle seized, and their women and children driven home by the Hovas, and sold as slaves in the public market; while towns and villages were left in ashes, and vast tracts of country desolated and without inhabitants. Among the flower of the male population of Ankova their wars were terribly destructive. Old men speak of the numbers of light-coloured, vigorous youth of the province of Ankova, who in the armies of Radama and his successor left their homes never to return. These men speak also of the resemblance originally in figure, in flowing hair, and in complexion, of the general population of Imerina, so different from the mixture of races in the capital and the suburbs at the present day.

The Supreme Ruler of the universe can educe good out of evil; and calamitous as, to the then existing generations, the transition from a state of comparative independence and self-government to one of enforced obedience under a military and alien sovereignty may have been at the time, it may ultimately prove to have been the best, if not the only means of uniting the people under one rule, and preparing the way for their becoming, under a wise, just, and enlightened government, a united and prosperous people.

Radama was in many respects a remarkable man. His natural sagacity, clearness of perception, and vigour of thought often enabled him intuitively to comprehend the utility and value of the new objects brought under his notice. The physical strength of Europeans at times greatly astonished him. Witnessing, on one occasion, the comparative ease with which the English smith, while engaged at his work, removed a heavy anvil which neither the king nor any of his attendants could lift from the ground, he exclaimed, "These would be dangerous people to fight with!" But Radama estimated the intelligence and skill of the foreigners far higher than their physical strength, their riches, or political power; and while stipulating with the British agent for the means of conquering the country, he earnestly implored aid in the acquisition of knowledge for himself and his people.

The earliest use which the king made of the friendship of the English was to send a number of youths to them for education, and to ask for instructors in useful arts as the means of elevating the people and developing the resources of the country.

Compared with Europeans the Malagasy were uncivilized, though in some respects they were greatly in advance of the tribes inhabiting the adjacent coast of Africa,* or Mosambique, the natives of Australia, or the South Sea Islanders; and they had already attained some of the important elements of a higher civilization. Most of the races had an

---

* A foreigner once remarking to Radama that if the people did not avail themselves of the means of instruction, they would be like the Mosambiques, for the Malagasy and the Africans were the only nations who could not read and write, he replied that he would rather not be king at all than rule over such an ignorant people.

organized civil government. They were a nation of agriculturists and herdsmen. The flesh of the ox constituted their chief animal food, and though some of the tribes, such as the Sakalavas on the west coast, cultivated arrowroot, or a species of pulse, and though fruits were abundant, rice was with most of them the staff of life, and constituted their daily food. Oxen and rice were also, after the abolition of trade in slaves, their most important articles of export.

The climate of Madagascar is warm, yet all the inhabitants, above the very poor, are decently, and some of them now richly clothed. Large herds of cattle fed on their plains, or were fattened in their pens or stalls, yet the people never clothed themselves with their skins.* Caterpillars or worms of different kinds feed on the leaves of indigenous or exotic plants, and spin delicately fine or coarse silk, which is cleaned, and coloured with native dyes. This silk is spun in simple looms, of Indian or Arabian origin, woven not unfrequently with beautiful and curious patterns into rich and gorgeous dresses for the nobles of both sexes, and for the higher classes in Madagascar generally. Cotton is grown throughout the country, and a species of nettle yields a tenacious fibre resembling hemp, which is also manufactured into strong and durable woven cloth, worn by the farmers and middle classes, wrapped round the body by day, and spread over

* The skin of an ox killed for food is not removed before the carcass is cut up, but is either left on until the meat is cooked, or is taken off and cooked separately.

them as a counterpane by night. The leaflet of the large, majestic rofia palm is slit into threads and woven into cloth, which is used for many purposes, besides furnishing almost the only clothing worn through life by thousands of the slaves.

The native iron is of excellent quality, and the people have long been accustomed, by a rude and simple process of smelting, to render it available for two of the most important purposes of life—the supply of food, and the means of defence. No plough is used in the country, but watercourses are cut, and the fields are dug and prepared to receive the seed with spades manufactured by the people out of native iron. The head of the spear, their national weapon, originally the fire-hardened and pointed end of a stick, then a shaft armed with a kind of porcelain or burnt clay, has now for many generations been made of iron, the use of which is reported to have been introduced by the Hovas, and first employed in their conflicts with the Vazimba, or earlier inhabitants of the country. Sentence of death was sometimes inflicted on military criminals by cutting off their heads with the edge of a spear. Knives, axes, and other articles of iron were in use amongst them before their acquaintance with the English.

Measured by our European standard the Malagasy might be deemed ignorant and barbarian; but a people whose chief food was rice and beef or poultry, whose clothing was silk, cotton, flaxen, or other woven cloth, who built houses with walls of wood or stone, who fortified their towns and villages with walls and moats, and the entrance to which was through stone-built gateways, of which numerous examples still exist, who possessed iron implements of tillage and weapons of war, could not be considered destitute of the material elements of a higher civilization, nor unworthy of the highest efforts of Christian philanthropy.

The outward circumstances of the people were, at the period now under review, better than their morals or their religion, and the former had been for some time progressively deteriorating. Their earliest forms of government appear to have been patriarchal and simple, and the social morals of the people who had retained their earlier simple habits of life were superior to those of their successors, to whom increase of riches and power had brought the greatest changes.

The introduction of foreign weapons, especially firearms, chiefly by the slave dealers, stimulated the inhabitants around the harbours and in the interior centres of population to frequent forays amongst the outlying villages, or to more formidable expeditions, chiefly for the capture of slaves; and these habits of life had introduced a government of military despotism among several important tribes at the time when Radama became sovereign of the Hovas.

This ruler, favoured by the subsidies from England, soon overran the entire country, and became the acknowledged, if not the actual sovereign of the whole. As such he claimed the country with its produce as his property, and the inhabitants as his dependents and servants, holding their lands, however extensive, by virtue of his consent, and only during his pleasure. The inhabitants of the provinces retained their own social and general regulations, but Radama's word was supreme law throughout the land, and he claimed the power of life and death over the entire population. In the exercise of this onerous authority he associated with himself men of high rank and reputed wisdom, but his own will was always finally supreme. The exercise of this system of absolutism was occasionally mitigated, within the range of the king's personal influence, by the public and material encouragement with which he rewarded industry and stimulated improvement; but such encouragement was regarded as selfish when it was found that the government monopolized the advantages of every improvement, which was prized not as a source of additional benefit to the people, but as a means of enriching the members of the government, increasing the revenue, or augmenting the army.

The national revenue, not then large, was derived from the spoils of war, the produce of the soil, customs dues at the ports, profits on trade, a sort of poll tax on slaves, a portion of the fines levied by the judges, the property of criminals, the *Hasina*, or acknowledgment made on appearing before the sovereign, and the *fanompoana* or government service required from all classes. The most skilful artisans in the country, goldsmiths, silversmiths, manufacturers of most expensive silk lambas, or mantles, were forced to perform without pay all the work in their respective crafts required by the government; and when, shortly afterwards, the lay members of the mission taught the men and youths to work in iron and wood, to construct machinery, tan leather, to weave with English looms, to make bricks, and burn lime, all who learned were also required to work for the government without wages. Even the women and children whom the wives of the first missionaries taught needlework became thereby government servants.* A few were probably sensible of pleasurable emotions arising from the acquisition of knowledge and skill so useful, but the increased demands for unrequited labour to which these attainments subjected their possessor prevented all enthusiasm, and retarded their extension among the people.† These, and other unrequited labourers

* An unexpected and somewhat amusing illustration of this kind of government service occurred in the preparation of my outfit for my first journey to the capital. The Governor of Tamatave had sent for my service, a few days before I was to set out, a light and convenient palanquin; the government smith had repaired the ironwork, but it had no cover to keep out the rain, and I was a little amused when, soon after daylight the next morning, two middle-aged females, apparently superintendents of the rest, followed by three-and-twenty young women, came with sewing apparatus, to fit the covering of my palanquin.—"*Three Visits to Madagascar,*" p. 271.

† I was once putting up some bookshelves in my room, assisted by a native servant whom I had hired from his owner, and who was attentive, obliging, and honest; when, having marked the length of a shelf on the board, I held out the saw and asked him to cut it off; but he drew back, observing, "I have work enough without wages already, I don't wish to become a carpenter.'

for the government, as well as the soldiers, were all free men.

When Captain Le Sage visited Antananarivo in 1816, Radama's fighting men, drawn from the several districts to the province of Ankova, amounted probably to 20,000. These consisted of the ordinary peasantry of the country, led by their local chieftains, under the supreme command of the king or his officers. The English envoy had been accompanied by thirty men to show the Hovas the weapons and manœuvres of foreign soldiers, and two of these had been left with the king to train his troops after the European manner. The appearance and the march past of these in the following year, before the king and Captain Stanfell, did not indicate any change. Radama's military force, though at that time inferior in number, if not in efficiency, to that of the Sakalavas and others, was afterwards largely increased, and armed to a great extent with muskets. The troops received no pay, and only occasionally articles of clothing. In distant expeditions they depended on the provisions they might find, and at home on the fruits of their own exertions, and on the labour of their relatives. Cowardice in the face of the enemy, or desertion, was punished with burning alive; sometimes, as a mark of favour, the culprits were shot before they were burned.

If the civilization or barbarism of a people is shown by its laws and their punishments, the Malagasy would seem to have been barbarian at the time of our early acquaintance with them. The usages of more enlightened nations existed in the appointment of judges, and the open courts in which the accuser and the accused, with their witnesses, were confronted. But it was seldom more than form; the integrity and virtue requisite to its practical value were wanting. Reverence for the sanctity of an oath, respect for truth, and judgment according to evidence, rarely characterized their judicial proceedings.

The simplest forms of justice never attended the use of the tangena or poison. This fearful ordeal, employed to prove the innocence or guilt of persons accused, sometimes of purely imaginary crimes, could be made, by the preparer of the poison, to inflict at once sentence and execution on its unhappy victim. So frequent was the use of this appalling ordeal, that it was supposed that one-tenth of the population drank it in the course of their lives—some twice or thrice,—and that one-half of those who drank it died. Thus, besides the misery and poverty imposed on survivors, three thousand persons, mostly in the prime of life, perished every year from this monstrous device, which superstition, policy, and greed inflicted on the people.*

Radama, humane and considerate as he generally was, felt no obligation to respect life when he was offended. A slave one day attending at table had the misfortune to break a dish. The king ordered an officer near him to take the man away, and see that he never committed the offence again. The

* "History of Madagascar," vol. i., p. 487.

officer called the man out, returned soon afterwards, and, in answer to the king's inquiry, said he was dead. Equally summary death was inflicted afterwards by the king's widow, when a female slave, pouring water on the queen's hands, spilled a small quantity on her dress. It needed only a look and a sign from the sovereign, and the poor girl was taken away and put to death.

Nothing among the Malagasy was more repugnant to every humane feeling than the cruelty of their punishments, and the barbarity with which they were inflicted. Fourteen crimes, the chief of which comprised the several varieties of treason, were punished with death, inflicted in almost as many different ways. Some of these punishments were fearfully agonizing and protracted, especially burning by a slow fire, flogging to death, starving to death, and crucifixion. The more ordinary methods were spearing, beheading, hurling over a precipice, suffocating in a pit with boiling water, and dashing out the brains, as when sentenced by the tangena to death. No proceeding could be more revolting than their behaviour to the culprits before execution, or the treatment of their bodies afterwards. The execution of criminals was a sort of public holiday, to which adults and children repaired; and familiarity with such spectacles doubtless contributed much to the hardness of heart, and want of all humane feeling so often manifested in the shedding of blood and the infliction of suffering.

Although the administration of justice was seldom

pure, and often regulated by the ability and willingness of the suitor to bribe the judges, the frequency with which the latter were appealed to showed that the people were quarrelsome, or exceedingly fond of litigation.

Domestic slavery, which has prevailed from a remote period, was, when compared with that of the West Indies or America, comparatively mild, but it was still slavery. The master exercised entire control over the slave and his offspring. He could sever all the natural ties of human life, and extract for his own benefit, or sell to others, all the labour his slave was able to perform. The male slaves cultivated the ground for their masters, and also fetched wood from the forest. They were by some masters treated with great cruelty. I once saw a boy about fifteen years of age, with a rough heavy iron collar on his neck, working with a number of other boys or men carrying firewood. Another slave whom I saw working near the same place had an iron collar round his neck, with pointed iron spikes six or seven inches long fixed in the collar and standing up by the sides of his head.*

Certain labours in the culture of rice were performed by female slaves, but they were chiefly employed in household occupations; also in dressing and spinning cotton or hemp, weaving it into native cloth for articles of dress, making rush and other baskets, and preparing the fibre of the rofia and other trees for being woven into cloth. Married slaves

* "Three Visits to Madagascar," p. 143.

occasionally live in sincere affection towards each other, and manifest great fondness for their children, but are liable to be separated by one of the parties being sold and sent away, never to return. The children belong to the owner of the mother; and the

charge of an infant, whose advent is welcomed by the owners as an increase to their property, is added to the mother's ordinary labour, perhaps interrupted only for a week, after which a slave-mother may be seen working in the fields, or bringing home a large jar full of water on her head, carrying at the same time her child on her back.

Though the punishments of the female slave were less severe than those inflicted on the men, they were at times painfully irksome and degrading. I one day

entered a house in which a number of female slaves were carrying baskets of cotton, prepared for spinning, from one room to another, and as they passed along, I saw one young girl who had a couple of boards fixed on her shoulders, each of them rather more than two feet long and a foot wide, fastened together by pieces of wood nailed on the under side. A piece had been cut out of each board in the middle, so that, when fixed together, they fitted close to her neck, and the poor girl, while wearing this instrument of punishment and disgrace, was working with the rest.

Some of the nobles own 200 or 300 slaves, and where their masters are rich and prosperous the bondage is comparatively easy, though the slave can possess no property, and has no rights. Some idea of the estimate in which they were held may be gathered from the answer of Radama, who, when the British agent proposed a money compensation for the loss of the profit on the sale of slaves, replied, "They are not worth their keep to us." Though the work of the slaves is comparatively light, slavery is a calamity and a curse both to master and slave. One of the great evils arising from it was, and still is, the dignifying of idleness as belonging to freedom, and the degrading of labour by making it the badge of slavery. Few free men, except the very poor, ever engaged in any regular employment, or, except a small class of traders, sought to increase their means by their own exertions. The continuance of slavery will be one of the most formidable barriers to the civilization and improvement of the people, as well as a source of increasing weakness to the free portion of the nation, if its continued existence does not actually lead to their ultimate subjection, and the loss of their country to a more free and powerful race.

The mental faculties of the Malagasy are often active and clear, though necessarily limited in their range of operation, and those of the Hovas are, in this respect, superior to the rest of their countrymen. Many were earnest questioners, gladly welcoming additions to their knowledge and materials for thought. Some cherished a passion for calculation, seeming to be arithmeticians by intuition; but the delight of greater numbers was in *miady varotra* (the battle of bargaining), in which they are occasionally clever, and always eager; and although spending much time and labour for but little profit, they are better pleased than with equal gain without disputation.

Whatever may have been the morals of the quiet and peaceable tribes when the English first penetrated the interior of the country, those of the Hovas were revolting and depraved. Courtesy, propriety, and seeming sincerity characterized their ordinary social intercourse, but these semblances of virtue rendered only more offensive the vices which they concealed. The moral difference between truth and falsehood was often not perceived. In many of their communications, especially with foreigners, truth was only accidental. Deception, especially if advantageous, was approved, and at times rewarded as a virtue; and truth, if unfavourable, condemned as a weakness, and a crime to be punished. The advantage to be gained was chiefly considered, and the love of truth for its own sake seemed unknown. The practice of bribery in the administration of law destroyed the value of evidence, and often gave judicial sanction to perjury. Few felt any obligation to speak the truth when falsehood would serve their purpose better; and the habit became so strong that at times they neither believed each other nor themselves.

Honesty, so nearly allied to truth, was scarcely more regarded. The honesty which tradition ascribes to their ancestors, in the security of goods in the

market, has long ceased, if, indeed, it was ever more than a myth, and the number and severity of the punishments inflicted by law for theft, which was often attended with murder, show its frequency and danger. The police, or watchmen, patrol the capital every night, and the house and premises of every person of property in Imerina are surrounded by a high wall of burnt clay, armed along the top by several lines of firmly fixed, sharp-pointed pieces of bone or hard wood, for greater protection against thieves.

The custom of burying with the dead the treasures they most valued while living, and placing money in the mouth of the corpse, necessitates the careful guarding of the dead until the tomb is made secure. Funeral observances always ended with feasting, and at the interment of a rich chieftain, forty or fifty oxen have been sometimes slaughtered. On these occasions it was customary to fix the bullocks' skulls, with the horns attached, on poles set up near the tomb, round which a low fence of horns was sometimes also fixed. This practice of placing the treasures of the dead in their tombs, and depositing in one grave the bodies of successive generations, probably caused the size and solidity of many of the native sepulchres. The remarkable square-cloistered and ornamented tomb at Isotry, which the father of the late, and the present prime minister prepared for himself, occupied nine years in building.* The smallest tombs were from three to six yards square. The nobles erected their own tombs during their lifetime. Tombs often occupied conspicuous places, and I have seen near some of the villages nearly twenty in a line on each side of the road.

* It is reported that during the building of this tomb, he whose body was to be placed there requested his sons to open the door occasionally after his death, and let the sun shine in upon him.

The accompanying illustration from a photograph represents the tomb which a noble of wealth and influence had built near the capital, and in which he was interred a short time before my last visit. The contents of a grave were not considered safe until the tomb was finished, and the entrance walled up. A

chief who died while I was at the capital, was buried in a large sepulchre, which had a stone in the doorway, and earth heaped up against it. An armed watch was appointed until the masonry should be finished. But during the second night ten men began removing the earth, preparatory to robbing the grave, but fled when fired upon by the watch. The graves of those who are comparatively poor are violated for the sake even of the graveclothes, or for the few small pieces of silver placed in the mouth of the corpse.

The morals of the people were most clearly seen in their domestic life. Families appeared to live together in peace and good-will towards each other, though in outbreaks of passionate rage the Malagasy was at times savagely cruel. Parents, as a rule, were fond of their children, though parental influence was weak, and control rarely exercised. Radama's father had, for special military reasons, made drunkenness a capital crime, and the sobriety of the people at that time contrasted favourably against the intemperance with which foreign commerce has since cursed the inhabitants, especially in the neighbourhood of the ports.

The licentiousness of the people was at the same time almost universal. Chastity seldom existed except among the females protected by early betrothment; but in the other sex it was neither esteemed nor expected. The marriage tie, loose and brittle as it was, prevailed among all classes, and was usually arranged by the parents with slight regard to the children, who were generally too young to have any opinion on the subject. The early age at which marriages were contracted, often with little previous acquaintance and no mutual attachment, rendered the tie extremely insecure, and often useless as a safeguard of virtue, or a check to immorality.

Whatever may have been the relation of the sexes with regard to equality of numbers in former times, such had been the destruction of life among the men, caused by sickness and want of food during the frequent distant and protracted wars of Radama and his immediate successor, that it was estimated that the women were as three to one of the entire population, a proportion which could not but be unfavourable to the morals of the people. Concubinage was adopted by all whose means were equal to its expensiveness, and proved a constant source of misery, and of quarrels and litigation between members of the same family, as well as of frequent divorce and of ever-increasing demoralization, producing a state of misery and impurity of which civilized and Christian communities can form no adequate conception. But it is as remarkable as it is cheering to know that there were, during the same period, marriages of choice and affection, in which husband and wife remained united in loyalty and love to each other throughout life, notwithstanding the fearful prevalence of vice in the general community.

The Malagasy might be described, in a sense, as a religious people. The name of God was in constant use amongst them. "May God bless you" was a frequent acknowledgment of favour, an expression of thanks, or a parting salutation. The term by which God is most frequently expressed signifies Prince of Heaven—literally, prince of fragrance or perfume. Another term also used means the source or cause of possession. But neither of these words was associated in the minds of the people with any idea of the true God as revealed in the Bible. They were used to designate the spirits of departed men, especially those of former sovereigns, or persons of renown. The idols, or other objects of religious homage or fear, were called God, and very naturally some of the great Creator's works. The sun, moon, and stars, certain mountains, the grand phenomena of nature, thunder, lightning, earthquakes, and hail, were said to be God. Also the genii, or demons, spiritual agents of good or evil inhabiting the invisible world, were thus designated. The ruling sovereign was called the visible God. Anything new which they were unable to comprehend was spoken of in the same manner. I once heard the production of some photographic likenesses which I had taken ascribed to God. There was, in its ordinary use, no moral signification or principle of true religion associated with the word God.

The Malagasy had no idea of the immortality of the soul as revealed in the Scriptures; but their first religious belief, as is the case with most unenlightened races, appears to have been in the separate existence of the human spirit after death. The earliest tradition of any worship relates to that which the Vazimba, the supposed aborigines of the central parts of the island, offered to the spirits of the dead. The tombs of this primitive race are most scrupulously preserved, and are still used for religious purposes. They frequently crown the summit of a lofty mountain, where at times the inhabitants of the surrounding villages assembled to offer sacrifices at the tomb to the spirits of the Vazimba.

But there was still a craving after a nearer and more defined object of worship than a disembodied spirit in an invisible world; and the material household god, together with the idols of the individual members of the family, were the next constituted objects of trust and worship. Subsequently the heavenly bodies, certain valleys and mountains, in which idols were kept, or in which renowned men had lived, were deemed sacred and worshipped. The spirits of their ancestors, and those of the ancestors of the reigning sovereign, were objects of the highest religious regard.

The so-called national idols were of comparatively modern origin, being an extension of the principle of household worship, introduced from political motives by successive rulers. representing themselves as the fathers of the people. There are fifteen of these in Ankova, two of which were supposed to preside over the entire kingdom. The chief is Ra-ke-li-ma-la-za (renowned, but small). His influence is supposed to render the sovereign invincible and universally victorious, as well as to protect against crocodiles, sorcery, and incendiarism. The next is Ra-ma-ha-va-ly (able to answer). He is called God, sacred, and almighty, able to destroy or restore life, to control the thunder and lightning, and to give or withhold rain. He is also credited with a sort of omniscience from which nothing can be concealed. The whole serpent tribe were said to be his servants. This idol was also a sort of Malagasy Æsculapius, to whose care the health of the province was confided. When sickness prevailed, or was threatened, the idol was brought in procession to the capital, where the inhabitants, together with thousands from the surrounding country, knelt in silence, with bared head and shoulders, in one vast assembly, while the idol was carried to and fro, raised on a pole above the kneeling multitude, the attendants accompanying the idol bearing a horn filled with honeyed water, which they sprinkled on the people, and assured them of safety.

The primitive worship of the Malagasy was simple and spiritual. The Vazimba neither made images nor associated charms with their religious rites. A plain stone fixed upright at one end of a tomb, or a simple mound of earth and stones raised on the site of a grave, often in the midst of a grove, was their temple and altar. Their worship, the most esteemed in the country, combining homage and invocation, was accompanied with sacrifices of oxen, sheep, and poultry, the blood and fat of which were offered on the altar, and the rest eaten by the worshippers. These were the only sacrifices offered in Ankova. In former times, in the southern part of the country, human sacrifices were offered, not the captive, the slave, or the lowest members of society, but the highest and best, the chiefs or nobles, as most acceptable to the idols supposed to dispense the fruits of the earth, and to give prosperity to the people.

The belief in a sort of fetishism, sorcery, or divination, has been a source of the widest misery and crime, and has often enjoined the iniquitous and deadly poison ordeal, which is deified and invoked as the trier of innocence or guilt under the name of Rai-ma-na-man-ga, and has probably destroyed more lives and inflicted greater suffering than any other single cause in Madagascar.

But the most direct power over the people was the sikidy, or divination, which, in different forms, prevailed throughout the island. Believed to have been received from a supernatural source, and regarded as the will of God, the influence of the sikidy extended over both worlds, affecting gods and men, as well as the unquiet ghosts which left their graves to disturb the living.* The most baneful influence of the diviners was their pretending, by calculations based on the age and position of the moon at the period of birth, to reveal the destiny or *vintana* of every newly born infant, thus deciding, whatever its rank or parentage might be, whether its life should be preserved or destroyed. The decisions were believed to be those of God, and though determined by a table of divination which might be worked almost like a game of chess,† were received by the people as their fate.

---

* When it was reported, soon after the death of Radama the First, that his ghost had been seen near his country palace, dressed in an embroidered scarlet uniform, which had been buried with him in his tomb at the capital, and mounted on one of his favourite horses which had been killed at his funeral, priests, offerings, and the diviners were sent to inquire the cause of his appearance, and to prevent his ghost causing further alarm to the people.

† "History of Madagascar," vol. i., p. 431.

Such were the external aspects of heathenism in Madagascar, and such were some of the objects of its worship, but their name was legion. The whole land was full of idols. Their imagined power was supreme and resistless over every individual, from birth to death; and the effect of their delusions was to darken the mind and deprave the heart. The tendency of idolatry was to enslave its votaries, as well as to shroud in hopeless and impenetrable mystery all that would be after death.

The most intelligent and zealous worshipper of the idols invested them with no attribute of virtue or goodness, ascribed to them no intelligence or principle such as could impart worth and dignity to human character. The idols offered no aid in achieving the great purposes for which man has been created and his race perpetuated, nor tended to raise him above the selfish and grovelling instincts of animal existence. The great difference which they recognised between their idols and themselves was the possession, by the former, of supernatural power. That power their moral cowardice made them fear, and their selfishness made them covet, in order that they might be feared by others, or be able to destroy all who opposed them.

While I was residing at the capital eighteen criminals were publicly, in the presence of thousands, sentenced and beheaded in one day, and on another day fifteen fell beneath the executioner's spear. Observing to an intelligent officer that the thought of those days always filled me with horror, he remarked more than once, "Those were days of *power*. Every heart in Antananarivo felt that power, and was filled with fear." This remark probably expressed the native idea of the supernatural power belonging to the objects of their worship—a power to fill the heart with fear, a power to kill.

Improvements from other countries were at first opposed by the idols, and everything new excited their hate or their fear. Some were said to have a great antipathy to muskets and gunpowder, especially after one of the keepers had been shot in battle, while cheering on his comrades, and bearing the idol on his shoulder.

The idols also were mean and covetous beings. No appeal was ever made to their compassion. Money payments were connected with all the transactions in which their idolatry was associated.

The knowledge of divination is believed to have been imparted to the Malagasy by one of their renowned idols,* and wherever the sikidy was employed, the diviners must be paid. The preparers and the administerers of that deadly draught received

---

* This idol was supposed to reside in a cavern in the rocky part of a lofty mountain thirty miles from the capital. In the part where his altars were fixed there is a reverberatory echo, in which probably originated the belief of audible answers being returned to those who visited the cavern and saluted the idol. Radama I. visiting this spot on one occasion saluted the idol, and was answered by a low, solemn voice. The king then offered his hasina, or present of money, when, a hand being slowly moved forward to receive it, he seized the hand, exclaiming, "This is no god. This is a man!" and gave instant orders to his attendants to drag out the impostor.

money for their work. When the parties who drank the poison were pronounced guilty, and barbarously murdered, and even when their wives and children were sold into slavery, all their property was confiscated; half belonged to the king, the remainder being the perquisite of the executioners, while all the expenses of the trial were exacted from the family or relatives.

This brief notice of the social and moral condition of the people, and of the superstitions and idolatries of the country, will enable us to form a more correct opinion than would otherwise be possible of the encouragements, as well as of the appalling, and, to us, invincible antagonism by which Christianity was confronted on its entrance into Madagascar. It will also show the combined and organized forces which so fiercely disputed every step in its advance, and enable us more clearly to comprehend the marvellous victory which God, by the gospel, has achieved among the people, and which ranks among the most remarkable triumphs of Christianity in this our nineteenth century.

CHAPTER II.

Arrival of the first missionaries on the coast of Madagascar—Fearful ravages of illness and death—Renewal of the mission at the capital under the auspices of Radama—The English language taught in the first schools—Radama's letter to the Missionary Society—Alarm of parents respecting their children—The native language reduced to writing—Arrival of missionary artisans—The native language taught in the schools—Commencement of public Christian worship on the Lord's day—Wide extension of education—Increasing attendance at the Sunday services—Singing introduced into Christian worship—Arrival of the first printing press—Review of the first ten years of the mission—Death of Radama—Assassination of his successor and friends—Ranavalona placed on the throne—The character and reign of Radama.

Towards the close of the last century, the recognition of the duty of Christians to communicate the knowledge of Christ to the heathen nations, was revived by the divine Spirit in the religious communities of our own country, and attention was soon afterwards directed to Madagascar.

In 1814 the Rev. J. Le Brun, born in Jersey, educated in the Missionary Seminary at Gosport, was sent to Mauritius with a view to commencing his labours in Madagascar or in Mauritius, as divine Providence might open his way. He remained in the latter island, and devoted a long, blameless, and benevolent life to the education and spiritual welfare of the slave population, accompanied with a large and lasting measure of the divine blessing. In Mr. Le Brun a number of unhappy slaves from Madagascar found a kind and faithful friend, whose concern for the spiritual welfare of their countrymen terminated only with his life. Sir Robert Farquhar, Governor of Mauritius, recommended the directors of the London Missionary Society to send missionaries to Madagascar, with assurances of all the encouragement he could give.

Two years after the first intercourse of the English with the Hovas, the mission appointed by the society reached the shores of Madagascar with the word of God, the gospel of salvation, a peaceful means of moral and spiritual power and blessing, directed to a higher and nobler end than any ever before known among its inhabitants.

Encouraged by an experimental visit to the coast of Madagascar in August, Messrs. Jones and Bevan proceeded soon afterwards with their wives and children to the port of Tamatave, and were welcomed with joyous salutations by the chiefs and youths who had, during the former visit, been their scholars.

But this attempt to settle among the people proved fearfully disastrous. The season was the most unhealthy of the year, clouds and rain darkened the heavens and deluged the earth, while a fatal malaria spread over the long-desired and seemingly inviting shore. Mrs. Jones and Mr. and Mrs. Bevan, with two children, landed in the country only to sicken, suffer, and die. It was in the hearts of these missionaries to labour for the Malagasy, and thus to consecrate their lives to their divine Lord; and the sacrifice was doubtless accepted, though to offer it was all that was allowed to them.

Bereaved, afflicted, and alone, the surviving missionary removed to Mauritius, devoting his attention, as returning health allowed, to preparation for resuming his appointed work. In the autumn of 1820 he embarked under favourable auspices, in company with the British agent, for Madagascar; and, on reaching Tamatave, commenced the journey through the unhealthy part of the country before the destructive fever had appeared. Early in October the travellers reached An-tan-an-a-ri-vo, the capital, where, after marching through lines of English-trained soldiers, Mr. Hastie was publicly received in great state by the king, who cordially welcomed Mr. Jones, his missionary companion. The treaty for the abolition of the slave trade, which, though ratified by the English Government, had in the meantime been repudiated by the officer at Mauritius, required the king's earliest attention; but by the judicious efforts of Mr. Hastie he was induced to re-enact the prohibition of the traffic, much to the satisfaction of the peaceable and respectable portions of the community.

Radama had, in the meantime, been made acquainted with the more remarkable effects of the operations of the London Missionary Society in the

South Seas, and no sooner had the British flag been hoisted at the palace to announce the ratification of the treaty, than the king sent a message to Mr. Jones encouraging him to remain in the capital, with a promise of countenance and protection for any other missionaries with their wives and families who might come to his aid.

Before the end of the year, the missionary publicly commenced his great work of teaching. It was a truly small beginning, for he had only three scholars. Little did he think how soon the number would be multiplied by more than thousands. The small company increased daily, and a new school-house being soon required, the foundation of the building was publicly laid, and sprinkled with sacred water by the king himself, who gave this public testimony of his respect for the missionary as a means of promoting his usefulness among the people.

In the course of the ensuing year the solitary labourer was cheered by the arrival of Mr. Griffiths, sent from England to his assistance; and when afterwards the wives of the missionaries and an English child arrived, being the first ever seen at the capital, they awakened lively interest and curiosity, especially amongst their own sex, and were treated with much kindness.

The numbers and progress of the scholars increasing, a second school, with sixteen pupils, was opened by Mr. Griffiths, while the missionaries' wives commenced teaching the females needlework, and the making of articles of clothing for themselves. All that the missionaries were yet able to do was to impart to the children the mere elements of instruction; but the increase of their scholars encouraged them to persevere.

A singular misunderstanding occurred before the end of the year. The missionaries arranged for a short holiday, on the occasion of their first Christmas at the capital, and gave the children permission to remain at home for a few days. So great, however, was the change which had taken place in the minds of the parents, many of whom had at first suspected ulterior motives on the part of the king and the missionaries, in their endeavours to obtain pupils, that they now considered the teaching likely to prove advantageous to their children, and without seeking any explanation, they called a public meeting, and complained of the teachers withholding instruction from the children. The complaint was made known to the king, who sent to inquire why the teaching was interrupted, adding that if the children had not behaved well they should be corrected. Explanation satisfied the king, and the missionaries in due time resumed their instructions.

When Mr. Hastie was about to return to Mauritius, Radama announced that he intended to send twenty youths—ten to Mauritius, and ten to England —for education, and invited parents who were willing to send their children to bring them to him. A large number came; and one chief was so eager to send his son that he offered to give three hundred dollars, a large sum in those days. When the king heard of the offer, he asked what the chieftain was really willing to give. He replied that he would give at once half the sum he had mentioned. "Then," said Radama, "as you are evidently in earnest, your son shall go free. I will pay his expenses." This proceeding, highly characteristic of the king, reveals in part the secret of his great influence over the people, as does also the following occurrence, relating to the same event.

One of the youths selected, afraid of the sea or fond of his home, although perfectly well on the previous day, declared he was sick, and unable to go; on hearing of which the king ordered him to receive fifty lashes, and to be hung by the thumbs on a high pole in sight of all the people. The order was sufficient, and was one of the many evidences given by the king that he intended the conditions of the treaty to be strictly observed.

After concluding the treaty, the king sent Prince Ratefy, the husband of his eldest sister, as ambassador to London in 1821. The youths selected to be educated in England accompanied him, and were placed under the care of the London Missionary Society, the English Government defraying the cost of their education. The prince was also the bearer of a letter to the directors of that society, requesting additional missionaries, and men to teach the people the useful arts of civilized life. In compliance with this request, Mr. Jeffreys and four artisans, competent to teach the people useful arts, were appointed to Madagascar, and sailed in the same ship with the prince and his attendants on their return. The king expressed his gratification at the arrival of the Englishmen, and a third school, under the care of Mr. Jeffreys, was commenced, with twelve pupils.

Education was, however, still pursued under difficulties. The unfounded suspicion of some of the people, that the missionaries were not altogether different from the white men who had formerly sought for slaves at the capital, was revived during the absence of the king, excited, it was said, by the return of Prince Ratefy without the children he had taken with him to England; and a number of the parents not only refused to send their children to school, but, in order to prevent their being taken there, actually hid them in underground rice-pits, where several died from suffocation. The king's mother, in some respects a worthy mother of such a son, caused an order to be published in the market that any one raising false reports should be sold into slavery, and that those who were guilty of suffocating their children in the rice-holes should be put to death. This removed, for the time, objection to the attendance at the schools.

The unreasoning fickleness and suspicion of the natives were among the slightest of the difficulties with which the missionaries had to contend. Unacquainted with the language of the country, they commenced their noble work by teaching the children English, and with such success that, at a public examination of the school in 1822, in presence of the king and his attendants, the first class in the school read in English the whole of the VIIth chapter of the Acts of the Apostles, translating parts into their own language.* But the teachers, necessarily dissatisfied with the limited extent to which they could instruct the youth of the country in a foreign language, had been long engaged in providing the means of more rapidly teaching them through the medium of their own. That language was exclusively oral. It had never existed in a written form, and when commencing its acquisition, the missionaries had no predecessors whose philological investigations could assist them. No Malagasy alphabet, grammar, or vocabulary had ever been written.

It is sometimes said that the best way to learn a language is to undertake to teach it. This generally implies the use of the aids above mentioned; but the missionaries had to attempt the treble task of learning, constructing, and teaching the language of the people at the same time. In prosecuting this work the letters of the English alphabet were used, so far as they were available, to express the sounds of the native tongue, the French sounds being given to the vowels, and the Arabic figures used to express the numbers. The orthography was simple, the Malagasy syllables consisting, for the most part, of consonant and vowel, or diphthong, and the words invariably ending with a vowel.

For all the purposes of society in a corresponding state of civilization to that of Madagascar, the lan-

* Mrs. Jeffreys' "Journal," p. 108.

guage was sufficient and ample, often capable of expressing the nicest shades of meaning with brevity and precision. The king, who was himself learning English from Mr. Hastie, and French from Mons. Robin, his secretary, was much interested in the great work of giving to his own language a written form, and amused at the several changes in the appearance of the words before the best mode of spelling them was determined, though perplexed sometimes by the different sounds attached to the same letter in the English language; in consequence of which he issued an order that in the Malagasy language no letter should have more than one sound. Notwithstanding the unremitted attention of the missionaries, it was two years after their arrival before they finally decided on the Malagasy alphabet, which has ever since remained unchanged by foreigners, or by the thousands of natives by whom it has since been used.

Education had now become so popular that an adult school was, under the auspices of Radama, opened in the palace yard, in which the officers of the army and their wives, to the number of about three hundred, were instructed by Mons. Robin, the king's secretary. Besides daily teaching, the children attended at the school on Sunday for catechetical instruction and reading the Scriptures, and were also present on that day during the worship of the missionaries and artisans. Early in 1824, several of the best scholars were, with the king's consent, employed in teaching schools in the adjacent villages;

and these were so successful, that, in order to make teaching more effectual by training native masters, the king proposed that three separate schools should be united in one central model and training institution, under the instruction of Messrs. Jones and Griffiths, in a large building adjoining the residence of the latter, and that the wives of the missionaries should continue to teach the females.

The native language was used in the school, and only forty of the most advanced scholars continued the study of English, in which some of them attained a degree of proficiency which enabled them not only to read English books, but to translate several small publications into their own language, which were afterwards printed and used by the scholars.

Public worship in the native language was now held every Lord's day in the large school building, and adult natives were invited to attend, but very few accepted the invitation. The spirits of the devoted servants of Christ were often stirred within them as they listened to the conversation of the people, or passed by the recently anointed pagan altar at which sacrifices had been offered, or mingled with the multitudes wholly given to idolatry; and yearning over their delusion and danger, the missionaries spoke to them, as opportunity offered, of the living and the true God. Few appeared to be in the slightest degree interested in their statements. Some were offended at the implied disparagement of their idols; and others appeared to be afraid of the displeasure of both priests and idols, or of the malignant spirits whom discussion on these subjects might provoke. The priests generally avoided the missionaries, and it was pretended that their presence in the capital was offensive to the idols.

At the same time the increasing number of scholars cheered their teachers. There were two thousand under instruction, and the growing interest which some began to manifest in relation to the claims of the idols, and the teaching of the New Testament respecting the only Saviour of men, inspired hopes that from among them the firstfruits of Madagascar might be gathered unto Christ.

The Malagasy children, many of them quick, attentive, and earnest, accustomed to all kinds of conversation, and freely to express their opinions on every subject, often manifested a precocious intelligence and strength of opinion unknown at so early an age in more advanced communities. On such minds the new and wondrous revelations of the Bible could not but make a deep impression, even before they might perceive the issues to which these revelations would lead. They began to think lightly of the idols and their worship, to speak disparagingly of them amongst themselves and in their families, and hesitated not to treat without reverence the altars of the Vazimba, or the curious and beautiful trees considered sacred which were often planted around their graves.

One of the native teachers in a village school was struck to the ground by a savage chieftain for speaking to the children disparagingly of the idol of the place. Some of the parents expostulated, and entreated their children not to speak against the idols; but still the children answered that if to please their parents they should say they believed in the idols, it would be a lie, and they could not do it; they had been taught to speak the truth. The behaviour of the children was reported to the king, but he dismissed the complainants, telling them to mind their work and leave the children to mind their lessons.

Radama himself had recently shown that the decisions of the sikidy were but slightly regarded by him when they opposed his own will. He had a short time before returned with his army from a campaign, and, on approaching the capital, learned that the diviners had declared that he must halt outside for a number of days; but, determined to show them that he would enter the capital when he pleased, he marched straight to his palace, without halting in the suburbs as the diviners had directed. This public act on a great occasion was but one of many in which Radama had shown that, however frequently he might, for state purposes, follow the pretended directions of the idols, he was at least sceptical as to their existence or power, and his conduct could not fail to affect very powerfully the minds of his more intimate companions, as well as others.

Shortly afterwards, when the people of a so-called sacred village applied to the king for a piece of scarlet cloth for their idol, he replied, "Surely he must be very poor if he cannot obtain a piece of cloth for himself. If he be a god he can provide his own garments."

The missionaries, who, since the opening of schools in the villages, had divided their Sunday labour between preaching in the large building in the capital, and visiting the schools for the purpose of addressing the children, were encouraged both by the progress in the schools and the attendance at the chapel, where the congregation at times exceeded a thousand persons, the queen and one of the king's sisters being frequently present.

The Malagasy are passionately fond of music. The children, early taught to sing, were now often heard in the streets of the city, as well as at home, singing the hymns they had been taught in the school. The king not unfrequently went to the school to hear them sing, reading to them the first line of the hymn. While the progress of the children greatly encouraged the teachers, it taxed their energies to provide lessons and books that should nourish and extend their growing intelligence. Their teachers were especially anxious to impart to them the elements of religious truth; and as their own progress in acquiring the language increased, the missionaries translated detached portions of the sacred Scriptures, which were then read in the schools, and used in the sabbath day services by the missionaries and their pupils.

The king, who had been absent with his army, returned at the close of 1824, and having heard repeated complaints of the rapid increase of the scholars, and of the offence which the teaching of the religion of the foreigners had given to some of the people, sent officially to the missionaries to say that they were going too fast; that the people would not hear of any God but their own, nor of any religion except that of their forefathers; and he requested that the schools might advance more slowly, or he should not deem his kingdom safe. This expression of the king's views, and his having prohibited the collecting of the children for public worship, produced considerable fluctuation in the attendance of the scholars for a time. But the missionaries commenced a prayer meeting in the native language, which a number of the scholars readily attended, and several united, with much simplicity and earnestness, in praying to the true God for the blessing of the Most High on themselves and their countrymen. These valuable services were afterwards extended to the village schools, where several of the teachers presided with great propriety.

One great difficulty in teaching had been the want of books. All the Malagasy lessons hitherto attainable had been manuscript copies of those prepared by the missionaries, and transcribed by the advanced scholars; yet, notwithstanding the willing industry of the best writers, the supply had always been inadequate. Most gladly, therefore, did the missionaries, in 1826, welcome the arrival of a printing press, the first ever seen in Madagascar, which promised an easy and adequate supply of books. The king, gratified by the establishment of the press in his dominions, not only directed the missionaries to select six youths to work permanently as printers, but encouraged the people again to send their children to the existing schools, and authorized the opening of others. With devout gratitude to God, the missionaries also welcomed the renewed attendance of the children at the public services on the Lord's day.

Death had repeatedly diminished the feeble band of devoted labourers, but others had arrived to occupy the vacant post. Mr. Johns, accompanied by Messrs. Cameron and Cumming, followed by Mr. Freeman and Mr. Canham, had arrived to strengthen the mission before the close of the ensuing year.

All the brethren who were engaged in teaching useful arts to the people united heartily with those appointed to preach the gospel, attending the prayer meetings, imparting religious instruction on the Sunday, and earnestly endeavouring to diffuse the knowledge of the Redeemer among all classes.

Radama was often absent from the capital in the fearfully destructive wars which followed his first victories, and the officer left in charge as governor of the capital during his absence, appeared to rejoice with the missionaries in the progress of their great work. The public examination of the schools in February, 1828, was the most gratifying ever held. The one small school in the missionary's room, commenced in the end of 1820 with three scholars, had, in less than eight years, increased to thirty-two, in which four thousand youths and children were receiving Christian instruction. The temporary governor of the capital ordered a kabary on the day on which the report of the schools was read. He was present on the occasion, and in addressing the parents of the children, and the head men of the districts, in the king's name, reminded them of their obligations to the white men, several of whom, he added, had died in working for them and their children, and whose bones now rested in adjacent graves far from the land of their fathers. Urging all to more diligent attention to instruction, he closed by directing that those who had completed their period of instruction should still attend the services on Sunday, and the monthly examinations.

The existing and prospective value of these schools, together with the worship of the true God associated with the teaching, was greatly enhanced by their being extended over the several districts of Ankova. Still more important was the fact that there were large numbers of educated persons amongst the general population; and that, taught by these, numbers of young and adult persons, relatives or companions of those who taught them, had learned reading, writing, and arithmetic without ever entering any school. The extent of education, and the value attached to it, had never before been equalled.

Although the printer sent out by the Missionary Society was seized on the journey with fever, and died within a month after reaching the capital, the missionaries, assisted by Mr. Cameron, set up the press and printed lessons and school books. On the first of January, 1828, they sanctified the day by putting to press the first sheet of the Gospel of Luke, wishing, as they expressed it, "thus to hallow the new year of our missionary labours by this service, in opening the fountain of living waters in the midst of this parched ground, and," as they add, "with prayer that the healing streams may transform the wilderness into the garden of the Lord." Besides the rapid extension of education, the missionaries reported that their chapel was well attended thrice on the Lord's day.

No native of Madagascar had yet avowed faith in Jesus Christ, or desired publicly to declare his discipleship by receiving baptism. The intelligence, earnestness, and devout feeling on religious subjects manifested by some, inspired the hope that they were not far from the kingdom of God; and as the sovereign's approval was required before any one could thus unite with the Christians, Mr. Jones explained the subject to the king, endeavouring to ascertain his views. Soon afterwards, at an examination of the schools, Radama, though unable to attend, sent an official message, urging those whose time in the school had expired to seek further instruction, and to continue to attend public worship on the Sunday; adding, that if any persons wished to be baptized or married, they were at liberty to act according to their own judgment.

In order to extend the knowledge of the youths who had left school, as well as that of the more advanced scholars, a course of lectures was delivered to a numerous attendance. The first was on the being and perfections of God. Many of the youths wrote down the leading ideas presented, and others proved the retentiveness of their memories by their correct recitals of the great truths of revelation thus exhibited before them, and impressed on the heart and conscience.

Such were some of the results of the first ten years of the Christian mission in Madagascar. The time was brief, but its achievements lasting. Christianity had been presented in the simplest form to minds in the most unsophisticated state. It had been taught to the young. Its effects had been experimental and preparatory. So far as its highest object, the conversion of the soul was concerned, it had been barren of results; but as illustrating the harmony of divine providence with the purposes of divine mercy, it had been most conclusive. The light of divine truth had pierced a state of society enveloped in an atmosphere of moral darkness, intensified and polluted by monstrous forms of depravity and crime, as well as agitated and confused by witchcrafts, sorceries, divinations, and abominable idolatries.

The first pure, clear light of Christianity, faint, it might have been, as the dawn of the morning, had touched and enkindled in the minds of some a loathing of the vileness and falsehood of the native priestcraft, and a yearning after something more sure and true than the pretended responses of a billet of wood, or than the brainless vagaries and cruelties of astrology and divination. Truth, though as yet only a narrow point might have penetrated their minds, was too bright and clear to be extinguished by any agency that idolatry could employ, and too strong to be resisted. It had opened to itself an avenue to thousands of young and expanding minds. Its own inherent vitality and its divine origin constituted its protection against coming assaults or conflicts, and afforded guarantees for future victory. It was now approaching a new, a severer, and more protracted ordeal, in which, with greater suffering, it should achieve triumphs more transcendently glorious.

The constitution of Radama had never been robust, though vigorous, and it had been injured by the fatigue and exposure of camp life in unfavourable regions, as well as by attacks of fever; but more especially by intemperance, irregularity of life, and indulgences destructive to health. He was ill for many months during the last year of his life, seldom being able to attend to public business. He was seen only by his officers, latterly only by two intimate friends and his attendants; and he died on the 27th of June, 1828, at the early age of thirty-six years. The officers acquainted with the fact were unprepared for prompt action, and his death was kept secret. He was every morning reported to be better, and the band played every afternoon in the palace yard, as usual, to prevent all suspicion. This delay in mustering his friends and proclaiming his successor was their ruin.

In the meantime, a young officer attendant on

Radama's friends informed Ra-na-va-lo-na, one of his wives, of his decease. She sent secretly for two officers, her own partisans, and proposed to give them the highest offices in the army, and great rewards, if they would place her on the throne. The parties all knew that this could only be accomplished by the instant and copious shedding of blood considered most sacred; for Radama, having no son living, had nominated Prince Rakotobe,* the eldest son of his own sister and of her husband Prince Ratefy, to be his successor. The young prince, then in his eighteenth year, was popular, and the nation regarded him with affection and hope as their future sovereign.

The two officers to whom the proposal had been made agreed to attempt, at whatever cost of life, to secure the throne for the queen. They gained over to their purpose some of the priests and the judges, and then collected the troops in the capital under their command. Two days after the death of the king, a kabary was held for administering beforehand the oath of fidelity to whomsoever the king might be pleased to appoint to be his successor in the government. In the meantime, the young prince whom the king had designated heir to the throne was seized at night, hurried away to an adjacent

* This young prince was the first scholar sent to the first school, in 1820. He continued the friend, and occasionally the pupil, of the missionaries till his death; and they had reason to believe that his mind had been enlightened by the teaching of the Scripture, and brought under the influence of the love and faith which saves the soul.

village, and removed afterwards to a greater distance, where, by the side of a newly made grave, after granting his request for a few minutes to commend his spirit to God in prayer, they thrust their spears through his body, covered up his corpse in the grave, and returned to the capital.

The two divisions of the troops under the command of the officers engaged by the queen were led into the courtyard of the palace, where the officers, judges, priests or idol-keepers, and others, assembled on the morning of the 1st of August. To all these it was announced that *the idols* had named Ranavalona as successor to Radama, and their allegiance was claimed. Four officers of the late king's bodyguard replied that Radama had named Rakotobe and Raketaka, Radama's own daughter, as his successors. They had scarcely spoken before the spears of the soldiers around laid them dying on the ground. This act appeared to decide the question; and amidst the roar of cannon and the shouts within the palace yard Ranavalona was proclaimed queen.

An immense concourse of people were assembled in the capital on the 3rd of August, when it was officially announced that Radama had "retired;" that, according to the appointment of his father, Ranavalona was to be his successor, to whom all were required to take the oath of allegiance. Another and superior building was added to the line of the tombs of former kings in the palace yard; and on the 13th of August the remains of the late sovereign were deposited in their last resting-place, after which the strangers from the provinces returned to their several homes.

Considering the early age at which Radama was called to the throne, his reign, though short, had been rich in benefits to his country. His abolition of the slave trade, which saved his people from insecurity, plunder, and hopeless captivity, had closed one of the great slave markets of the world; the relations of friendship into which he entered with England, and the opening his ports to the commerce of civilized nations, inaugurated a new era in the history of Madagascar. The extension of the supremacy of the Hovas over a large portion of the country, though attended with fearful misery and destruction of life, may possibly issue hereafter in a united and prosperous people, under an enlightened and humane government. The introduction of letters, and a written language, together with the extension of education, and the employment of the printing-press, were benefits, the worth and influence of which are only beginning to be perceived.

Radama's abolition of the destruction of children born on unlucky days, and his frequent exposure of the craft and covetousness of the priests, as well as the jugglery of the diviners, saved the lives of multitudes of infants, and weakened the power of superstition among the more intelligent of the people. But, greatest of all, the introduction, during his reign, of Christianity into his country, his protection of its ministers, though personally resisting its claims, and refusing all teaching but that of his own heart;

though barren of spiritual good to himself, has proved a lasting and incalculable blessing to his countrymen. He had been raised up by the Supreme Ruler of the world at a peculiar period of his country's progress to introduce great changes, and to prepare the way for others greater still. His work was done, and he retired. His place was occupied by others who were to direct and urge the nation along the dark, impious, and fearfully retrograde course on which they were entering.

CHAPTER III.

Destruction of Radama's family—Drafting of scholars into the army—Appeal of the queen to the idols at her coronation—The New Testament and other books printed—Attention of the people to religious teaching—Baptism and partaking of the Lord's Supper by the first converts—Disapproval of Christian fellowship by the government—Formation of the first churches of Madagascar—Officers, soldiers, and scholars in the government schools forbidden to receive baptism or unite with the church—Christian officer accused of witchcraft, and subjected to drink the ordeal of poison—Masters forbidden to allow their slaves to read—Conversion and death of a young slave—Refusal of Christian soldiers to acknowledge the idols—30,000 readers, the result of ten years' educational labour—Idols rejected—Description of a Malagasy idol—Evidences of the power of the gospel among the people—Efficiency of native agency—Disastrous end of a teacher of a new religion.

AFTER the royal funeral, a season of national mourning was appointed. The ordinary occupations of life ceased, every amusement was forbidden, all classes were required to divest themselves of their ornaments, men, women, and children, throughout the land were ordered to make bald their heads, and clothe themselves in rags and sackcloth. The men, except those employed in the rice-fields, sat or slept away the weary days. The women, bald-headed and wailing, went, by order of the Government, to the place of the tomb of the departed to weep every day, some with unaffected grief for the dead, most of them from terror of the living.

But although teaching and learning, being classed by the government with amusements, were forbidden, and, with the exception of attention to the rice crops, idleness was enforced on the people, the government, released from public business, seized this season of general inactivity to strengthen their position, and arrange their plans for the reaction which they had united to create. Notwithstanding the booming of the artillery, the shouting of the troops, and the sworn oath of thousands, the occupant of the throne, to which a passage had been opened by the murder of its rightful heir, felt no safety in that elevated position so long as a single male member of the family of the late king remained alive, and only one female member of the family had been allowed to live.

One of Radama's cousins escaped to the Comoro Islands. The noble and high-spirited mother of the king was sent to an unhealthy part of the country, where she suffered a lingering and agonizing death from starvation in prison. Radama's eldest sister, and her husband Prince Ratefy, her brother's ambassador to England, both died by the hand of the executioner, the wife and mother in a manner fiendishly barbarous. The king's brothers and his uncle were starved to death in prison, and suffered such agony, that when no longer able to speak, they sometimes, by look and gestures, most affectingly but

vainly implored their guards to put them to death.*
Radama's early companions, faithful and trusted
generals, or governors of provinces, were shot. Their
only crime was having been true to their sovereign.
Such a commencement of the new reign augured ill
for Madagascar. It filled the minds of the people
with dismay, while it darkened the prospects of the
missionaries and their friends.

Forbidden to teach or preach, the missionaries
engaged earnestly in the preparation of elementary
and other books, and especially in translating the
New Testament, a work already commenced. In
the meantime Mr. Baker, an intelligent missionary
printer, having arrived, application was made for
such a number of youths to assist in printing, and
also in transcribing, as Radama had granted to aid
the missionaries in the work. The government
having decided that transcribing and printing were
neither learning nor teaching, the aid was given, and
a large supply of books provided.

After a cessation of six months, the government
ordered a limited number of schools to be opened in
villages in which no idol was kept; but the teaching
in these newly opened schools had scarcely commenced, when seven hundred of the teachers and
senior scholars were drawn for the army. This proceeding confirmed the suspicions of many of the

* One reason assigned for the infliction of this cruel death was
an unwillingness to shed royal blood, which was considered sacred;
hence members of the reigning family were put to death by some
process by which the shedding of their blood might be avoided.

parents as to the purpose for which the government collected the children in the schools, and so increased their disinclination to send them, that the numbers in attendance were one-half less than in former years. The next public act of the government was to discontinue the treaty with England, and inform the British agent appointed after the death of Mr. Hastie, that the queen did not feel herself bound by the treaty with Radama, and could not receive him as the agent of the British government; that she declined receiving the equivalent for loss in giving up the slave trade, but did not intend to revive the traffic. The presence of the British agent had been a restraint from which they wished, in future, to be free.

At the coronation of the queen on the 12th of June, 1829, in the presence of many thousands of people, after standing on the sacred stone, and having been declared by the representatives of the army to be sacred as their sovereign, Ranavalona took two of the idols in her hand, and thus addressed them:—" I have received you from my ancestors. I put my trust in you; therefore support me." The queen then returned the idols, which were covered with long pieces of gold-embroidered scarlet cloth, to their respective keepers, by whom they were held at the front corners of the platform on which the throne was placed, inspiring with superstitious awe the assembled multitudes. In her coronation speech to the people the queen declared that Radama had received the crown on condition that she should be his successor, and that she did not change, but would add to what Radama had done. Many who heard this speech, and remembered by what means she reached the throne, must have felt that truth received but little regard from the queen in her words to gods or men.

In the month of October of the same year, a fleet of six French ships entered the harbour of Tamatave, and opened fire on the battery, from which the Hova forces retired to Ivondro, whence they were driven, and the French moved on to the next northern port, where the resistance they met with obliged them to proceed to the Isle of St. Mary, still further north. An embassy was sent from the capital, and by entering into negotiations, the French were kept on the coast until the fever made such ravages amongst them that before the close of the year they sailed finally from the island.

Alarmed by the attack of the French, and apprehending its renewal in greater force, active military preparations for defence were urged forward, public homage and offerings were at the same time presented to the idols, and great efforts were made to revive the confidence of the people in the superstitions of the country. The movements of the government were directed by the pretended orders of divination, and the iniquitous ordeal by poison was restored in all its force. According to the direction of the diviners, the queen proceeded to the sacred city of Ambohimanga, the abode of one of the idols to which she had appealed at her coronation, carrying with her a large number of her jewels and other valuables, which she offered to Rafantaka, one of the idols of the reigning family. A number of civil and military officers were required to drink the poison at the capital, and a general purification of the country from any concealed crimes by which it might be polluted was ordered to be made; and by this murderous ordeal many hundreds of innocent Malagasy were sacrificed.

The attitude of the French, and the practical value of the efforts of the European artisans, probably suggesting the desirableness of the goodwill of the English, the authorities were induced to show a slight degree of favour towards the missionaries. Mr. Cameron, who was engaged in the construction of machinery and other works, had six hundred youths constantly under his charge, and devoted much attention to their spiritual welfare. A small addition was made to the number of the schools, while the missionaries were allowed full liberty to teach and preach, as well as to carry forward their great work of translating and printing the Scriptures, and preparing Christian books. In 1830, besides large numbers of other books, they completed the printing of five thousand copies of the New Testament, besides two thousand single Gospels. Well might the devoted missionaries rejoice in the completion of these works. This was the good seed which should be sown far and wide into many hearts, as into a virgin soil, for entrance into which they had by education prepared the way; and where, under the vivifying influence of the Holy Spirit, it should germinate, and bring forth fruits of holiness which should be unto everlasting life.

The portions of the Scriptures now provided were read by numbers in Imerina, and the distant provinces, where many who had been pupils of the missionaries now resided. These were not the only signs that God was working with His servants. "Conversation on the subject of religion," writes Mr. Baker, "is frequent among the natives, and the preached gospel reaches with impressive force the consciences of some. We have under our superintendence two thousand five hundred children, and with this charge it behoves us to feel our responsibility,—'Whatsoever thy hand findeth to do, do it with thy might.'" The existing place of worship became too small, and a second and larger chapel was erected at Am-ba-to-na-kan-ga (Guinea-fowl rocks) in the northern suburbs, not far from the government workshops. A suitable room was also engaged in a central part of the capital, where English and native preachers proclaimed the gospel to the people.

In the meantime a number of the natives, intelligent and earnest seekers after truth, had for some time received special attention and teaching from the missionaries, who rejoiced in the evidence which a number of them gave that they understood the nature and extent of the claims of the gospel, and had experienced its transforming power in their own hearts. Permission was given by the queen to

F

all her people who wished it, to be baptized, to commemorate the death of Christ, or to enter into marriage engagements according to the custom of the Europeans. The families of the missionaries, and the lay brethren associated with them, had already been united in Christian fellowship, and on the 29th of May, 1831, the first Sabbath after the queen's permission had been received, twenty of the first converts to Christ in Madagascar were baptized at Ambo-din-an-do-ha-lo (the lower part of the place of public assemblies); and on the following Sabbath, eight individuals, by receiving the same ordinance, at Ambatonakanga, publicly renounced paganism, and avowed themselves disciples of the Lord Jesus Christ, and at both places united in partaking of the Lord's Supper.

Two of the converts were husband and wife. The former had been celebrated among the heathen, but both were to become distinguished among the Christians. The man, now past the meridian of life, had possessed great influence among his countrymen as a diviner, and supposed revealer of destiny, and had been enriched by his art. A young friend had spoken to him on the falsehood and sinfulness of divination, persuading him to make himself acquainted with the true inspiration which God had given unto men, and urging him to visit the missionaries. The new and divine doctrines which they taught filled his mind with wonder and reverence; and there is reason to believe the divine Spirit impressed the truth deeply on his heart.

From Photograph by Rev. W. Ellis.

AMBODINANDOHALO.

Shortly afterwards he publicly destroyed his emblems of superstition and instruments of divination, with the exception of two, which, as proofs of his sincerity, he delivered to the missionaries. He then took his place among the scholars, commencing with the alphabet; and urged by motives, as delightful as they were strong, he continued without intermission as a scholar until he could read with correctness that Word which makes wise unto salvation. His wife seemed to have experienced the same divine change, and after twelve months of blameless Christian life the missionaries rejoiced to receive them amongst the first publicly admitted to the fold of Christ in Madagascar. At his baptism he received the name of Paul, of whom he had read so much in the New Testament, and he was frequently designated, in reference to his former life, "Paul the diviner."

The statement of motives contained in a letter of another of these early Christians to the missionary, shows how clearly he comprehended the requirements of a disciple of Christ. "I desire," he writes, when applying for baptism, "to devote myself, both soul and body, to Jesus, that I may serve Him in all things according to His will; and I pray God in thus giving myself to Jesus to assist me by His Holy Spirit, that I may love Jesus with all my heart, my spirit, and my strength—that I may serve Jesus even until I die."

The example of these baptisms stimulated inquiry among others, and much of the time of the missionaries was passed in the welcome and soul-gladdening employment of directing the inquiring minds of those who sought to take upon themselves the name of the Lord Jesus. Forty or fifty individuals, including some persons of rank, occupying responsible situations under government, usually attended these meetings of the converts with the missionaries. The public forsaking of the idols brought some annoyance and reproach upon the Christians, chiefly from their relatives, but this was cheerfully borne; and, compelled by the ardour of their love to the Redeemer, and their concern for the souls of others, they were accustomed to hold meetings in their own dwellings, for reading the Scriptures, conversation, singing, and prayer. By the divine blessing on these and other means, the members of the churches had been largely increased.

Some who, as already stated, held office under the government, and others who were allied to the reigning family, had desired publicly to declare their faith in Christ; but learning that such a step would be disapproved by the sovereign, they did not deem it safe to present themselves for baptism. A law existed, though not often enforced, prohibiting the use of wine in Imerina, and after the first administration of the Lord's Supper, a message was received from the queen, stating that it was contrary to law for any native to drink wine, after which water alone was used in this commemoration. The members of the government who were opposed to Christianity, having heard that several persons belonging to the army, and pupils in the schools, were receiving instruction previous to being baptized, orders were sent by the officers of the army forbidding the soldiers and the pupils in the schools to receive baptism, and also forbidding those who had been admitted to Christian communion to unite again in that ordinance. The soldiers were silent spectators when the ordinance was next celebrated,—viz., on the first Sunday in November, 1831, and after that time no one in the army or a pupil in the government schools was allowed to be baptized, or to unite in the communion of the church.

Although after the first baptism, those who had thus avowed their renunciation of heathenism and adherence to Christ, were received to the Lord's Supper, no church was formed until August in the same year, when a Christian brotherhood was organized among the worshippers at Ambodinandohalo, and shortly after at Ambatonakanga. The members on these occasions gave and received the right hand of fellowship, and agreed to a simple declaration of faith and order, including the chief evangelical doctrines, and, declaring the word of Christ to be the law of the church, securing to the people the admission to and exclusion from their fellowship. It was further stated to be the duty of every communicant to seek the edification of the church, and the extension of the gospel amongst their countrymen. Believing themselves that the word of God was the only true and safe ground of Christian faith and rule of Christian life, the missionaries were chiefly concerned that their converts should comprehend clearly this great foundation truth, and were content to leave minor questions to be determined by that rule as they might arise. Thus, by the loving care of the divine Redeemer, and with fervent prayer, as well as with trembling hearts, when they looked at surrounding darkness and at the immediate future, but in firm and joyous faith, the foundations of the Martyr Church of Madagascar were laid, thirteen years after the messengers of Christ had landed on the shores of that country, and eleven years after the commencement of their labours in the capital.

In the following year the schools, by order of the government, were collected at the capital for public examination, after which the proficiency of the scholars was commended in an official message from the queen, which also directed them to continue attending the teaching of the missionaries. About the same time an assemblage of the people was convened, on the completion of a canal cut under the direction of the missionary artisans, for bringing the waters of the river Ikiopo into a lake at the north of the capital, which had been converted into a reservoir for the government mills erected under the superintendence of Mr. Cameron. On this occasion a message was also delivered from the queen, expressing her Majesty's sense of the great value of the mission to the nation. These repeated testimonies in their favour, occurring at the time when the efforts of the missionaries for the spiritual benefit of the people were so encouraging, inspired a hope that the Most High might be influencing the rulers of the land to afford additional facilities for the prosecution of their great work. But all such hopes were fallacious, and only like gleams of sunshine which sometimes momentarily break through openings in the darkening clouds which precede the gathering storm.

The missionaries soon learned that the increase of the Christians was offensive to the government; that the endeavours of one devoted Christian to bring others to the knowledge of Christ had, notwithstanding his rank and influence, caused his impeachment on the charge of witchcraft, in consequence of which he had been ordered to drink the tangena; through which ordeal of death God had mercifully preserved him, to the great joy of the Christians. The missionaries found also that their educational efforts were only valued as they served to supply better qualified officers for the army, in which any Christian tendencies rendered their possessor liable to suspicion, and proved a barrier to his promotion. The prohibition to unite in the commemoration of the Lord's Supper, originally enforced against the government pupils in the schools and the soldiers, was now extended to the whole native population. Those already admitted to the church were not allowed to unite in the communion, and all others were forbidden to join their fellowship.

Another edict of the government, scarcely less discouraging to the Christians, was issued shortly after the examination of the schools. By this, every master was forbidden to allow a slave to read, on pain of forfeiting such slave and being himself reduced to slavery. Every slave was at the same time forbidden to learn to read and write under the heaviest penalties. The blessed influence of Christianity had already been the means of bestowing that spiritual liberty wherewith Christ makes free on some who were in bonds to their fellow-men. Among these one remarkable instance was conspicuous. A slave boy had learned to read while attending his young master to the school. The reading of the Scriptures had been the means of his becoming a sincere and humble believer in Christ, in whom he had publicly avowed his faith by receiving baptism in the close of 1831. He had seen in the missionary printing office the tract "The Poor Negro," with a frontispiece representing the negro in the attitude of prayer; and wishing to cultivate the disposition to pray, he gave, when baptized, his adopted name, Ra-Poor-Negro, as that by which he wished to be known. He continued to increase in knowledge of the Scriptures, in enjoyment of the gospel, and in usefulness amongst his own class, which form a large portion of the population of Madagascar. His death, which occurred a short time afterwards, was to all around him as remarkable as the change in his life had been. No one who has not stood by the bedsides of the dying heathen can form any adequate idea of the darkness, sorrow, and dismay which often attend their last hours. The Malagasy fever seized this Christian slave, and quietly terminated his life; but his most frequent expressions were, "I am going to Jehovah-Jesus, Jesus is fetching me. I do not fear." These words, "I do not fear," were the last he uttered in this world.*

The inhabitants of the conquered provinces had shown no attachment to the present occupant of the throne, or to the existing government; and rumours of hostile intentions against the Hovas were, without adequate, or even any foundation, frequently circulated in the capital. Large bodies of troops were also repeatedly sent, avowedly to reduce the disaffected to obedience, but most frequently to prevent future trouble by destroying those who might become enemies, and enriching the invaders with the spoils of their country. These troops were to a large extent officered by young men who had been pupils of the missionaries; and not a few in the ranks, as well as among the officers, and large numbers of slaves, and other camp followers who attended the fighting men, were Christians, and carried with them their books, especially their New Testaments.

The chief commander of one of these expeditions was a zealous votary of the idols, and before the army left the capital he ordered one of the national idols to be borne aloft through the lines, followed by the priests bearing vessels filled with consecrated water, which, in the presence of thousands of spectators, they sprinkled on the soldiers as a means of security and success.

In this army were a number of Christians who,

* An interesting narrative of Ra-Poor-Negro was afterwards prepared by Mr. Baker, and published by the Religious Tract Society.

through their officers, requested permission to be absent from the ceremony, as they could not, without doing violence to their consciences, unite in any act which implied belief in the idols. The general granted their request, but added that Rakelimaza would have his revenge. On entering the country they had gone to subdue, the forces were arranged in three divisions, the central and largest body of men being commanded by the general, in the midst of whose troops the idol was carried to the battle. The Christians were placed in the most exposed position, where it was probable they would be the first to fall. The two other divisions of the army were victorious, and took considerable spoil; but the central and strongest force, in which the idol was present, was defeated with the loss of about 1,000 men, 400 or 500 of whom were regular disciplined troops. This was a loss unprecedented in the wars between the Hovas and other races, and the division returned with broken ranks and no booty; lowered in the estimation of other sections of the army, and of the general community.

The Hovas seldom returned without spoil. In some instances it was reported that they brought home 10,000 youths, women, and children, who were sold into slavery. If only half that number were brought away, the slaughter of the men must have been great, and many tracts of country must have been left desolate and without inhabitants.

The conduct of the Christian soldiers in this, as in other campaigns, was truly honourable. Though equally exposed with others, and at times more so, they were always ready and prompt at every call. They were also distinguished by their consideration and kindness towards the vanquished, as well as by their honesty and the moral purity of their conduct. They availed themselves of suitable opportunities for holding meetings in each other's tents on Sunday, and at other times, for reading the Scriptures, singing, and prayer. Many of their comrades heard the word of God at these small camp gatherings for the first time, and afterwards became sincere and exemplary converts to the Lord Jesus. On more than one occasion, when the army returned to the capital after a period of absence, the Christian soldiers visited the missionaries, accompanied by a number of their comrades who had forsaken the superstitions of their country, had become disciples of the Saviour, and were seeking recognition amongst His people.

Other armies were organized and sent forth, and so determined were the government to keep up the strength of their military force, that every scholar above thirteen, and many scarcely more than twelve years of age, were drafted into the army. To prevent being left childless, parents purchased slave children, whom they sent to the schools as their own. The missionaries knew that they were only tolerated for the sake of the service which the teachers and artisans rendered to the government, and could not but regard as tokens of divine favour, in their anxious work, the large numbers of adults and children who, in 1833-4, voluntarily sought instruction, to enable them to read for themselves the sacred Scriptures.

The educational efforts of the mission had now been continued for fourteen years, and the scholars, though few at first, had rapidly increased, until the number under instruction at one time exceeded 4,000, who were all taught reading, writing, and arithmetic. It was estimated that from 10,000 to 15,000 Malagasy youths had passed through the mission schools during the period under review;* and if each of these only taught one relative or friend to read, the number of readers would amount to 30,000.

The recently awakened attention to Christianity had increased the number of readers, for the first aspiration of every one under religious impressions was to be able to read God's own word. Every Christian who could read was a voluntary and earnest teacher of others, for they all knew that the continuance of their opportunity was uncertain; but few even of the inquirers, excepting the aged, remained for any length of time unable to read. The addition of these to the number already specified, would, before the close of fifteen years after the opening of the first school, exhibit considerably more than 30,000 readers spread over different parts of the country. To supply these, large portions of the Bible had been translated, and, with liberal aid from the British and Foreign Bible Society, printed in the

* "Narrative of Persecution in Madagascar," by Johns and Freeman, p. 75.

native language. 2,500 tracts had also been printed by ready and generous encouragement from the Religious Tract Society; and these, besides school books, had been distributed amongst the people.

How wonderful and striking had been the course of Divine Providence in relation to the extension of the kingdom of Christ in this part of the world! The missionaries would have preferred more preaching and less teaching, but by no other course of action could so large a number of the people of Madagascar have been enabled to derive from the word of God spiritual nourishment, and strength of faith for the coming season of trial and suffering.

The missionaries had made frequent visits to the adjacent villages, for the purpose of encouraging the native Christians, and preaching to the heathen. Increasing numbers afterwards cast away their charms, and burned their idols; others came to the missionaries for further instruction, bringing the rejected idols as evidence of their sincerity. Among these was one belonging to several families. This idol had been a source of wealth to its possessor by the sale of small pieces of wood, which, having been hung about the idol, were afterwards sold as charms against fever, and other causes of danger. The central piece of wood which forms this structure is surrounded by shorter pieces, and by hollow silver ornaments, called crocodile's teeth, from their resemblance to the teeth of that animal. Amongst these are brazen ornaments, which were occasionally anointed with what was regarded as sacred oil, or other unguents, used in the consecration of charms, and other emblems of native superstition. This object of so much misplaced trust had belonged to the head man of the village, whose son had disposed of the charms; and such was the imagined power of these charms that an ox was often given as the price of one. The missionaries, when preaching in the village, spent some time in the family to which the idol belonged, and when the son visited them afterwards, they gave him a copy of the New Testament, which was made instrumental in his conversion to God; one of the first public evidences of which was the discontinuance of the sale of the charms.

It had never been difficult, since the commencement of the existing government, to obtain accusations against any one favourable to Christianity; and this young officer was accused to the queen of having practised witchcraft, in consequence of which he was required to drink the poison-water, that his guilt or innocence might be proved. His family, anxious to obtain a favourable issue, wished to employ the diviners. But the accused refused to allow of any employment of divination, declaring that it would be sin in him to allow it to be supposed that he believed it to be entitled to the slightest confidence. He repeated his declaration that he was innocent, and said, as he was condemned to the ordeal, he committed himself to God; and by the result of the ordeal he was pronounced free from the crime which had been laid to his charge.

The effect of his deliverance induced his family to seek Christian instruction, and to unite in Christian worship.

When the young officer was sufficiently recovered from the effects of the tangena he visited his family, and was rejoiced to find them seeking to know God. His father and the chief villagers gave up the idol to the young man, who stripped it of its ornaments, and buried it, but afterwards dug it up, and accompanied by one of the older inhabitants of the place, took it to the missionary,* with a request that he would visit the village, and instruct the people more fully concerning the true God.

Another instance is scarcely less instructive. A married couple who had applied to a maker of idols to furnish them with a household god, went to his house to receive it on the appointed day. It was not made, but promised in the evening. They agreed to wait; and the man went to the forest, and brought home the branch of a tree, and prepared the idol, leaving the fragments of the wood scattered near the fireplace. In the evening he asked his visitors to take their meal of rice with him, and they saw him put some of the small branches of the bough, out of which their idol had been made, into the fire to boil the rice. Having

* This idol, of which a representation is given on the next page, was sent to England, and deposited in the museum of the London Missionary Society. The rings and bandages are of fine silver chains. The ornaments on each side, called shark's teeth, are of silver, and hollow. They were filled with oil or other unguents used in anointing the pieces of wood used as charms.

paid about two dollars for their new god, they returned home. Shortly afterwards, a young Christian calling at their house was led to read to the wife that

part of the forty-fourth chapter of Isaiah,—"With part he roasteth roast, maketh a fire, warmeth himself, and the residue thereof he maketh a god."*

* "Narrative of Persecution," p. 54.

The woman was astonished at the exact description of what she had herself witnessed. The reading of this passage was instrumental in convincing her of the truth of the sacred volume; she abandoned her idol, and afterwards became a true disciple of the Saviour.

Loss of health obliged Mr. Jones to return to England, and three other missionaries had recently been ordered by the government to leave the country. Those who were left knew that they were only allowed to remain for the sake of the advantages which the government derived from artisans, by whom from one to two thousand youths had been taught useful kinds of skilled labour;* but as, towards the close of 1834, the government proposed to enter into fresh engagements with Mr. Cameron, the missionaries were encouraged to hope that they might be allowed to continue their great work.

Besides the preaching stations visited weekly, two large congregations met for worship every Lord's day in the capital. Nearly two hundred persons had applied for admission to Christian fellowship, and Bible classes had been formed for the regular perusal of the Scriptures.

The richest measure of spiritual prosperity yet vouchsafed to the mission marked the close of the year 1834. In reviewing the past, and surveying the existing state of the mission at this time, the brethren thus wrote to the directors:—" We look on with wonder and gladness, and are often prompted to exclaim, 'This is the finger of God!' The diffi-

* " Narrative of Persecution," p. 79.

culty still remains of ascertaining the number under religious impressions. But we have reason to think that several are savingly converted unto God, that many more are perfectly convinced of the folly of idolatry and divination, and that great numbers are awakened to inquire. The preached word is listened to attentively, and the Scriptures are earnestly sought and diligently examined. There are several prayer meetings held in the town during the week; and a spirit of prayer exists and increases among the natives. These meetings are commenced and conducted by the natives themselves, at their own residences, and they consider themselves as acting on their own convictions,—at the movement of their own minds, and from a consideration of present obligation to employ the means in their power for spreading around the knowledge of God, and of eternal life. God appears to manifest His purposes of mercy to this people by raising up an agency of His own from among themselves to carry on His own work, thus supplying the exigences of His cause by their unexpected instrumentality; and so compensating for our lack of service." *

Similar awakenings were at this time experienced in villages and districts sixty and a hundred miles distant from the capital, where the worship consisted chiefly of reading the Scriptures and prayer. Applications from these remote places for books, especially for the Scriptures, were frequent and numerous.

It must not be supposed that there were not at

* "History of Madagascar," vol. ii., pp. 484-5.

this time causes for anxiety and alarm. The following occurrence was one of the most mournful and perilous of these. A priest of one of the government idols, having heard from a native Christian, himself a converted priest, of the gospel of salvation by Jesus Christ, was deeply impressed, attended public worship at the mission chapel, returned to the village where he resided, and earnestly endeavoured to persuade the people to adopt his newly acquired religious views. Regarding him as deranged, they treated his endeavours with levity. He again visited his friends at the capital, who advised him to learn what the word of God taught before he attempted to teach. The advice did not please him, and he said that God taught him independently of the Scripture. He returned home and became the itinerant teacher of a new faith, comprising the resurrection from the dead, the general judgment, and the happiness of the world when wars should cease and universal peace prevail. In about two years this man had drawn after him about two hundred followers, and had also associated the worship of his idol with that of the true God. The great danger of the movement arose from his declaring that although he did not teach out of the Book, his religion was the same as that taught by the missionaries; his moral conduct was irreproachable.

In the autumn of 1834 this deluded man sent a second time to the queen, stating that he had an important message to deliver to her. The officer to whom the application was made known was also told that the followers of the priest were numerous.

They were summoned to the capital, and the queen sent messengers to meet them on the road, and to say that if the message they were coming to deliver was not true, they must return and abandon their opinions; but if true, they were to come forward and deliver it. They affirmed that it was true, and advanced, being about two hundred in number, to the capital. When the officers and judges went and asked what they had to say, they answered that they had a message from God, that the queen would be sovereign of all the world; that the dead would rise, and the living never die; that all would then live peaceably and happily, for there would be an end to the tangena, divination, murder, wars, and contentions. "God has told us these things, and God cannot lie. We offer," they said, "to forfeit our heads if what we say is false."

The conversation or examination continued for two or three days. In relation to the assertion that all mankind were derived from one source, the officers asked, "Do you mean to say that we and the Mosambiques are from the same parents?" They replied that the queen and all the human race descended from the same parents; and it was supposed this answer helped to seal their doom. Most of the two hundred remained firm to their word, but some withdrew. About midnight, after their statements had been concluded, the queen sent and put the priest and three of his principal followers to death. They were placed with their heads downwards in a rice-pit, boiling water being then poured on them, and earth afterwards thrown in until the pit was filled up. Seventeen of these men were compelled to take the tangena, under which eight of them died; the rest were all sold into slavery and their property confiscated, yielding to the queen, officers, and judges several thousands of dollars.

Although this combination of deluded men was destroyed, the event tended to excite suspicion against Christianity and its adherents. Such was the displeasure of some of the heathen party as to its progress, that spies were sent to the several places of worship to report any expressions in the addresses of the preachers which might be construed as injurious to the government; and declarations respecting the resurrection and the last judgment were reported unfavourably to the queen. The unwillingness of the Christians to abstain from work on days sacred to the idols worshipped by the inhabitants of the village in which they resided, also gave offence to the heathen. A young man who had been forced to desist from work on the idol's day, and who was overheard expressing his opinions respecting the objects of their worship, was, on the pretended order of the idol, sentenced to be cut to pieces, or the rice crop would be destroyed. This was reported to the queen, who did not gratify his accusers by his execu-. tion, but ordered him to drink the tangena, and in a short time after swallowing the poison, the supposed proofs of his innocence appeared, to the great disappointment of his enemies, and the grateful joy of the Christians. When, a few days afterwards, the young man came from one of the villages to the capital in a palanquin, as was customary on such occasions, a large number of Christians wearing white lambas joined the procession. From a distance the queen and some of her officers beheld with great astonishment the large procession. The queen inquired what it meant, and did not seem pleased when informed that it was a procession of Christians accompanying one of their number who had been declared innocent by the tangena.

CHAPTER IV.

Christian refusal to offer heathen sacrifice—False accusation of preaching sedition—A national assembly summoned—Christian worship declared unlawful—Missionaries forbidden to teach Christianity—Christians required to accuse themselves—Books to be given up—Stedfastness of the Christians—Their noble confession before the judges—Midnight meetings for prayer—Translation of the Scriptures—Compilation of dictionaries—Translation of "Pilgrim's Progress"—Last missionaries leave the country—Accusation against Rafaravavy and her companions.

IN the duties of subjects, of members of society, as well as in the social relations of domestic life, the Christians were in general so blameless, that the chief judge, before whom the accusations of other crimes besides rejection of the idols were preferred, bore a noble testimony in their favour when he dismissed their accusers with the declaration, that offences against the idols must be carried before the queen, and that no charge could be sustained against the Christians on any other grounds. It was only in relation to the homage and obedience demanded for the idols, and the superstitions associated with them, that the adherents to the new faith were found wanting. ' In reference to these the government and its agents found that the simple and sincere faith of the Christians endowed its possessors with a passive but invincible power—the heretofore unknown power of enlightened conscience armed with truth—before which they were helpless. It was also seen that, sustained by this power, the Christians opposed to the claims of the idols an unfaltering firmness and willingness to suffer, which filled their persecutors with rage and hate, and urged them to engage the highest earthly and invisible powers in their destruction.

Instances of the stedfast obedience of the Christians to the requirements of their faith occurred with increasing frequency; these were brought under the notice of the government, and were, with criminating additions, made known to the sovereign. One instance may suffice to show the requirements urged on behalf of the idols. A young chief, nearly related to a high officer of the government, was appointed guardian of an idol. This young Christian was told by the chief who had adopted him as his son, that at the approaching national festival the queen would present an ox to the idol, which he must kill as a sacrifice, and must eat part of it in honour of the idol, burning some of the fat as incense before it. His refusal to do this greatly incensed the chief against him, and against the teaching which caused him to refuse the homage required by the gods of his country.

The Christians were not ignorant of the crimes laid to their charge, nor of the endeavours of the priests and chiefs to excite against them the anger of the queen. An unusual seriousness pervaded their public and social gatherings; and seldom had larger or more deeply attentive audiences been seen than those which crowded the places of worship on the Sabbath days at this time. From the families of the immediate connections of the sovereign to those of the humblest slave, might now be numbered some among their relatives who were disciples of the Saviour. The large assemblies gathered for worship, the earnestness of the native preachers, and the serious attention of the people, were peculiarly offensive to the priests and their adherents, who carried the reports of their spies to the palace.

About this time the chief who had failed in his purpose to destroy by tangena the young Christian who had refused homage to his idol, went to one of the evening meetings for worship, where an excellent sermon was preached by a Christian slave, from Josh. xxiv. 14, 15. The chief returned, and according to his own interpretation of the sermon framed his accusation. Jehovah, whom they were exhorted to serve, was the first king of the English, and Jesus Christ was the second. By the gods whom the fathers of the Jews had served was meant the queen and her predecessors. On this iniquitous perversion of his words, the loyal Christian teacher was represented as preaching treason to the people.

The informer then went successively to three of the principal officers of the government and, weeping for effect before one of them, asked, it is said, for a spear to destroy himself, that he might not live to see the calamities coming upon his country. Encouraged by a message from the queen, he declared that certain persons in and around the capital were changing the customs of their ancestors, despising divination and the idols of the queen. "They hold," he added, "assemblies in the night, and deliver speeches, without permission from the queen. Beyond this, they urge all present to serve Jehovah and Jesus Christ; and these meetings are carried on by slaves. We cannot see the end of these things. The queen knows, and she alone, what is best to be done; but we fear these people, who have become so friendly with the English, will attempt to transfer the kingdom of the queen to them."

Ratsimanisa, the chief minister, laid this accusation, with his own confirmation of its charges, before the queen on the following day, when, it is said, the queen burst into tears of grief and rage, and wept for a long time. She then swore, by the name of the highest spiritual power to whom she could appeal, that she would put a stop to these things with shedding of blood. From that time the most profound silence reigned in the palace; the music was no longer heard; all amusements and dancing were discontinued for about a fortnight; the court appeared as if overtaken by some great calamity, while uncertainty and alarm pervaded all classes of society. An edict was issued requiring the people from the surrounding country, even to a child of a cubit high, to assemble at the capital on Sunday, the first day of March.

In the meantime, preparatory to the great assembly, a private order was given to write down a list of the houses in which meetings for prayer were held, and the names of all who had been baptized. The next day four officers met in the courtyard of the palace, when the names of the baptized, and a list of the houses where meetings had been held, were given in. The queen was astonished at their number, appeared exceedingly violent against the Christians, and swore in the name of Andrianimpoinimerina that she would put to death the owners of the houses. Two officers who were present spoke in favour of the Christians, recounting the benefits which the teachers of Christianity had conferred on the country, and stating that the death of the Christians would be a loss to the nation. Other chiefs were consulted about the desirableness of putting some to death in each district; but they expressed their disapproval of such a measure. The queen thanked the officers for their advice, and promised to consider it.

On the Sunday previous to the great assembly the chapel at Ambatonakanga was crowded. A judge who went there in search of his daughter, fearing she might suffer from being seen with the Christians, was surprised at the numbers, and afterwards remarked, "You will never see such an assembly there again." On the same Sunday evening, the queen, passing by the chapel and overhearing the singing of the Christians, observed, "These people will not be quiet until some of them lose their heads."

Two days after the list of houses used as places for prayer, and the names of the baptized had been read to the queen, the Christians assembled at Ambatonakanga for their usual week-day service; a native Christian preached an impressive sermon from the peculiarly appropriate text, "Save, Lord; we perish." It was the last public discourse ever delivered in that building.

While the Christians were thus employed, the missionaries went to the house of Mr. Griffiths to receive a communication from the queen, and a letter was presented to them by the chief minister, containing the following important announcement:—"That which has been established by my ancestors I cannot permit to be changed: I am neither ashamed nor afraid to maintain the customs of my ancestors. And with regard to religious worship, whether on the Sunday or not, and the practice of baptism, and the existence of a society,—these things cannot be done by my subjects in my country. But if there be knowledge of the arts and sciences, that will be beneficial to my subjects in the country, teach that; for it is good."

In acknowledging the letter the missionaries thus expressed themselves:—"We are exceedingly grieved respecting your word, which says religious worship is not to be performed by your subjects. For we know and are assured that the word of God is beneficial to men, and the means of making them wise, and that it renders illustrious and prosperous those kingdoms which obey it; and this teaching of ours the Word of

God, together with teaching the good dispositions, and the arts and sciences, are the purposes for which we left our native country.

"We, therefore, most humbly and earnestly entreat of your Majesty not to suppress our teaching of the Word of God, but that we may still teach it, together with the useful arts and sciences."

Morning had scarcely dawned on the first of March when the report of cannon, intended to strike awe and terror into the hearts of the people, ushered in the day on which the will and the power of the sovereign of Madagascar to punish the defenceless followers of Christ was to be declared. Fifteen thousand troops were drawn up, part of them on the plain of Imahamasina, and the rest in two lines a mile in length along the road leading to the place, where it was estimated by some of the missionaries that at least a hundred thousand persons were assembled. The booming of artillery from the high ground overlooking the plain, and the reports of the musketry of the troops, which were continued during the preparatory arrangements for the kabary or proclamation, produced among the assembled multitude the most intense and anxious feelings. At length the chief judge, attended by his companions in office, advanced and delivered the message of the sovereign, which was enforced by the chief officer of the government. After expressing the queen's confidence in the idols, and her determination to treat as criminals all who refused to do them homage, the message proceeded, "As to baptism, societies, places of worship distinct from the schools, and the observances of the Sabbath, how many rulers are there in this land? Is it not I alone that rule? These things are not to be done, they are unlawful in my country, saith Ranavalomanjaka; for they are not the customs of our ancestors, and I do not change their customs, excepting as to those things alone which improve my country.

"Now, then, those of you who have observed baptism, entered into society, and formed separate houses for prayer (or worship), I grant you one month to confess having done these things, and if you come not within that period, but wait to be first found out and accused by others, I denounce death against you, for I am not a sovereign that deceives. Mark, then, the time; it is one month from yonder sun of this Sabbath that I give you to confess, and this is the method you are to adopt. The scholars at Ambodinandohalo,* and those at Ambatonakanga—and not those only, for there are scholars in all these twelve principal towns,—and the scholars that have not opened separate houses, but at the appointed schools alone have worshipped and learned, these are not condemned, and these are not to confess; but those who have opened other houses, these are to accuse themselves.

"And those who have been baptized, whether they have worshipped in other houses or not, these must also accuse themselves, and those who have entered into society.

* The large central school, used also as a place of worship.

"And you, the civilians and soldiers that have been attending the schools for worship, and especially such as have opened other houses for worship, and been baptized, and entered into society, and kept the Sabbath, come and accuse yourselves on these accounts, for I the sovereign do not deceive; but if any come first and accuse you, I denounce death against you, and I do not deceive, saith Ranavalomanjaka.

"And I moreover announce this to you, saith Ranavalomanjaka: Here are your slaves that you have been teaching to write, and who have gone to the houses of prayer, and others who have gone to the schools, and especially that have been baptized; all these must also come and accuse themselves.

"And again, as to your mode of swearing, the answer you are giving, 'It is "true!"' and when you are asked, 'Do you swear it?' the answer is 'True.'

"I wonder at this. What, indeed, is that word 'True'?

"And then, in your worship, yours is not the custom of our ancestors; you change that, and you are saying, 'Believe,' 'Follow the customs,' and again you say, 'Submit to Him,' 'Fear Him.'

"Remember, it is not about that which is sacred in heaven and earth, that which is held sacred by the twelve sovereigns, and all the sacred idols, that you are now accused; but it is that you are doing what is not the custom of our ancestors; that I abhor, saith Ranavalomanjaka."

Two officers from one of the provinces then came

forward, and, after the usual expressions of loyalty, declared that the things of which her Majesty disapproved had been done in ignorance, not in disobedience. They then enumerated the friendship reciprocated between Radama and the English, with the advantages the nation had received from the industry, intelligence, and good conduct of the Christians as subjects. After which they begged the queen to accept an ox and a dollar as a fine or offering for what had been done, and a pledge of its avoidance for the future. These addresses appeared to give very general satisfaction.

Rainiharo, the commander-in-chief of the army, then advanced and spoke as follows:—" Respecting those who have received baptism, who have abstained from certain common practices, who have said, 'Follow its laws, do not fight,' who have reviled the holy idols, kept sacred the Sabbath, &c., unless those who are guilty of these crimes come forward by this day month to accuse themselves, we the hundred thousand (meaning the whole of the army) shall destroy them; for they have done these things of their own accord, without asking permission of the sovereign and consulting their officers. Unless, therefore, they come forward by this day month to accuse themselves, we are ready, Ranavalomanjaka, to cut off their heads."

Before the meeting separated the judges agreed to convey the proposal on behalf of the people to the queen, and the multitudes retired from the ground. The firing of cannon the next day announced that a royal message would be sent; but any hope which the presentation of their appeal might have inspired was destroyed when the officers, at the appointed time, arrived and announced to the anxious and expectant crowds that Ranavalona refused their peace-offering and their petition. The officers then further announced that, instead of allowing a month, during which they might accuse themselves,* the queen now ordered that within one week from that day every class of people, soldiers, citizens, scholars, artisans and slaves, should separately, as classes, and individually, repair to the appointed authorities, and acknowledge or give in a written statement of the offences they had committed. And further, that there might be no mistake about the consequences of neglect, the queen's message added, "Against those who do not come within that period, I denounce death." Then, after specifying the officers who had been appointed to receive their accusations, and the crimes that were to be acknowledged, the speech closed with the following warning :—" Remember that next Sunday is the last day, and unless you send in your names by that day you die wilfully." Whether or not the queen at this time intended to execute her threat, the government were evidently seeking to impress upon the people the enormity of their crime and its fearful consequences.

A special message was the same day sent to the

* The government wished it to be considered clemency on their part to give the people the opportunity of confessing their offences, as in such cases half the punishment was usually remitted.

H

missionaries, ordering them to refrain from communicating to their scholars religious instruction in any form and at all times; but lessons on chemistry, &c., such as Mr. Cameron was at that time giving to a class of young men, were allowed. Besides the scholars, the twelve senior teachers who had united in Christian worship were required to accuse themselves of having done so; and although they pleaded Radama's authority, they complied, stating that they "dare not oppose the sun;" to which the queen replied, "It is well that you do not dare to contend with the sun, but that you come to confess your guilt, and to crave pardon. It remains with me now to choose your punishment, and I will do with you as I will do with the others, for I shall show no partiality among my subjects."

There were few families in or around the capital in which some of its members were not involved in the accusations required, and no adequate conception can be formed of the deep concern and agitated feelings of the people during the remaining days of that fearful week. The utterly unfounded accusation against the Christian teachers, of preaching sedition and inculcating disloyalty, was often reiterated, and plausibly represented by some of the officers as hostility to the queen personally. This offence was also rendered more heinous by being directed against the deified spirits of her ancestors, and her own pretensions as the visible deity on earth. Treason and sacrilege were the highest crimes known,—both were included in the charges against the Christians, and were therefore represented as requiring the shedding of blood.

In a state of society like that then, or even now, prevailing at Antananarivo, an ordinary untroubled exterior does not conceal the strength or depth of the agitation within. All is visible and unrestrained. The missionaries learned more of the life and power of the mighty forces aroused by the results of their divinely appointed work, than they had ever conceived of before, or could otherwise ever have understood. The heathen, especially the priests, were now vigilant, active, hopeful, if not joyous, as they seemed to think the day of vengeance from their gods, and the hour of their triumph was come. The Christians and their teachers had sources of grief from among their occasional associates, as well as from the proceedings of the government. Some who had at times appeared in their assemblies, now consorted with the heathen and plunged into wickedness. Others denied having believed in Christ, or made excuses for their association with His people. These were the chaff among the wheat.

The great body of the disciples felt no hesitation as to what was their duty, and were only anxious to discharge it. They gave themselves to prayer, and when appearing before the judges, faltered not in their testimony. They declared that they meant no evil, and had done no evil to the queen or her kingdom, in the reading of the Scriptures, prayer, and observance of the Sabbath. They prayed, they added, to the God of heaven and earth to prosper the queen's reign.

One exemplary and honoured Christian being asked by the judges how many times he had prayed, replied that he could not tell; but for the last three or four years he had passed no single day without praying several times to God. When further asked how he prayed, he answered before enemies and friends, that he confessed his sins to God and asked forgiveness, imploring God's help that he might live without sinning, and be prepared for eternal happiness. He also asked, he said, the same blessings for his family and friends, for the queen, and all her subjects; and added, "I ask all these things in the name of Jesus Christ, for we receive nothing from God but through His Son Jesus Christ, who died for sinners." The judges observed that such prayers were very good, but as the queen did not approve of them, they ought not to be offered in her country. This faithful and devoted man, at the same time, spoke much to the judges of the holy Saviour who died for the guilty, and while he did so was treated with attention and respect.

Although prayer had been forbidden, it was never more sincere and earnest than at this time. One faithful company of believers met every midnight in the vestry at Ambatonakanga for prayer, and long afterwards remembered the consolation and strength they had found in those midnight hours when drawing nigh unto God. And God drew nigh unto them. At one of these midnight meetings, a queen's officer of high rank presented himself as a friend, and was welcomed; and when asked afterwards why at this perilous time he joined the Christians, he replied that he perceived so much injustice in the kabary, that he determined to join the injured party, and that after having attended a few times the meetings of the Christians, he resolved that their God should be his God. That as to accusing himself, he was determined not to do it until he was convinced that in attending their meetings he had done wrong. This noble follower of Christ proved faithful to his Saviour, and a true friend to the Christians, with whom he afterwards suffered.

The word of God was indeed precious to the Christians in those days. A number of Christian women, whose husbands had gone to the city to give in their accusations, communed with each other, and were sad as they sat together in the house of one of their number. Late in an evening of this week a Christian friend entered the dwelling, and listened to the tale of their sorrow. He endeavoured to cheer them, presenting before them the promises of God's word, the faithfulness and love of their blessed Lord, and urged upon them prayer; he also read to them the forty-sixth Psalm, prayed with them, and left them trusting and cheerful. These women, one of whom was sold into slavery on account of her faith, remembered that evening with grateful feelings, and long afterwards declared that they had seldom since, in hours of depression, failed to find consolation and support in reading that psalm and in prayer.

After much distress on account of the cruel, revolting, and nameless brutalities which it was reported were to be inflicted on the Christians, the day which had been regarded with such strong but opposite feelings arrived; and on the morning of the ninth of March the queen's message was brought by the judges and officers to the assembled people. The offences of the Christians were recited, the punishment due to them declared, especially the exhortations to the people to "Believe in Him," "To follow Him," &c.; adding, in reference to the scholars, "Now for all this evil which you have done in my country, I would have so dealt with you that you should never have had power to do good or evil again, had not the cries and entreaties of Imerina, viz., the people of the province, prevented me." On hearing the intercession of the people, the queen accepted their offering and money, and refrained from inflicting punishment, but added, "Your lives alone will be sufficient the next time." And with regard to Christianity, after enjoining prayer to the objects of national worship, the message was thus closed:—"If any change this mode of worship, I will punish them with death, saith Queen Ranavalona."

The fear inspired by this threat was deemed sufficient. None were put to death or sold into slavery, but about four hundred officers were reduced in rank, and fines paid for two thousand others. Although life was not taken, the purpose to extinguish Christianity was firmly determined on. The week after the queen's message had been delivered, every person who had received books was ordered to deliver them up, without retaining even a single leaf, on pain of death. This order was severely felt, few obeyed it literally, and in the distant provinces scarcely at all; the books given up, being regarded as English property, were returned to the missionaries.

So far as opportunity offered, the missionaries continued privately to impart consolation and encouragement to the Christians; but their opportunities were few, and the peril to the people great. Notwithstanding this, the converts continued to increase, and their spiritual improvement was rapid. The ordinance of the Lord's Supper was at times privately administered to them. Their endeavours to learn to read the Scriptures were unremitted, and the receiving a copy of portions of the Scriptures afforded unspeakable joy. Some walked sixty, some a hundred miles to obtain one. Not a few who received parts of the sacred volume at this time found it afterwards, in the lonely forest or the desert mountain, a fountain of living water, and a storehouse of bread from heaven.

The missionaries had never supposed that all who attended their preaching believed in Christ; but as faith cometh by hearing, they had rejoiced in their attendance, and prayed for their conversion. Though grieved that the faith of some had failed when the day of trial came, the native Christians, as well as their teachers, were still more deeply afflicted when they heard that the evasions and excuses of those who had sought thereby to escape punishment, had been made the occasion of all being stigmatised as cowardly and false. It was reported that one chief who had visited their chapels as a spy, declared that when he heard the Christians singing, "I am not afraid to die," he thought it was so; but that when he afterwards heard them accusing themselves, and begging for their lives, he knew that they were as much afraid of death as others, and "had been singing lies." Indeed, he added, he did not believe there were any true Christians in Madagascar.

The advantages conferred by teaching the youth of the country to work in wood and iron, especially the latter, were highly prized by all classes. Excellent iron abounds in several parts of the country, and the people, with great patience and labour, and by a rude and simple process, melted the ore mixed with charcoal in stone or clay pits, or kilns, covered over with clay, providing the blast by pistons worked by hand in hollow trunks of trees. We have already stated that they were able to construct a number of rude but useful articles before the missionaries arrived, but the greater variety of workmanship and excellent finish which the English smith taught them, were esteemed by many as among the greatest benefits which the mission had conferred on the people. Some hundreds of native youths had been taught by Mr. Chick, the intelligent smith associated with the mission, and all the ordinary as well as more complicated ironwork required in the water-wheel, and other machinery and buildings erected for the government, had been made by native smiths, under the direction of their indefatigable Christian instructor.

From Photograph and Sketch by REV. W. ELLIS.

IRON-SMELTING AND NATIVE SMITHS.

The government had also encouraged education and attendance on public worship, and it was not until it had been falsely represented that sedition was preached, that any hostility was manifested in that quarter. The threat of capital punishment doubtless alarmed a number in whom religious impressions were only faint and undefined; and although the great body of the Christians fearlessly confessed their faith before their judges, the ignoble use which had been made of the fears of others was probably not without its influence on the believers in future seasons of severer trials.

The stern prohibition against Christian instruction and worship throughout the country on pain of death, and the order to the missionaries not to teach religion in any form, had virtually brought the mission to an end. But one great work, the translation of the Old Testament, was still unfinished, and to its completion the missionaries now directed their undivided energies. Mr. Baker, assisted by the artisans, worked at the printing of the translation, until the whole was finished; and thus, by their last labour, the sorrowing missionaries conferred on the people the greatest boon which, next to the introduction of Christianity itself, Madagascar had received. Messrs. Freeman and Johns also compiled English and Malagasy dictionaries, which have proved highly serviceable to their successors, and are the only ones yet published.

The missionary could now neither open the chapel nor preach in his own house. No Christian could visit him without danger, and, except with extreme caution, they seldom entered his door. He could visit none of his flock in their own dwellings without exciting suspicion, and exposing them to peril. Under these circumstances the brethren could not but question the duty of remaining; more especially as the government pretended to believe that their teaching of Christianity had only been a cover under which they promoted political purposes. Their most judicious native friends also appeared to think that, for the future interests of the gospel in the country, it would be best that they should retire, at least for a season.

The government would gladly have retained the artisans, especially those who had taught them to work in iron and to construct machinery; but, as Christianity was proscribed, these Christian men declined the overtures of the government, and with blighted hopes and deepest sorrow, chiefly on account of the scattered and exposed condition of the infant church they had been honoured to gather, Messrs. Freeman, Cameron, Chick, and Kitching, left the capital in June, 1835, Messrs. Johns and Baker remaining for a season.

To these two mission families the ensuing year was a period of anxiety and distress rarely equalled, and perhaps never surpassed, in the missionary experience of modern times. The departure of the other missionaries failed to assuage the wrath of the government against the Christians. The servants of those who had left were subjected to the treacherous ordeal of the tangena, to prove whether or no they were exempt from any malign influence contracted by residing in the houses of the Christian teachers, and two of them died. The infant of another was destroyed by the queen's orders the day after its birth. The government became more oppressive. Sunday was desecrated by compulsory work and by public amusements; while vice, disease, and poverty increased among the people.

During this time Mr. Johns translated into Malagasy that inimitable itinerary of Christian life, "The Pilgrim's Progress." Six copies were transcribed, and distributed in manuscript among the Christians. The peculiar structure of the native language, in which names of persons are generally descriptive of some quality or circumstance connected with parentage, birth, or character, one name often comprising a complete sentence, favoured the transfusion into the translation of much of the spirit, truth, and beauty of the original. A copy of the translation was sent to Mr. Freeman, then in England, where it was printed and forwarded to the Christians, by whom it was joyfully received, and, next to the Scriptures, prized as their most valued treasure; at which we cannot be surprised when we consider the many graphic delineations of Christian life, as then existing in Madagascar, which that incomparable work contains.

Gradually the Christians sought out their fellow-believers, using the utmost caution before disclosing their own feelings to others. Sometimes a recognition was secured by reference to Jer. xxx.15,—"If I declare it unto thee, wilt thou not directly put me to death?" To which the answer would be a naming of the following verse:—" As the Lord liveth, which made us this soul, I will not put thee to death, neither will I give thee into the hand of those men who seek thy life." The Christians ventured afterwards to meet secretly in their own houses or in those of the missionaries, but more frequently they met on the summits of solitary mountains, whence they could survey the rocky hills, and brown or grassy plains, and observe the movements of men at a great distance. In such places they would give expression to their pent-up feelings by singing the praises of God their Saviour, and reading His blessed word, without fear of being overheard or disturbed by those hunting for their lives.

The application to teach and to print books being sternly refused, and a fresh persecution having again broken forth, and having received intimation that the government expected them to leave, the missionaries deemed it their duty to follow their brethren. Leaving with the native Christians about seventy complete Bibles, several boxes of the Psalms, Testaments, hymn-books, and others of different kinds—the chief part of which were buried for greater security,—and after many prayers, Messrs. Johns and Baker, the last of the missionaries, sorrowfully parted from their Christian brethren, and set out for the coast, in July, 1836.

The object of the persecution which now broke forth was a member of a family of rank and position, who had become a sincere disciple of Christ before the government had proscribed Christianity. Her name was Rafaravavy. She belonged to a family remarkable for zealous devotion to the idols and to the superstitions of the country. This distinguished lady had been awakened to a concern for her soul's salvation by the conversation of a native Christian. The missionaries had afterwards every reason to believe that her heart had been changed by the Holy Spirit, and that she had become a true convert to Christ. Before the suppression of Christianity she had obtained one of the largest houses in the capital, which she appropriated to Christian worship; and her simplicity of character and earnestness induced many to attend the preaching of the gospel.

Notwithstanding the punishment threatened by the queen, Rafaravavy and a few female friends occasionally met in her house on Sunday evenings to read and pray. On the 17th of June three of her slaves went to the judge and accused her of these practices. A Christian who heard the accusation hastened to inform her of it. She immediately placed her Bible and other books in a place of security, while her father, on hearing what the slaves had done, had them confined in irons. Rafaravavy, however, ordered them to be liberated, sent for them, forgave them, wept over them, and spoke to them of the mercy and forgiveness of God through Christ. Two of them afterwards became Christians, and one of them died for her faith.

The judge demanded the names of her companions, and, on her refusal to give them, reported her offence to the queen, who in great wrath exclaimed, "Is it possible that any one is so daring as to defy me? And that one a woman, too! Go and put her to death at once." Two of the queen's high officers, and a woman of rank and influence with the queen, pleaded for the life of the accused, on account of services which her father and brother had rendered to the State, and the sentence was deferred.

Rafaravavy had one small tract still in her possession. It was on the love and influence of the Holy Spirit. The expression of a devout Christian recorded in that small book—viz., "I will cast myself at the feet of Jesus, and if I perish, I will perish there;" to which some one had answered, "If you perish there, you will be the first that ever did, for sooner shall the heavens and the earth pass away than the Saviour reject any one coming to Him"— seemed to have made a deep impression on her mind.

On the day on which the last of the missionaries were to leave the capital, Rafaravavy, not knowing the hour at which she might be summoned by the executioner, went, at about three o'clock in the morning, to take leave of them. The interview was deeply affecting to both parties. Mrs. Johns afterwards remarked, "I shall never forget the serenity and composure with which she related to me the consolation she found in pleading the promises of God, and drawing near to Him in prayer." It was on the same day that, contrary to the expectation of Rafaravavy and her friends, the queen sent an officer to say that the services of her father had secured her pardon; but she must pay a fine, and if ever again guilty of a similar offence, life alone would then make atonement for her crime.

In order to avoid frequent interruption and danger, from the constant watch kept over her every movement by the emissaries of the government, Rafaravavy bought a house at Ambatonakanga; there a small company of believers, some even from the district of Vonizongo, many miles distant, occasionally met at night for prayer. Sometimes they travelled twenty miles to hold, on the top of a mountain, or in the hollows on its sides, their religious meetings, losing all sense of weariness in the freedom and security with which they could join in praise and prayer to God.

About twelve months after his departure, Mr. Johns visited the coast, and at Tamatave was gladdened by the arrival of four Christians with intelligence of their brethren in the interior. They reported that the mind of the queen remained the same in regard to Christianity. "It is thought," they wrote, "that we shall certainly forget the word of God now that we have no teachers. The queen does not know that the best Teacher of all, the Holy Spirit, is still with us." "We will go forward," they added, "in the strength of the Lord. If we confess Him, He will also confess us, when He shall come in the clouds to judge the world, and to present all that are His, blameless, before the Father for ever. We have opportunities of meeting on the mountains to sing and pray on the Sabbath. We have also three services in the capital during the week, after sunset. Our meetings are large, through the diligence of the disciples in conversation, in season and out of season; so that when we examine the state of 'Pilgrim,' we wish to be like him in 'progress.' All the Christians here are teaching others to read, there are ten learning with one friend, six with another, four with another, and the number is increasing. How much does the compassion of the Saviour console us now! We are filled with wonder at the work of the Holy Spirit; for it is He who persuades us to increase thus in love. The word is indeed true that says, 'I will send unto you the Comforter.' 'It is expedient for you that I go away.' Precious to us now is Jesus. He is our rock, our shield, our hope, and our life."

We have seen how, in a campaign in the south, the heroic faith of the Christian soldiers sustained them, when they refused to acknowledge the claims of the national idol carried in their ranks to the battle. They were threatened by their commanding officer with the vengeance of that idol, but trusting in God, they stedfastly advanced in the conflict where danger was greatest, and where the largest number were expected to fall. In another army that same faith was sustained by the love of Christ in the heart. In a letter to Mr. Johns from the Christians at the capital, speaking of the death of a Christian soldier who had fallen in an expedition to the north, the writer observes, "He was a beloved brother, and we frequently found great pleasure in

FAITH OF A CHRISTIAN SOLDIER.   113

his society. One of our friends who was with him in his tent when he died, having asked him if he had any fear, he replied, 'Why should I fear to die while Jesus is my friend? He hath loved me with an everlasting love, and I love Him because He first loved me. I am persuaded He will not leave me now, and I am full of joy at the thought of leaving this sinful world to be for ever with my Saviour.'" Some of the companions of this young soldier remarking that they never heard him mention the name of the Saviour without tears, and a missionary afterwards, noticing the same, having asked how it was, he replied, "How can I do otherwise than feel, when I mention the name of that beloved Saviour who suffered and died on the cross for me?" With such devout soldiers in the army, we cease to wonder that the military posts in Madagascar became centres of Christian light and blessing to many in the surrounding country.

CHAPTER V.

Arrest of Rafaravavy—Confession of Paul before the judges—A Christian's feelings on the way to execution—Fearful conflagration in the city—Postponement of Rafaravavy's execution—Arrest, examination, and execution of the second martyr—Torture of his wife—Flight of Rafaravavy and her companions—Perils and suffering—Honesty of Christian slaves—Flight of the Christians to Tamatave—Safe embarkation—Their song of praise to God — Welcomes in London and among the churches in England—Their return to Mauritius—Capture, torture, and execution of the praying people in the capital—Friendship among the Christians—Condition of the fugitives in Madagascar.

WHILE the Christian messengers from the afflicted church at the capital, and the missionary who had come to sympathize with them, were engaged on the coast in affectionate conference and prayer, their enemies at the capital, influenced apparently by the hope of profit, were active in their efforts to secure their condemnation. Two women, one of them related to the Christians, accused ten of the latter of meeting on the Sunday for prayer at the house of Rafaravavy. The chief officer of the queen, to whom the judges carried the accusation, declared with an oath, "Then they shall die! for they despise the queen's law." They were all immediately arrested.

Officers were repeatedly sent to Rafaravavy, chiefly to discover her associates, stating on one occasion that the queen knew who her companions were, but wished to give her the opportunity of telling the whole truth.*

This benevolent woman, careful of the lives of her fellow-Christians, answered, " If, as you say, the queen knows as well as I do, why do you ask me again ? " They then brought one of her companions who had confessed that she prayed with her, and when confronted with her Rafaravavy said, " We have prayed together; we do not deny it;" and when further asked, " Where have you prayed ? " she replied, " In our own houses, and in many other places. Wherever we went we endeavoured to remember God, and pray to Him." On being asked if they had not met for prayer at Akatso, a mountain, they answered, "Yes, but not there only. Wherever we went we remembered God, in the house and out of doors, in the town and in the country, or on the mountains."

The officers then proceeded to the other Christians already in prison, chiefly for the purpose of inducing them to name those not yet accused. They falsely told a young woman whose name was Ra-sa-la-ma, that the others had already given the names of all the Christians, so that it would be of no avail for her to refuse to mention those she knew. Influenced by this specious declaration, Rasalama mentioned the names of seven who had not before been impeached, and these, amongst others esteemed and beloved,

* The usual penalty was diminished when confession was made.

included Raintsiheva,, the diviner, known among the Christians as Paul. The seven were immediately apprehended, and the declarations—confessions, as they were called—of the whole were then laid before the queen.

The answer which the aged Paul had given to the judges afforded but little ground for his condemnation. He said, "I have certainly prayed to that God who created me, and has supported me, and is Himself the source of all good, to make me a good man. I prayed that He would bless the queen, and give her true happiness in this world, and in that which is to come. I asked Him to bless the officers and judges, and all the people, to make them good, so that there might be no more brigands and liars, and that God would make all the people wise and good." No wonder that some of the officers said there was no evil, but good in such praying. When the officers retired to confer on the course they should pursue towards these people, one of their number adduced the statement of Paul on behalf of the Christians, saying, "Let us do nothing rashly, lest we advise the queen to shed innocent blood. What is their guilt?" The chief officer replied, "They pray to Jehovah, to Jesus, to Christ;" and when one reasonable man said, "These may be with them but different names for one God, as we have several names for God," the minister replied, "The queen has forbidden any to pray to Jehovah, and having despised the commandments of the queen, they are guilty."

Fourteen days longer the Christians and their friends were kept in great anxiety, then an order was sent to the people in the market to go and seize the property of Rafaravavy. The first intimation which she received of danger was the rush of the rabble into her dwelling, seizing everything therein, pulling down the building, and carrying every part of it away. Meanwhile, four of the royal guard, usually employed in the execution of criminals, ordered Rafaravavy to follow them; and when she asked whither they were leading her, the answer was, "The queen knows what to do with you." They led her along the road leading to Ambohipotsy, where criminals were usually put to death; she therefore concluded that orders had been given for her execution. But the fear of death was removed, and the prayer of Stephen was repeatedly uttered by the way. In calling those eventful moments to her recollection she afterwards said, that she felt as if all relating to earth was ended, and wished her spirit was liberated from her body. One beloved Christian approached near enough for her to speak to him, and she asked him privately to go with her to the end, that if she were strengthened to bear testimony to the presence of Christ in her last moments, it might encourage any who might have to follow. He answered, "I shall not leave you, dear sister. Cleave to Him on whom you have built your hope." Another dear friend had before said, "Fear not, beloved sister; though there may be affliction here, there is rest in heaven." Shortly afterwards they entered a house belonging to one of the subordinates of the commander-in-chief, where she was bound in fetters, called by a name which signifies "causing many tears." One of the soldiers said to the smith who was riveting these on her limbs, "Do not make them too fast. It will be difficult to take them off, and she is to be executed at cock-crow to-morrow," the still and quiet hour often chosen for inflicting death on criminals.

But during the solemn darkness of those intervening hours of night the city was roused from its slumbers, and thrown into the wildest confusion of dismay, by the bursting out of a fierce conflagration, which burned down many of the dry, closely packed wood and thatch houses, and spread the greatest consternation among the people. The morning was dark, and clouds drifted across the sky, bearing innumerable fragments of burning material over the palace yard, and filling the minds of the beholders with terror. The officer in charge of the city, on seeing the confusion created by the fire, had issued an order to discontinue government service; and although the executioners had previously received instructions to put their prisoner to death, they now delayed the execution of the sentence until further orders. In reference to this occurrence one of the natives was afterwards heard to remark, "God is indeed the sovereign of life!"

On the day when Rafaravavy was taken to be put to death, the remaining prisoners were distributed amongst the chief officers or their subordinates.

Paul and Rafaravavy were placed in irons in separate houses, those two being considered leaders of the Christians. At the same time the officers and people were collected to hear the message of the queen, in which she said, " I will reduce them to perpetual slavery now. If I find out that they have companions, and have assembled in private houses, I will put them to death whenever they are accused."

Among the ten Christians in confinement was Rasalama, the Christian woman whom the falsehood of the officers had betrayed into revealing the names of seven of the Christians, who were now her fellow-prisoners. A relative having expressed her surprise that she should have accused her friends, since their praying had been unknown to the government until she mentioned them, she was deeply grieved on thus learning that she had been the cause of their arrest; and she was overheard to express her astonishment that the people of God, who had neither excited rebellion, nor stolen property, nor spoken ill of any one, should be reduced to perpetual slavery. She was also heard to say that she was not afraid when the Tsitialaingia came to her house, but rather rejoiced that she was counted worthy to suffer affliction for believing in Jesus; adding, "I have hope of life in heaven." Tsitialaingia, signifying " hater of lies," is the name of a round-headed silver lance, on which the name of the queen is engraved,* and also of the officer by whom it is carried. It is

* In the representation of Malagasy spears on the next page, that in the centre shows the form of Tsitialaingia.

the representative or emblem of the power of the queen, and seems to be regarded as endowed with supernatural means of detecting falsehood. It is borne by officers sent to arrest persons suspected or accused of crimes against the sovereign, and who are then said to be arrested by Tsitialaingia. The haft as well as the head of the spear or lance is of silver. When the officers bearing this spear reached the house of an accused person, the spear itself was fixed in the doorway, and as long as it remained in that position no one could enter or leave the house.

The offensive part of Rasalama's words was reported to the commander-in-chief, who commended the informer, and ordered the prisoner, who continued singing hymns, to be put in irons, and while thus suffering to be beaten. She said, "My life shall go for my companions. You say Rafaravavy will be put to death; but no, she will not die. I shall be killed instead of her." Her extreme agitation of mind, added to the feebleness of body produced by the cruel beating and severe sufferings, caused her friends to think that perhaps, for a short season, her mind scarcely retained its balance; but it was perfectly restored afterwards. She was ordered for execution the next morning, and on the previous afternoon was put in irons, which, being fastened to the feet, hands, knees, and neck, confined the whole body in a position of excruciating pain. In the early morning she sang hymns as she was borne along to the place of execution, expressing her joy in the knowledge of the gospel; and, on passing the chapel in which she had been baptized, she exclaimed, "There I heard the words of the Saviour." After being borne more than a mile farther, she reached the fatal spot, a broad dry shallow fosse or ditch, strewn with the bones of previous criminals, outside what was formerly a fortification, at the southern extremity of the mountain on which the city stands. Two or three hundred feet below this Malagasy Golgotha stretches the wide plain, spotted with villages, verdant with rice-fields, and irrigated by streams from the Ikiopa, which, issuing from the lofty Ankaratra, almost encircles the capital in its course to the sea on the west.

Here, permission being granted her to pray, Rasalama calmly knelt on the earth, committed her spirit into the hands of her Redeemer, and fell with the executioners' spears buried in her body. Earth and hell had done their worst. Some few of the bystanders, it was reported, cried out, "Where is the

God she prayed to, that He does not save her now?" Others were moved to pity for one whom they deemed an innocent sufferer; and the heathen executioners repeatedly declared, "There is some charm in the religion of the white people which takes away the fear of death." Her intimate companions were in prison or concealment, but one faithful and loving friend who witnessed her calm and peaceful death, when he returned, exclaimed, "If I might die so tranquil and happy a death, I would willingly die for the Saviour too." So suffered, on the fourteenth day of August, 1837,[*] Rasalama, the first who died for Christ of the Martyr Church of Madagascar, which, in its early infancy, thus received its baptism of blood. Such were the calm, quiet, but glorious triumphs of the grace and love of Christ which were witnessed in this world. But how dim and feeble, how utterly beyond all conception here, would be the vision which opened before the liberated spirit, and the transport which would fill the ransomed soul, when, set free by the executioner's spear, it was "absent from the body, present with the Lord"!

After the death of Rasalama, the other Christians under arrest, with two who had been absent at Tamatave when accused, were consigned to irredeemable slavery, but their wives and children were allowed to be redeemed by their friends. Two hundred, in all, were enslaved on this occasion. The aged Paul, who

[*] Letter from Rev. D. Johns, *Missionary Magazine*, February, 1838.

From Photograph by Rev. W. Ellis.

PLACE OF THE FIRST MARTYRDOM.

had been heavily ironed night and day, and guarded as a felon, became a slave of the chief minister, who sent him to field-work with four other Christian slaves. They were in the rice-fields all day and in irons all night, but had a hut to themselves; and the venerable servant of Christ proved a great source of consolation to his fellow-slaves, often repeating to them the forty-sixth Psalm, which he had committed to memory, and leading their minds to their divine and loving Saviour.

Rafaravavy, who had now been some months in irons, constantly guarded by soldiers, was, by an order of the queen, sold in the public market to the chief military officer; and he placed her in the charge of one of his aides-de-camp, who was a relative, and who treated her kindly, giving her liberty to go and come, so that her work was not neglected. During this period she had the happiness of spending much time with her husband, to whom she was greatly attached. He was a colonel in the army on the west coast, and having heard of her circumstances he obtained leave of absence for a few months to come to the capital.

Rafaralahy, a young man about two-and-twenty years of age, who had accompanied Rafaravavy herself, when it was supposed she was being carried forth to execution, and had witnessed the tranquil death of Rasalama, had been accustomed to receive a number of the Christians at his house, which was nearly two miles from the capital, for reading and prayer; and Rafaravavy, after her liberation, soon joined this little band of Christians. An apostate from the faith, a former teacher and friend of Rafaralahy, who had become his debtor for a sum of money, when asked to pay it, went immediately and accused his friend and benefactor to the queen's minister of holding meetings for religious worship in his house, giving the names of twelve persons who were accustomed to meet with him. Rafaralahy was arrested and put in irons, every effort being made to induce him to reveal the names of his companions. But he simply replied, "I am here, I have done it. Let the queen do as she pleases with me, I will not accuse my friends."

After being confined in heavy irons for three days he was taken out for execution. On the way he spoke to the officers of the love and mercy of Christ, and of his own happiness in the prospect of so soon seeing that divine Redeemer who had loved him and died to save his soul. Having reached the place of execution, the same spot on which Rasalama, nearly twelve months before, had suffered, he spent the last moments of his life in supplication for his country and his persecuted brethren, and in commending his soul to his Saviour. As he rose from his knees the executioners were preparing, as was customary, to throw him on the ground, when he said that was needless, he was prepared to die; and quietly laying himself down he was instantly put to death, his friends being afterwards allowed to inter his body in the ancestral grave.

Immediately after the execution of Rafaralahy,

his young wife, a quiet, timid woman, whom the Christians regarded as a believer in Christ, and his Christian attendant, were seized, bound, cruelly flogged, and threatened with severer punishment unless they revealed Rafaralahy's associates. They bore this torture until, overcome with pain, terror, and exhaustion, their power of endurance gave way, and they mentioned the names of those who had been present at the meetings for worship.

On the same day, at a short distance from the capital, in the quiet dwelling of a respectable civilian, three Christian women, all equally ignorant of the death and suffering which had been inflicted on their friends, were conversing with the master of the house, when a slave suddenly entered and gave a note to Rafaravavy, one of the three females. The countenance of the reader changed as she read and declared to her friends that Rafaralahy had been put to death, and his wife and companion tortured until the names of his companions had been revealed, including her own and the two friends then with her. Instant flight afforded the only possibility of escaping from certain death; and the three Christian women, leaving the house of their friend, travelled in company towards the capital. At the foot of Ambohipotsy, the place of execution, they stopped, united in prayer, bade each other farewell, and taking different paths, separated, not expecting to meet again on earth. The two women fled to distant parts of the country, and were not heard of for some time afterwards.

Rafaravavy entered the city, and after conference

and prayer with four of her friends, and sending in search of Paul and others involved in equal peril, they left the city at midnight. How imminent had been their danger they did not know until afterwards. A warrant for the death of Rafaravavy had been prepared the same evening, and the next morning the officers to whom it was confided had gone to the house of her master where she resided, and to every other house which she was known to visit, in order to seize and convey her to execution. Paul, and a nephew of Rafaravavy, an eminent Christian, were afterwards arrested and put in irons; but the government delayed putting them to death in hopes of finding Rafaravavy and her friend, and of striking greater terror into the minds of the people by executing at one time four of the Christian leaders.

Leaving the city under the darkness of midnight the fugitives travelled towards the west, and continuing their journey by the least frequented roads, they reached in the evening of the following day Itanimanina, more than forty miles from the capital, where the cordial welcome of friends added to the grateful joy which their preservation inspired. They had not long shared the protection and hospitality thus afforded, when a friend in the service of the government arrived to invite some of the Christians to seek shelter with him in a forest to the eastward of Ambatomanga, on the opposite side of the capital. From him they learned that their escape had caused a great stir in the capital, and that soldiers had been sent out in every direction to search for them. David, his wife, and Joseph returned with their friend to seek shelter in the forest. Finding when they reached the city that David's wife had not been accused, she remained there with her friends, while her husband and his companion proceeded to the forest. These men were distinguished Christians who had been sold into slavery on account of their faith, and were employed by their masters as traders, as was also another of those now under accusation. They had spent the last hours before their flight in packing up the goods belonging to their masters, making out clear accounts of all they had sold, putting the money in the package, and leaving it properly addressed for their masters. One of these, a high officer of the government, on opening the package and finding the property and money, was astonished, and said, "It is not customary for slaves when they run away to send back their masters' property. These people would make excellent servants if it were not for their praying."

Here, by moving from place to place for security, they remained for about three months, occasionally suffering for want of food, as their friend carried most of the rice on which they subsisted on his back from the capital, a distance of forty miles. Simeon, who was concealed for many weeks in a sort of stage or place for cooking utensils, built over the fireplace, in a native house near the city, afterwards shared their safety in the forest, and their suffering from scarcity of food.

With the kind friends who had opened their doors to the Christian fugitives, Rafaravavy found shelter for several weeks, sleeping under their roof at night, but retiring for concealment before daylight every morning to the hollows of an adjacent mountain. Venturing to return one evening before dark she was discovered, and her hiding-place reported to the chief minister at the capital, who sent eight soldiers to apprehend her. So unconscious was their victim, that two of the soldiers were within a minute or two of entering the house before its inmates had the slightest intimation of their approach, and Rafaravavy had only time to conceal herself behind a mat before they entered, stated their business, and inquired where she was. Every syllable they uttered she heard, and trembled lest her loud breathing should betray her. After a lengthened conversation the owner of the house went out, and the men, supposing he had gone to inform Rafaravavy, followed him, and thus allowed time for their victim to escape by another way.

The fact of affording shelter to the Christian fugitives involved their protectors in equal peril; and the arrival of the soldiers in the district rendering their own dwelling no longer safe, they became homeless wanderers with their friends. The perils through which they passed, through the weary and anxious weeks while hiding for their lives, rendered their privations and sufferings still more distressing. Sometimes they found that the soldiers had gone before them, leaving orders with the head men of the village to apprehend any women not belonging to that part of the country who might come amongst them. At other times the soldiers would be following along the same road, or a number would come upon them suddenly, causing some to run into the bush, and those unable to fly to seek concealment by plunging into some bog which might be near, in which they sometimes sunk so deep as to be unable to extricate themselves without help. Sometimes the soldiers would halt for the night in a village, beyond which, in order to avoid suspicion, the Christians did not proceed until the early morning, or, as they expressed it, before the light enabled one to " see the colour of the cattle." At one time Rafaravavy was concealed in an empty room with an unfastened door, before which while the soldiers who searched the house were standing, the master of the house, a friend of the Christians, succeeded in diverting their attention for a few moments in another direction, and thus the Christian escaped.

At times they were drenched by the falling sheets of tropical rain on the barren mountains over which they travelled in order to avoid being seen. Sometimes they slept among the large stones and boulders by the sides of the rivers, or lay concealed among the tall grass on the flat top of some ancient sepulchre. As they frequently travelled by night, they met with brigands and robbers, and on one occasion discovered that they had taken shelter in one of their caverns. Their preservation amidst dangers so imminent, during the three months in which they were wanderers in the country west of Antananarivo impressed them deeply with a sense of the ceaseless protection of their heavenly Father, and inspired hopes of their ultimate deliverance.

Not less remarkable and cheering was the evidence, which this season of exposure and danger revealed, of the extent and value of the influence which the Christian mission at the capital had spread over the country—the fruit of the past, the seed of the future. Except when inspecting the schools established by the government, the missionaries had seldom travelled beyond the suburbs. The first halting-place of the Christians who fled from the city, at the period now under review, was nearly fifty miles distant, yet they found Christian families who welcomed and sheltered them. And often during their wanderings over the western portion of Ankova, as well as during their subsequent journey to the eastern coast, they found Christian residents where none were known or expected, and more frequently in outlying houses than in the villages. Some of these Christians possessed portions of the Scriptures, and were able to read them. At one place these books of the Christians were preserved in a box, and buried in the ground. Even at the solitary houses it was found that the Sabbath was kept; and in some instances members of families more or less related to each other, but residing several miles apart, came together on the Sunday to unite in Christian worship. To the hunted Christians such gatherings were indeed like fountains in the desert, and from one to another they went as from strength to strength.

Equally cheering was the holy bond of brotherhood which united the Christians, thus scattered among the heathen, to each other in mutual confidence and love, alike in joy and in sorrow. Nor was the spontaneous affection with which they welcomed, sheltered, and helped on their way the brethren fleeing for their lives, less noble and generous. Late one evening, on entering a village, and hearing in one of the houses a great noise as of many persons talking, the fugitives passed quietly on to the house of a female friend, who was struck dumb by their appearance, but at length told them that soldiers were seeking them in every direction, that a party of them were at that time in the village, and in the very house in which they had heard the noise as they passed. "And where," asked this true friend in their hour of need, " shall I hide you to-night and to-morrow morning?" She afterwards concealed them in a pit near her house, the mouth of which was covered with thorn bushes. They remained there a night and a day, and then removed to a plantation of manioc, belonging also to their friend, where they found shelter for several days and nights. One day they saw, from this place of concealment, the accuser of Rafaralahy and eight soldiers pass close by in search of them ; but they remained undiscovered. After continuing here ten or twelve days, they left their protector and friend, to proceed to the residence of another friend a few miles distant. How honourable to the feelings and true to the spirit of Christianity was the conduct of this truly faithful woman, who, though she knew that her own life was imperilled by affording shelter to her fellow-Christians, did not recommend them to seek safety elsewhere, but unhesitatingly accepted the danger that she might honour her Saviour by protecting the lives of His people!

Another friend who had been deeply anxious, knowing how many were hunting for their lives, burst into tears of joy on their arrival at his dwelling, and provided for their safety. While sharing the hospitality and protection of this generous Christian family, they heard that Mr. Johns was at Tamatave; and as this offered a prospect of escape, they returned to the capital, which they reached in three days. Here, with the advice of friends, Rafaravavy and her companion Sarah remained in concealment, while the husband of the latter, with another Christian, set out for the eastern coast, in order to confer with Mr. Johns, if still there, on the possibility of their escaping from the country. Acting on the advice of Christians at Antananarivo, Mr. Johns had remained at Tamatave; he welcomed his Christian brethren, and, with a valuable friend, arranged their escape from the island. This friend placed the messenger from Rafaravavy in a place of safety at a distance from Tamatave, and sent his fellow-Christian back with letters to the fugitives to hasten to the village on the coast where their companion was concealed.

Notwithstanding all the aid their friend could give, those concealed in the forest suffered so much from exposure, sickness and hunger, that they made

THE TRAVELLER'S TREE (*Urania Speciosa*),
Showing the mode of obtaining water.

their way by short stages to the capital, where they obtained food and shelter. When the messenger from the coast returned with a letter to the Christians advising them to attempt to reach Tamatave, Rafaravavy, Razafy, and three others condemned to death on account of their faith, left their companions, and, accompanied by two friends as servants, commenced their last, and in some respects most dangerous journey. They did not venture, for four days and nights, to enter any house. Some of them were recognised on the road. Their steps at other times were so closely followed by travellers along the same road, as to force upon them the impression that they were either known or suspected, and were liable to be apprehended if not actually put to death.

Two days' journey had brought them to the precipitous Angova pass, after which they travelled through the rugged forest, the country of the beautiful rofia palm and the traveller's tree. On reaching Andevoranto, on the coast, their money being insufficient to hire a canoe and proceed by water, they travelled along the margin of the sea or the lakes, and walked along the deep, soft, sandy beach, until they approached the port of Tamatave, where, concealing themselves in the jungle, they sent the servants with a note to their friend residing there. They knew that in the neighbourhood of the port the soldiers were constantly passing, and the two days thus spent were among the most intensely anxious and exhausting they had ever known, for they had been three days without food. Their trust was in God, and they were not disappointed. When the messengers returned, the smile on their countenances revealed their success. Their friend was waiting for them, and would come in a canoe for them after dark.

The sun had not set when they proceeded to the appointed rendezvous. Shortly afterwards their friend came, and conveyed them in his canoe safely to his dwelling. They breathed more freely when they found themselves within protecting walls and beneath a sheltering roof; but felt scarcely assured of the reality of their position and treatment, so different from those which had marked every waking hour of the time since they had parted from their friends at the capital. The friend whom God had here raised up for their protection, was a military officer as well as a local judge, secretly also a believer in Christ; and he incurred equal risk with the fugitives by the shelter and help which he now rendered them. He received them with sincere kindness, set food before them, and they united together in reading God's word, and in rendering praise to their divine Protector. He informed them that, in consequence of arrangements with Mr. Johns, he expected a ship, and would see them safe on board. He told them also that his official engagements at the port would not allow him to be much with them, but he would leave them in charge of his nephew, who would supply their wants; and when he left in the morning, he directed that they should hold themselves in readiness to come at any time he might send for them. When the ship arrived, and had taken in her cargo, their friend sent a confidential messenger to tell them to cut their hair, and follow the guide he had sent to the port. The darkness of night was descending when they left the house and proceeded to the jungle near the sea, where their guide left them with anxiously palpitating hearts, while he informed those who were to take them to the ship. Friends soon came with a suit of sailors' clothes for each, which they put on in the bush, while another friend went to the landing-place to divert the attention of the guards.

The moment had now arrived when life or death seemed to depend upon the slightest movement. Noiselessly, and with almost suppressed breath, they proceeded to the water's edge, entered the boat, pushed off from the shore, passed over the rippling waters of the bay, and reached the ship. As soon as the last of the Christians was safely on the deck, the captain, rubbing his hands, addressed to them the welcome and assuring words of their own language, "Efa kabary" (finished is the business, or accomplished is the object). The Christians, as soon as they could realize their actual safety, and could command their feelings, asked permission to offer a song of praise to God for their deliverance, which being granted, the sailors and the captain listened with evident pleasure, while standing together on the deck the Christians thus gave expression to their devout and grateful feelings. The cool, fresh breeze from the land in the early morning wafted the ship out of harbour, and they reached Mauritius in safety on the 14th of October, 1838.

In about a month this little party were followed by the generous Christian friend who had arranged for their escape, and who afterwards found that neither his own life nor that of his nephew was safe in Madagascar, in consequence of the aid he had rendered to the Christians. By Mr. Johns, by their countrymen, by Mr. Le Brun, and other Christian friends, the liveliest gratitude was manifested on behalf of the rescued Christians, who afterwards proceeded, by way of the Cape of Good Hope, to England. Arriving in May, 1839, they were affectionately welcomed by the directors of the London Missionary Society, as well as afterwards by the friends of missions at a large and deeply interesting meeting in Exeter Hall.

Several of the Malagasy Christians had the privilege of becoming acquainted with a number of the friends of missions in London; they also visited, in company with one of their teachers, several of the churches in the country, and were not only encouraged by the kind interest manifested on behalf of Madagascar, but they secured the respect and esteem of those in our own country who witnessed their consistent spirit and deportment. Rafaravavy and Razafy deeply interested those of their own sex who, during their short stay in England, made their acquaintance. Both had been in comfortable circumstances in their own country. Rafaravavy inherited property, with which she served God; and her husband was a colonel in the army. Razafy's husband was a respected civilian. Both were distinguished, especially the former, by intelligence, urbanity, gentleness of demeanour, benevolence, and sincerity of character. All these qualities, purified and elevated by the fear and love of God, when associated with the imprisonment, torture, privation, and danger which these Christian women had suffered on account of their faith, made a deep impression on the minds of their friends, and is cherished still. They were witnesses for the gospel in Madagascar, and earnests of its future triumphs.

The Malagasy Christians, accompanied by Mrs. Johns, returned to Mauritius early in 1842, where a piece of ground was purchased at Moka, and a house built, in which she resided until her death. Here she gathered around her the destitute refugees from her own country, furnishing for them a secure and quiet home, while endeavouring by her teaching, example, and benevolence, to bring them to believe and trust in the Saviour, whose presence and blessing she had herself so largely experienced. Since her death her place has been a home for Malagasy Christians, as well as a missionary station, where Simeon, the last survivor of the refugees, still resides, labouring faithfully for the benefit of his countrymen. Mr. Johns, with whom Simeon had returned to Mauritius, maintained affectionate intercourse by letter with the Christians at the capital of Madagascar, and made frequent voyages to different parts of the coast, in the hope of saving some of them; but the difficulties proved insuperable, and in 1843 he sank under the influence of fever, fatigue, and anxiety. In his death the Society lost a faithful missionary and the native Christians a firm, true, and indefatigable friend.

Although a number of those who were seized after the public execution of Rafaralahy had been sold into permanent slavery, all these did not escape death. Ravahiny (the stranger), a young woman of considerable personal attractions, whom her husband had already divorced on account of her having become a Christian, was, at the time referred to, sold into slavery for life. Her father had for the same reason denied her the shelter of his roof. Her relations, all heathen, feeling indignant at her abandonment of the religion of her country, and disgraced by her present servile condition, endeavoured to compass her death. They applied to the chief officer of the queen to receive her among his slaves or his concubines, which required that she should be previously tried by the tangena, to ascertain whether she practised witchcraft, or used charms, which they pretended were possessed by the Christians. Though strongly opposed to the ordeal on account of the treachery exercised in its administration, she was forced to drink the poison, and perished under its effects—the third victim of the Martyr Church of Madagascar to the fierce hatred of the idolaters.

Shortly after this three Christian females, two of them wives of the companions of Rafaravavy, were accused of meeting together for prayer. The officer sent in the evening to apprehend them, found two of them reading the Scriptures. One of them escaped, and while the man was beating the other whom he had secured, her Bible fell from her dress. She was then taken to his house, and again beaten by six men to force her to reveal the names of her companions. This savage treatment of the woman failing to secure their object, she was taken next morning before the chief officer of the queen, and on refusing to give information about those who had associated with her in reading and prayer, she was ordered to be flogged until she did so. She bore the anguish and indignity of the public laceration of her body with unfaltering fidelity to her fellow-Christians, until, faint with pain and loss of blood, she swooned at the feet of her brutal torturers. After her recovery she was sold into irredeemable slavery, and was ordered to take the tangena, but saved her life by escaping before it had been administered. Those accused at the same time fled to the uninhabited parts of the country, and were not afterwards heard of.

The escape of the victims seemed to increase the destructive rage of their persecutors, and orders were issued by the queen to the soldiers sent in search of them, to bind hand and foot any whom they might find, to dig a pit on the spot, hurl them head foremost into the pit, and to pour boiling water upon them until they ceased to live. They were then to fill up the pit with earth, and continue their search for others. The reason assigned for this revolting barbarity in destroying the Christians wherever they might be seized, was the pretence that they could not have escaped so often had they not possessed some powerful charm, which might be exercised for evil to others, and which rendered it dangerous to bring them to the capital even for trial.

We have seen, in the instance above related, that the reception of Christianity, in the judgment of the heathen, severed the closest ties of social life, causing the husband to repudiate his wife and the father to expel his daughter from his house. On the other hand, Christianity exalted friendship to something far above the interchange of the ordinary courtesies and attentions of social life, making it a reality and a bond, than which no earthly tie was stronger or more lasting. Many of the Christians belonged to different clans, dwelt in different parts of the country, or occupied different ranks in society; but the possession of a common faith, the trust in one Saviour, the hope of one heaven, made their interest in each other here a proof of vital union unknown in the country before.

When Rafaravavy and her companions travelled forty or fifty miles from her home before seeking help or rest, they were received, sheltered, and provided for as if they had been the nearest relatives.

One of the marvels and causes of offence to the heathen was that the Christians were all of one mind, and always helped one another; and the trials through which they were now passing called into practical exercise, intensified, and purified the bonds of holy union by which they were united in love and interest in each other's welfare.

The number of Christians spread over the country was increased by those whom the growing severity of persecution forced to fly from their homes in the city, to seek shelter and food at a distance, or perish. All were deeply affected by the barbarous orders given to those sent out to seek and destroy them. " We have heard," was their remark, in a letter sent to one of the missionaries about this time, " of the orders of the queen respecting us, and the manner in which we are to be put to death if discovered. We still confide in the compassion of the Saviour. Can you do anything to rescue us? We think of the death awaiting us. 'The spirit is willing, but the flesh is weak.'"

In another letter to Mr. Johns they observe, " We state to you our condition, that, *if possible*, you may do something to relieve us. We say 'if possible,' for our Saviour himself employed this expression in His prayer to His Father,—' If it be possible, let this cup pass from Me!'" The brief postscript to this letter was, " Please send us some books; and farewell till death."

These are not the only occasions on which we may observe how the Christians habitually felt that every parting might be "till death." The three women, after praying together at the foot of Ambohipotsy before they separated, said, " Now we enter the city, then to the place of execution, where all will end with us in this world." The affecting language of David to Jonathan, when flying from Saul, " There is but a step between me and death," did but express the Christians' constant sense of the price at which they held their faith. Nothing confounded their persecutors more than the passive strength of the believers under suffering and death. The heathen knew of nothing stronger than the fear of death. They saw the Christians calmly meeting it rather than renounce Christ. The heathen acknowledged that the power which sustained the Christians was more than human, and when they heard the executioners declare that the new religion made those who received it not afraid of death, many would conclude that the foundation of their faith was, as the Christians testified, divine and true.

CHAPTER VI.

Attempt of the Christians to reach the coast—Their capture on the road—Remarkable escape of two prisoners—Execution of the rest—Influence of public executions on the people—Extreme affection of the Christian captives, and cheerful death of Christians at Vonizongo—Savage execution of Raharo and his friends—Death of Rev. David Johns—The Prince Royal's friendship to the Christians—His efforts in their favour—Kindness of Prince Ramonja—Severe persecution in 1849—Noble confession of the Christians—The faithful Ranivo—The burning of the nobles—The hurling over the precipice of the Christians—Vast number punished.

AT the hour of midnight, when the refugees who came to England were leaving the capital, Rafaravavy, disguised as a slave, went to the prison to take a last farewell of a beloved nephew who had been six months in chains. She found him sleeping in his fetters, and fearing her voice might betray her to his keepers, she silently pressed his manacled hand, and quietly departed. The young man, who was under condemnation as one of the leaders among the Christians, was deeply affected when made acquainted with this visit, the proof of the affection of one whom he never expected to meet again in this world. Others also, including Paul, were in prison, and some in concealment. Paul and his companion, being a short time afterwards declared innocent by the tangena, were set at liberty, but the former, on hearing that it was intended to put him to death secretly, fled and concealed himself.

Near the close of 1839, Joshua, an intelligent and eminently devoted minister among the Christians, was with eight companions discovered praying, and being threatened with the tangena, fled, and joined those in concealment, some of whom had been in peril for the last two years, and whose number now amounted to sixteen. Mr. Baker, and other friends in Mauritius, generously sent money for their support; Mr. Griffiths also being at that time at the capital in the capacity of a trader, and Dr. Powell, who had recently come to the capital, likewise assisted them. The latter, proceeding in the early part of the following year to Tamatave, offered to aid these Christians to escape from the country, if they could reach the coast. Their number now made safety increasingly difficult; and having, more than once, very narrowly escaped detection, it appeared to the Christians that their only prospect of life depended on their being able to escape from the country.

On the 23rd of May, 1840, these sixteen Christians left their places of concealment, and, under the direction of two guides chosen by their friends, commenced their journey to Tamatave. They travelled safely from the province of Imerina, through the next province, and entered the third province, in which they journeyed onward till they reached Ranomafana.

A short distance to the north of these celebrated

hot springs they were, in consequence of the misplaced confidence of one of the guides in a relative, to whom he had communicated the object of the journey, captured, and taken back to Beforona, where they were imprisoned for a fortnight, and then conducted to the capital for trial. When within about six miles of the city, a young woman, concealing herself behind one of the men, made her escape; finding a female friend, she was placed for safety in an unoccupied house, the doors and windows of which were filled up with stones; there she remained undiscovered until the guards had given up their search and resumed their journey, then, loosening her hair, she fled for her life northward, until she reached the house of a Christian, where she received welcome, shelter, food and clothing.

The rest of the captives, five weeks after the commencement of their flight, were brought to the foot of the capital, and lodged near a village called *Faliarivo* (a thousand joys). If the captors thought of the import of the name, what cruel mockery it was to detain in a place so designated these toil-worn captives on their way to sentence and execution! But if, during this same night, faith revealed to any of the Christians visions of glory at all resembling that which the martyr Stephen saw, how appropriate the designation of this, their last resting-place on their last journey!

The next morning the captives were brought into the capital, bound hand and foot with cords, and subjected to close examination, each one separately, during several days, to discover the names of other Christians, but all were true to their friends; and although there were probably more than two hundred Christians in the capital or the suburbs, none were mentioned. The guides implicated Mr. Griffiths; but the Christians, unmoved by the promises or the threats of the examiners, preserved by their silence the lives of their brethren.

The prisoners were then placed under guards in several houses until the sentence of the queen should be declared. A young man and a young woman, each bound separately with cords, were confined in the same house, with a soldier to guard them. At midnight, while the guards slept, the young man began to work with his teeth at the cords on his wrists, and ultimately freed his hands. He soon removed the cords from his feet. Then he examined the cords that bound the hands and feet of his fellow-prisoner, but found that although she was not, like the captives of ancient times, chained to the guards who kept them, yet the soldier in charge lay, while sleeping, upon the cord which bound her limbs. The young man then opened the window of his prison-house, and finding that the guards outside were sleeping, he passed out and ran to Analakely, where knocking at the door of a friend's house, he greatly alarmed the inmates, who started back in astonishment when they saw him, but recognising his voice, admitted and embraced him with joy. A military friend afterwards concealed him amongst the tents of some recruits recently arrived from the country.

During the course of my visit to Madagascar in 1853, in company with Mr. Cameron, I frequently met with the young man who had experienced this remarkable deliverance, and recorded my impression of the first interview in the following words:—

"While we were in the house of a foreigner, a Christian, whom we had expected to see, entered the place where we were sitting. After looking earnestly at each of us for a few moments, and almost mechanically giving us his hand, there came over his whole countenance such an expression as I had never before witnessed in any human being. It was not ecstasy, it was not terror, and yet apparently a blending of both, marked by an intensity of feeling but rarely witnessed. During the whole interview, which took place under circumstances of secrecy but great danger, there was a strange uneasiness, mingled with evident satisfaction, which can be seen only in times and positions eminently perilous, and which it would be difficult to describe.*

Mr. Jones, the senior missionary to Madagascar, as well as Captain Campbell, an English officer from Mauritius, were in the capital at the time when the Christian party were brought back. They had heard with sorrow of their capture, and contributed to the alleviation of their sufferings.

On the morning of the 9th of July the firing of cannons announced that a kabary was to be held at Imahamasina, where the troops under arms and a vast concourse of people began to assemble early.

* "Three Visits to Madagascar," p. 36.

Guns continued firing from the battery on the edge of the mountain overlooking the plain during the day; and towards noon the commander-in-chief and the chief officers of the government passed along the road to the plain, and on reaching the place to which the prisoners had been already taken, proclaimed before the multitude the following sentence passed by the queen on the Christians:—

"With respect to these people who pray and read the books of the foreigners, I have, says the queen, admonished them several times, yet they persevere to oppose my will. Some have been put to death, others reduced to perpetual slavery, others fined, and others reduced in rank, for praying and worshipping the God of the white people. But these continue to pray in spite of all I do; and not only that, but they have endeavoured to make their escape from the country. Sixteen of them were found and caught to the north of Andevoranto. Eleven are condemned to be put to death. Two out of the eleven have escaped. Nine are now to be conveyed to the place of execution; and one man who maimed himself that he might not be made a soldier. These part with me, and so I part with them. They forsake me, and I forsake them. Take them, and present them before the house of the white man." *

They were nine in number, and being, from want of food, too weak to walk, they were tied to poles, and thus carried on men's shoulders. Joshua, the

---

* Mr. Griffiths.

native preacher, seemed to recognise his former teacher as the procession of death halted, according to the orders of the queen, before Mr. Griffiths' house. All appeared to be engaged in prayer. A hallowed serenity, almost an expression of hopeful joy, irradiated the countenances of some. One young woman, in whom many were interested, spoke to the soldiers and executioners of the blessedness of trust and hope in Christ, as she was borne along the road, for the distance of a mile from the place where sentence had been pronounced, through the city to Ambohizanahary (village of God), a rugged hill nearly opposite the palace. There, in the attitude of prayer, these nine martyrs fell without a struggle beneath the spears of the executioners.

The head of the venerable Paul the diviner, and that of Joshua the preacher, were struck off, and fixed on poles near the spot, to warn others of the penalty that awaited all who forsook the idols of the country. The bursting of the cannon which was fired as a signal for the execution of the prisoners, and the wounding of the gunner, caused many of the people to declare that it was an omen of evil to the persecutors of the Christians.

The great body of the spectators were unusually quiet, for the people, if not friendly, were becoming less willing to inform against the Christians. Some occasionally succoured them, and not a few regarded with instinctive condemnation the cruelty and injustice with which they were treated. The spectacle of these public executions, regarded in association with the humble, cheerful confidence with which the Christians recommended the Saviour to those who were conveying them to death, for their own love and trust in that divine Redeemer, was the strongest demonstration of the truth and reality of their own religion which could possibly be given. And thus these fearful cruelties were made, under the influence of the divine Spirit, a means of increase and strength to the church which they were intended to destroy.

A message from the queen was sent by Tsitialaingia to Mr. Griffiths, who was accused of sending the Christians away, stating that because he was an Englishman she did not subject him to the penalties that would have been inflicted on a Malagasy, but ordered him to pay a fine for his head, a fee to the accusers, and another fine to the government; altogether about £30. He was also ordered to leave the capital in a fortnight, to depart from the country, and not to return. He finally left, not without considerable peril, on the 1st of September, 1840.

Although the government seemed to regard Christianity as a source of insecurity and danger, the removal of the Christians did not bring strength to the government, or peace to the people. The cruelty and oppression, corruption and greed of many in power, rendered portions of the population desperate, and tended both to fill the prisons with criminals and the borders of the uninhabited parts of the country with bands of armed robbers, which imperilled life and property. At the time when the Christians suffered, some hundreds of the people had been accused of different offences, and were awaiting trial.

After the death of the Christians, little was said about Christianity, but much was thought. To have spoken favourably of those who had been put to death would have been treason, but many pitied, and no one blamed them. The unfaltering faith and blameless lives of the believers, the blessed hope which brightened their future, and which no present sufferings could overcloud or destroy, the benevolence, love, and truth which marked their course, were patent to all and acknowledged by many. The good confession some had witnessed, their meek, uncomplaining submission, and the hopeful prayer which occupied their last moments, contrasted with the parade of power put forth in connection with their execution, sunk into many hearts, and were already producing deep ponderings as to the cause of the difference between the character and influence of Christianity and of heathenism. God was by this means as much unfolding the nature of His kingdom, and preparing the hearts of His people for its reception, as by the most active efforts of the preachers of His word. The votaries of idolatry, by the manifestations of its character and influence which their treatment of the Christians produced, were at the same time loosening its hold upon the people, and thus removing one great impediment to their acceptance of the gospel of salvation. Had the Martyr Church in its earliest years not been thus severely tested its faith would have been feebler, and its witness for God would have been less conducive to the subsequent triumphs of the gospel in Madagascar.

But the lives already sacrificed, and the severe bondage inflicted on the Christians, failed to appease the anger of their persecutors, whose restless endeavours to destroy them greatly increased their peril. The soldiers in search of them were so numerous, and had become so well acquainted with their hiding-places, that concealment became daily more difficult. Those who fled to the desert and forest were at times in danger of starvation, or of being carried off by the armed bands of robbers which infested the uninhabited parts of the country.

We do not wonder that although the faith of these Christians did not fail, they were bowed down by their affliction. It creates no surprise that their places of meeting were less numerous, and more difficult of access, and that fewer of the Christians were able to attend them. These were the darkest days which had overtaken them. They were destitute of all earthly consolation; and nothing, during the entire progress of the gospel among them, shows more clearly the presence and care of the divine Saviour, than the stedfastness of their faith, and the actual additions which, even under these circumstances, were made to their numbers.

The Christians in Vonizongo, a district in the west, having heard that some of the Sakalava chiefs to the north-west were willing to receive the Christian teachers, sent two of their number, Ratsitsambahina and Raberahamba, to visit them. On their return, these men were captured by the guards on the frontier, and while their companions in the province escaped, they were sent to the capital for trial. There they were cruelly treated to induce them to name their companions. To a Christian friend, who brought them food while they were in prison, they managed, unperceived, to whisper a message of affection to their fellow-believers, and the assurance that, whatever they might suffer, they would not reveal the names of their companions; and they kept their word.

On their trial these Christians declared to the judges that they went into the Sakalava country of their own free will, to try to soften, by the teaching of the word of God, the hearts of the people who stole their cattle and committed violence in the country; that they prayed and read the Book, but all was done in loyalty to the queen and for the good of the country. They were sentenced to die, and sent back to their own village to be executed.

These men had been soldiers, and manifested not only holy confidence in God, but cheerful courage in death. They were both executed in the public market on Sunday, the 19th of June, 1842. When led forth to be executed they took leave affectionately of their friends, saying, "Farewell, beloved friends, God will cause us this day to meet with Him in paradise." The heathen spectators were struck with awe and astonishment at the manner in which these Christians met their death. Their fellow-believers spoke of them as only having ascended to heaven before their companions. The heads of these first martyrs of Vonizongo were severed from their bodies and fixed on poles in a public place; but the sequel seemed to show that the ghastly skulls served rather to perpetuate in the minds of the people the constancy of the Christians, than to deter others from receiving their faith.

Three months after these events Antananarivo witnessed a fearful illustration of the blind and sanguinary wrath of the queen against the Christians. Some unknown person affixed, during the night, on the wall of a house in the capital, a paper—a leaf of the New Testament—with Matt. xxiii. 13 underlined: "Woe unto you, scribes and Pharisees, hypocrites! for ye shut up the kingdom of heaven against men: for ye neither go in yourselves, neither suffer ye them that are entering to go in." When the queen was told what had been done she was extremely angry, and issued a proclamation, requiring the person who had been guilty of the offence to accuse himself within four days, declaring that if the offender did not confess within that time, and was afterwards discovered, he should be cut into pieces as small as musket-balls.

No one having confessed at the expiration of the appointed time, Raharo, a Christian, who had been baptized and had been one of the head teachers in the government schools, together with several others, was arrested. Raharo was ordered to take the tangena, under which he died. Ratsimilay, another

Christian, having endeavoured to save him from the ordeal, was put to death, as was also Imamongy; and their bodies were cut into small pieces, and afterwards burned. No evidence whatever was produced to show that either of these young men, or any of the Christians, were connected with the affixing of the obnoxious paper. It seemed as if they had been seized on account of their being Christians, and of having been educated. There were many excellent writers in the capital, who were neither Christians themselves nor friendly to those who were, and parts of the New Testament, in manuscript or print, were accessible to all. It is scarcely possible, considering the consequences and the probable results of so daring an act, to believe that any Christian could have been guilty of it.

In the following year Madagascar lost one of its most sincere and devoted friends in the death of the Rev. David Johns, a laborious and self-denying missionary, who cheerfully consecrated his life to the spiritual welfare of the Malagasy. When driven from Imerina, Mr. Johns made several voyages to the western coast of the island, seeking to secure shelter or the means of escape for the Christians, and to spread the gospel among the people. While thus employed he died, in the fiftieth year of his age, at Mosibe, in August, 1843. Besides ordinary missionary labours, Mr. Johns wrote some of the native hymns, which the Christians still delight to sing, and translated "The Pilgrim's Progress" into their language, a book which, next to the Scriptures, proved a source of instruction as well as unspeakable consolation to them during their long night of persecution and suffering. These efforts on their behalf, together with his own gentle, affectionate, unselfish spirit, endeared him to the Malagasy, amongst whom his memory is still fragrant. A grateful tribute of respect was paid to the work of the deceased missionary by the commander of H.M.S. *Isis*, Sir John Marshall, to whom he was personally known, and who erected an appropriate monument over his grave in the island of Nosibe, occupied by the French, whose hospitality and kindness had soothed the last hours of the English missionary.

God did not leave His people in this season of their weakness without encouragement. They were not at this time harassed by impeachments or arrests, and were astonished as well as cheered by continued accessions from the heathen. One great affliction was a want of the word of God, for a supply of which they most earnestly applied. Speaking of their Sabbaths, they said, "We always go to some hill or valley far away. We leave home on the Saturday, and on Sunday meet together and offer our worship to the Lord. It is only the men who can thus go to a distance, and this makes us feel on account of the sorrow of those who cannot go. Still we do not faint. Hitherto we have been safe, for God has hidden us under the shadow of His wings; for though many hear about us, and see us, they say, 'These people pray,' and do not inform against us, but compassionate us."

In the course of divine providence light often appears in the midst of unusual darkness; and at this time light and hope from an unexpected quarter arose in the midst of desolation. An officer who often had business at the palace was occasionally accompanied by his nephew, who was a Christian. The young visitor was noticed by Rakotond-radama,* the prince royal, then in his sixteenth year, only son of the queen, and heir to the throne, who soon entered into conversation with him.

Emboldened by the frank and genial bearing of the prince, the young visitor after a time spoke to him of the faith of the Christians, and the prince became deeply interested in the subject. About the same time a young Christian, who had been baptized among the earliest converts, became distinguished as a fearless and faithful preacher of the gospel, even while severe penalties against Christianity were threatened by the queen. The spirits of the disciples were revived, their activity renewed, and large audiences were gathered, who not only listened with attention to the young evangelist, but publicly avowed themselves disciples, to the number of a hundred or more. The visitor of the prince spoke of these meetings, and at his suggestion he attended them, was deeply impressed, and repeated his attendance. After a time the earnestness of Ramaka, or, as the Christians called him, Rasalasala (the bold one),

---

* The name of the prince is a compound word, Rakoto signifying *young*, or the young one; Radama, the name of his reputed father. The name signified young Radama, or Radama the youth.

and the effects of it on his mind, were such that he declared himself desirous of being more fully instructed.

As the prince had a separate establishment of his own, he arranged for Christian teachers to go to his house every evening, when he was not otherwise engaged, to pray and to explain the Scriptures to him. During the same period he often attended the meetings for public worship on the Sunday. From his earliest years the prince had manifested an instinctive horror at the reckless shedding of blood and destruction of life. The sufferings of the Christians had also excited his compassion, predisposing him to befriend them, and to regard with favour their more humane and merciful faith.

Before the close of the year in which the prince had associated himself with the Christians, an accusation was brought to the government against them, with a list of one hundred names of persons who had disobeyed the queen's law by attending meetings for prayer. The list was given to the prime minister, who, discovering among the accused his own aide-de-camp and relative, destroyed the list, and only twenty-one were proceeded against.

On behalf of these accused Christians the prince pleaded with his mother so effectually, that none were sentenced to death. Nine were ordered to drink the tangena, under which one died. Five were sold into slavery, two escaped, and the rest remained in chains. Severe and iniquitous as this punishment was, the Christians were filled with thankfulness that the lives of so many had been spared. In their letters at that time they ask the missionaries to thank God for giving them such a friend as the prince had proved, and to implore on his behalf divine protection and blessing.

If, without that work of the Holy Spirit which alone can change the heart, the prayers of the Christians could have secured the implanting of new and holy principles in the heart of the prince, he would have become a disciple in heart and life, as well as in sympathy and aid. As it was, however, we are not surprised at the gratitude which the friendship of the queen's son inspired; for though the Christians could not see him frequently, and could only meet for worship in the night, or in solitary places, and were followed even then by spies, who reported their names to the government, they add in their letters, "But thanks to the prudent mediation of the prince, the things reported by the spies proceed no further." "The prince," they observe, "comes regularly with us in the woods on Sunday for worship, and often takes some of us home to explain to him the word of truth."

Among the intimate friends of the prince, and one of the companions of his youth, was Prince Ramonja, his cousin, the son of his mother's eldest sister, and the brother of Ramboasalama, his rival. Prince Ramonja, Radama's senior, was a man of gentle spirit, strongly attached to the prince, and a great favourite with the queen. By the conversation of the teachers he was induced to unite with the Christians. He allowed them to meet for worship in his houses, and was, for a number of years, one of their most powerful and devoted friends.

Simultaneously with these favours the great Head of the Church raised up another valuable friend, less powerful, but equally devoted to the welfare of the Christians. The prime minister sent a nephew, to whom he was much attached, to their meetings, with instructions to write down the names of all who might be present. The young officer went, but told the Christians the object of his visit, and advised them to return immediately to their homes, lest harm should come. When his uncle, on his return, asked for the list, he replied, "There is none." "Why," said the uncle, "have you disobeyed my orders? You must lose your head, for you also are a Christian." The young man quietly replied, "I am a Christian, and if you will you can put me to death; but I must pray." After a pause, natural affection triumphed, and the uncle said, "Oh no, you shall not die." Thus again, by the holy courage of this young man, the Christians were delivered.

To the effect of this discovery by the chief officer of the government, together with the continued influence of the prince with his mother, may be ascribed, in part at least, the leniency shown to the Christians, and the welcome accessions to their numbers. Not a few residing in country places repaired to the mountains, amongst which the Christians were in concealment, to ask instruction, and to unite in their worship. The believers who had been put in chains were kept in their own houses, under guards of soldiers; but their friends and others had free access to them. With these the prisoners conversed, and prayed, and praised the Lord. They read the Holy Scriptures, explaining and enforcing their saving truths. The Christians declared that sweet were their bonds when so employed; and God blessed these sermons delivered by preachers in chains. Numbers received the word in love and faith; and some, even among the soldiers appointed to guard the prisoners, were also converted to Christ. Gradually, by the kindness of the keepers, or the consent of the authorities, the chains of the prisoners were loosened, and finally ceased to be fastened on their limbs. Writing of this period (1847-8), the Christians observe, "The Lord hath taken away their chains;" and they add, "This great power in favour of the gospel fills the minds of the people with astonishment."

The employment of the imprisoned Christians was preaching the word, and repairing such copies of the Bible and other books as remained in their possession. Scarcely any want was more keenly felt amongst them than that of books. Most of the educated Christians employed themselves in copying out, so far as their materials would allow, portions of Scripture, and other books. The eyes of some were seriously injured by close application to this work in their places of concealment. I brought home no memorials of the persecutions in Madagascar more deeply affecting than some of these fragments of Scripture, worn, rent, fragile, and soiled by the dust of the earth or the smoke in the thatch, at times when they had been concealed, yet most carefully mended, by drawing the rent pages together with fibres of bark, or having the margins of the leaves covered over with stronger paper.

This welcome season of rest, refreshment, and strength, derived from accessions to their number, confirming their faith that God was working with them, was but a preparation for severer trials. After about two years of comparative calm and progress, the heaviest storm of persecution yet endured burst upon the church. On the 19th of February, 1849, two houses belonging to Prince Ramonja, which had been used as places of Christian worship, were demolished, and the materials carried off as spoil. Eleven Christians were seized and put in chains. A kabary, or public meeting, was called at Andohalo. The substance of the message from the queen was, "I have killed some, I have made some slaves till death, I have put some in long and heavy fetters, and still you continue doing that practice. How is it that you cannot give up that?" (praying).

Two Christians answered, "Reverence for God and His law prevents our giving up praying." One said, "Our prayers will bring good to the queen, to her subjects, to her kingdom, and to ourselves who offer them. When the fruits of the earth are ripe, and we live to the end of the year, we rejoice and pray *

---

* There are specific words for praise, homage, and thanksgiving; but the native word for *pray* generally is used to signify worship. The places of worship are called prayer-houses.

to God to bless the queen, and the kingdom, and ourselves."

A week afterwards the Christians, throughout the districts of the province, were ordered to accuse themselves at the appointed place in each district. The queen's message sent by the officers and judges, to whom confession was to be made, was this,—" I give these praying people time to accuse themselves; but it is not for their sakes that I give them time, but for the sake of Imerina; and were it not so, I would put them all to death, for they do the things which I hate."

At Vonizongo, when the judge urged the people to take the oath which recognised the idols, and to implore the prescribed curses on themselves if they violated it, Rabodomanga stood forth and said, "I do not pray to wood and stones, nor to the mountains. Unto God alone do I pray, for He is great. He cannot have associates" (other gods). One of the officers said, "You wretch! will you not pray to the spirits of the ancestors and to the idols?" The heroic Christian woman answered, "I do not pray to these: it is God alone that I serve" (in worship).

The message from the queen, on which the gathering in the district had been ordered, was to give the Christians an opportunity of accusing themselves, that she might inflict on them a less punishment than death. But the proposals of the judges, and the answers of the people, show that the commissioners were not so much concerned about the people accusing themselves, as they were to induce them to take the oath. The Christians regarded the oath as invoking the idols; their refusal, therefore, was expressed in their declaration that they should not or could not worship billets of wood, but "God alone." One of these added, "For He alone is worthy to receive religious honour and praise."

Rainitraho, a noble, a descendant of one of the most distinguished sovereigns of the country, replied, "God has given none to be worshipped on earth, nor under heaven, except the name of Jesus Christ." "Fellow!" exclaimed the officer, "will you not worship the departed kings and the idols which raised them up?" To which the stedfast confessor replied, "I cannot worship any of them, for they were kings given to be served, but not to be worshipped. God alone is to be worshipped for ever and ever, and to Him alone I pray." This faithful Christian sealed his testimony to Jesus Christ with his blood in the flames. After his answers, one of the officers from the capital interfered, saying, "Let us stop the examinations, lest all the people declare as these have done." The advice was adopted, and no others at Vonizongo were then required to take the oath.

The first Christian to whom the officer proposed the oath at Analakely, answered, "I shall not pray to stone and wood. Steps are made with stone, and houses built with wood, and the idols are only cuttings of wood. Why should I worship them? for unto God alone should men offer prayer and worship."

In reference to the charge that the Christians

were not loyal subjects because they condemned quarrelling and fighting, Mary said, " If our enemies say they (viz., the Malagasy) will not fight, it is not the Christians at all that they speak of, for against the enemies of the queen and her country the Christians will fight. As for stones, and wood, and the idols, and the mountains, God has not given them to be prayed unto ; for they are things without life. But God is the Lord of heaven and earth, and of all things ; and for these reasons I do not pray to things without life."

One of these last Christians, on being questioned, said, " I believe in God, for He alone can do all things for me ; and I wish to obey whatever He commands me ; but as to swearing by the queen, or by one's father or brother, a lie is a lie still, whether you swear to it or not. I believe in God, and put my trust in Jesus Christ, the Saviour and Redeemer of all that believe in Him." This woman was then put in chains, with her companions, to await the queen's pleasure.

Ranivo, an interesting and beautiful young woman of good family, about whom much interest was felt, and whom the queen wished to save, when questioned, said, " I cannot serve the idols: God alone will I serve as long as my life shall last, for God has given me life and spirit, a higher spiritual life to worship Him, and for that reason I worship God."

Rainisoanaly, the examining officer, then said, " Perhaps you are not right in your mind, or ill; or perhaps you are under some charm, and you should consider well lest the queen should not like you, and you should destroy yourself for no purpose."

Ranivo replied, "I am not deranged, nor am I suffering from any illness." Then addressing her father, who was present, she exclaimed, "You indeed love me, O father, but God has given me a spirit to worship Him, and I should be filled with dread if I were to cease to pray to Him; therefore I shall not cease to worship Him, lest I should die everlasting death." Then the officer said, "Bind her," as he had ordered them to bind the others.

Of two others, whom they asked where they had preached and who were their companions, one said, "I preached in my own house;" and both said, "It would be sin against God to betray our friends, and we cannot do that." The officers then left, saying as they went, "These are stubborn and obstinate people."

The trials were now ended, and the multitude separated until the morrow, when sentence was to be pronounced. The captives in chains spent this their last night on earth in their respective prisons, guarded by the soldiers, their keepers. Their communings with their own spirits, with their divine Lord, on the eternity they were so soon to enter, it would be profane to make the subject of conjecture. Their brethren in Christ, whose limbs were still unbound, met together an hour after midnight to pray. The firing of cannon at break of day agitated the hearts of thousands, and while the firing of the guns continued at intervals through the morning, the multitudes gathered at Analakely. The preachers, teachers, readers of the Scriptures, and worshippers of God were conducted to the plain, and each class of offenders were placed by themselves.

But the sight which most deeply penetrated many hearts, and stirred their inmost feelings, was that of the true, stedfast confessors who had refused to bow down and worship the idols of Ranavalomanjaka. Outwardly there was everything to repel, or to awaken pity. Each Christian man and woman was fastened with cords to two poles, their bodies wrapped in torn and soiled pieces of matting, in token of their degradation, their mouths filled with rag to prevent their speaking of the Saviour; yet these eighteen, the noble, the civilian, the slave—all equal now, children of God going to glory—formed, as they were borne along—the young and faithful Ranivo walking alone at the end of the illustrious line—the grandest procession which the sun of Madagascar had ever shone upon.

On reaching the appointed spot these Christians were placed on the ground, the soldiers encircling them with their spears fixed in the earth. And then, accompanied by their escort, and marching to the sound of military music, with all the solemn pomp belonging to their rank and duties, the officers and judges, with their attendants, arrived, and delivered the message of the queen, which was as follows:—

"I, the queen of Madagascar, say that no religion whatever, excepting that of Andrianampoinimerina and Radama, and the customs of your ancestors, shall be ever introduced and practised in this my country: anything else is totally rejected by me. Had I not ordered the followers of the new religion to inculpate themselves, they would soon overturn the country, and all the people would follow them. I consider them rebels; therefore I tell you how I have punished them, as the spirits of Andrianampoinimerina and Radama have revealed to me."

This short fragment of the speech exhibits clearly what were the principles on which this fearful persecution was sustained—the determination of the queen that no other religion than that of her ancestors should exist in Madagascar; the extent to which Christianity would have increased, had she not interposed—" all the people would follow them;" and the declaration that in their punishment she acted under the inspiration of the deified spirits of her ancestors. The sentences of the queen upon the offenders, who were divided into classes according to their rank or their crimes, were then officially announced.

The four nobles, two of whom were husband and wife, were sentenced to be burned alive at Faravohitra, the last village on the northern end of the mountain on which the city is built. The fourteen others of inferior rank were sentenced to be hurled from the edge of Ampamarinana, a rock to the west of the palace, and their wives and children to be sold into irredeemable slavery.

The remaining sentences included labour in chains for life, inflicted on one hundred and seventeen persons, with public flogging on one hundred and five of their number. Fines, equivalent to one-half of their value if sold into slavery, were imposed on sixty-four. A fine of three oxen and three dollars was inflicted on one thousand six hundred and forty-three persons, for attending Christian worship. Prince Ramonja, holding high rank in the army, was, for the same offence, fined one hundred dollars, and reduced to the rank of a common soldier. One of the officers of the palace was deprived of his rank and fined fifty dollars; as were all other officers in the army or the civil service of government, and reduced to the lowest grade. The total number of those on whom one or other of the sentences was pronounced on this occasion amounted, at the least computation, to one thousand nine hundred and three, but by some accounts it is nearer three thousand.

When the sentences had been pronounced, "cannon were fired at intervals during the forenoon, and when all were finished, the soldiers struck up their music, beating the great drums and the little drums to agitate and terrify the prisoners." But the Christians condemned to die began singing one of their native hymns, commencing,—

> "Ary misy tany soa,
> Mahafinaritra indrindra."
>
> (There is a beauteous land,
> Making most blessed.)

Then the soldiers took up the four nobles and carried them from the plain up the hill-side to Faravohitra, a place on the highest part of the hill. As they were carried along they commenced singing another of their own simple and expressive hymns, the first verse of which begins—

"Hod' izahay Zanahary."
(Going home are we to God.) *

The last verse, which might have been written for that hour, is—

"When we shall die
And depart from this earth,
Then increase our joy;
Take (us) to heaven,
Then rejoice
Shall we for evermore."

Enemies and friends would alike understand the feeling and the significance of this hymn. It was the expression of the assurance of their hope, full of immortality, and it was a triumphant answer to the slander of one of the most implacable of their persecutors, who had declared that when they sung this and similar hymns they were singing lies, for they were as much afraid of death as others.

Thus they sung until they reached the spot where one large pile of firewood was built up, and they were then fastened to stakes a little above the wood. When the pile was kindled, and the flames were rising, they prayed and praised the Lord. Among the utterances then heard by those around them were these,— "Lord Jesus, receive our spirits—lay not this sin to their charge;" and, as if visions of the future triumphs of the Lord were given to their departing spirits, one

* The lines are translated literally, not according to rhythm or metre.

was heard to exclaim, "His name, His praise, shall endure for ever and ever."

Once, if not more than once, the falling rain extinguished the fire, which was rekindled; and to one of the sufferers the pains of maternity were added to those of the flames. While their spirits were thus enduring and praying, a large and triple rainbow, the sign of God's promise and faithfulness, was stretched across the heavens, one end seeming to rest upon the spot whence the martyrs' spirits were departing. Some of the spectators, to whom the phenomenon appeared supernatural, fled in terror; but one, who faithfully remained to the end, records of the Christians, "They prayed as long as they had any life. Then they died; but softly, gently. Indeed, gentle was the going forth of their life, and astonished were all the people around that beheld the burning of them there."

The transactions on the plain of judgment were ended. Liberty and life at the price of apostasy had been offered, and by some few, occasionally associated with the Christians, it had been accepted; but by the great body of the accused, amounting to between two and three thousand, it had been deliberately declined. Sentence against the followers of Christ had been pronounced. And, as in general the punishment immediately follows the passing of the sentence, nothing now remained but its infliction. The criminals of highest rank, in whose veins the blood of kings was supposed to flow, had already been sent away to die. In the same order and manner in which they had been brought to receive judgment, the remaining fourteen confessors were now taken along the public roads, through the agitated and deeply affected crowds in the city, to Ampamarinana, the Tarpeian rock of Madagascar. Here, on the top of a lofty precipice, at the edge of the western crest of the mountain on which the city is built, the matting wrapped round their bodies was removed, but their arms remained pinioned, and their ankles were bound with cords. Thus bound they were taken, one by one, to the edge of the precipice, and either pushed, or laid down and rolled, or kicked over the downward curving edge, whence they fell fifty or sixty feet, when, striking a projecting ledge, they bounded off and fell amongst jagged and broken fragments of granite lying at the base of the precipice, one hundred and fifty feet below the edge from which they had been hurled. Life was generally extinct. One distinguished Christian, when the matting in which he was wrapped had been removed, is said to have asked permission to stand and view once more the scene before him. His request was granted, and after looking at each familiar object, he remained silent a few minutes, as if in prayer; then, forced over the precipice, he was heard singing a Christian hymn as his body descended to be crushed and broken in death.

Ranivo, belonging to the tribe or clan from which the reigning family trace their descent, and whom the queen, anxious to save, had ordered to be placed so that she might see the other Christians thrown from the fearful height, was then led by the executioner to the edge of the rock, and directed to look down upon the mangled bodies of her friends. Her relatives entreated her to take the oath, save her own life, and please her sovereign. But she begged that she might follow her friends, as she could not take the oath. A member of her own family expostulated, but failed to shake her purpose.* The executioner then struck her on the face, saying, "She is insane, take her to her parents." The mangled and scarcely lifeless bodies of those thrown from the precipice were dragged along to the spot where the nobles were burnt, and consumed in one vast pile, the lurid flames of which, with whatever feelings they might be regarded from the windows of the palace or the dwellings of the high officers, were intended to spread awe and terror among the inhabitants of the numerously peopled villages around from which they were visible.

* This member of her family afterwards told me that he, with other officers of the palace, went to see the execution of the Christians, not believing until then that they were not afraid to die. Of the subsequent life of this faithful Christian woman I possess a most interesting memoir by her nearest friend. She was faithful unto death.

CHAPTER VII.

Severity of Prince Ramonja's punishment—Convict labour of Christian officers—Kindness of the princes to the Christians—Numbers of the Christians—Voyage of Messrs. Cameron and Ellis to Madagascar—Opening the ports to foreign commerce—Second visit to Madagascar—Protracted intercourse with Christians from the capital—Visit to Mahavelona—Correspondence with Christians at the capital—Andriambelo—Midnight meetings with the Christians—Want of the Scriptures—Third visit to Madagascar—Arrival at the capital—Reception by the government—Statement of the object of visit—Interviews with the prince and Ramonja.

THE day after the execution of the Christians, the fines in money and cattle, which had been inflicted for minor offences, were, on the petition of the officers and people, reduced one-half; but the payment of even this mitigated penalty was sufficient to reduce many to abject poverty. Whether it was supposed that any latent tendency towards Christianity existed among the people is not known, but the whole of the non-Christian community, gathered in the capital, were required to take the oath of allegiance to the sovereign and the idols before they were permitted to return to their homes.

It has already been stated that the heaviest fine levied was imposed on Prince Ramonja. He was also treated with extreme severity, being not only reduced to the grade of a common soldier, but subjected to unusual hardships. He had been accustomed to wear as comfortable clothing as the highest in the land, but was now allowed only the common light thin lamba, little more than a waistband or girdle, and with only this covering was frequently appointed to night duty, at a time of the year when a thick woollen dress would have been acceptable to Europeans.

The prince royal, his friend, often went to visit him, and wept at the sight of his sufferings. The prince also sent him food from his own kitchen, but it was included among the rations served out to the party to which he belonged, and was shared with all in common. The effects of the treatment which this benevolent and kind-hearted prince experienced at this time remained through the remainder of his life, during the greater part of which he was an invalid. But under all his own sufferings he remained the faithful friend, the wise counsellor, and the fearless advocate of the Christians.

Prince Rakoto himself was at this time powerless, for he had been accused by the prime minister to the queen of reading the Bible and attending the meetings of the Christians for the worship of God. But the queen, who was probably not ignorant of the fact, is said to have replied, " Oh, Rakoto is young, he does not know what is proper, and he is my only son."

It has been already stated that Ramboasalama, Ramonja's brother, was the rival of the prince royal in his claim to the throne. This arose from the queen, at the time of her coronation, not being then herself a mother, having declared that her nephew, who was then standing by her side, should be her successor. Although this declaration was not repeated after her own son was born, her nephew never relinquished his claim; and after the prince royal had shown some leaning towards the Christians, the hostility of Ramboasalama became more determined and violent. He also became the chief supporter of the idols, and was one cause of the extreme severity with which the Christians were treated.

Some Frenchmen residing at the capital, after the expulsion of the missionaries and the departure of the artisans, had proposed to the queen to introduce a number of European works, amongst others the manufacture of glass, including looking-glasses, as well as the foundry of cannon. These works were commenced at a place called Mantasoa, about twenty miles from the capital, and a large number of Christian officers who had been deprived of their commissions, and had been serving in the ranks for three quarters of a year, were, as an additional punishment, sent as convicts under heathen taskmasters to quarry, dress, and carry granite stones, and construct a large stone building at this place. They were not allowed to have the habitation, food, and clothing which their means would have enabled them to provide. Their labour, which was excessive and severe, was continued after the period when their first sentence expired. They were then sentenced to drag

Native farmer, and bearer or servant.   Hova officers.   P. 177.

large heavy logs of timber from the forest, the severest labour known in Madagascar. In 1852, Ramboasalama and the heathen party proposed that they should be again sentenced to the same severe labour; but the prince and some of the officers opposed him, and they were released. It was when pleading the cause of these Christian officers that the new commander-in-chief, who had succeeded his father in that office, remonstrated before the queen with the officers of the government, saying, "They have suffered twice over the punishment to which they were sentenced. Why should they be sentenced again? The thunderbolt does not strike twice." Their friends prevailed, and they escaped the repetition of the misery and toil.

During my first visit to Madagascar I saw a number of these men at Tamatave and Mahavelona, where many of the Christians found a secure asylum, and was deeply affected by the narrative of their sufferings and privations. Two of them, represented in the accompanying plate, were officers who had endured this punishment. The officer in the striped silk lamba had suffered in an earlier persecution. The taskmasters of the officers employed in quarrying and carrying large stones, seemed to have treated them with great cruelty. The tall man with his hat in his hand, a gentle-spirited and most estimable Christian, an aide-de-camp of the prince, once removed his lamba, and showed me the large scars of the deeply cut wounds on his shoulders, produced by the heavy rough stones they were obliged to carry for the building. The work was afterwards abandoned, and the place is now a ruin.

Prince Ramonja, whose health suffered greatly, was, after a time, released from his severe punishment, and became an officer of the palace. The Christians speak of him at this time as "a wise and faithful friend, who truly loves the Lord Christ Jesus." To him they had recourse when in difficulty for counsel, as well as in times of danger for protection. He not only attended their meetings, but notwithstanding the reproaches of his family, spoke without fear to the queen and his own relations of the gospel of Christ. The queen's regard for her sister, his mother, saved him from suffering on that account.

There was no denunciation at this time of the queen's determination to extinguish Christianity; but every fortnight when the soldiers of the district were mustered at parade in the capital, an order from the queen was read, enjoining the utmost vigilance in officers and men in searching or spying about the houses and villages to detect and seize any engaged in reading or worship. Under these circumstances, the friendship and encouragement of the prince and of Ramonja must have been to them of unspeakable value. Both these princes spent large sums of money in sending succour to the Christians. Rakoto also on one occasion went to the place where a number of recently captured Christians were confined, set them free, and ordered their keeper, if called to account, to say that he had released them.

The gospel was still proscribed at the capital, but the disciples enjoyed comparative freedom in the provinces, continuing still to increase in number in the country districts. Their secret meetings in the city were more numerously attended; and these gatherings were rendered deeply affecting by the occasional presence of some who ventured to come secretly from their places of concealment, and of others who, notwithstanding their having been sentenced to chains for life, were sometimes able to join in the midnight worship of their brethren wearing their chains. These were not massive rings and bars of iron, such as those by which the Christians were bound together, but lighter iron chains, reaching from an iron band fastened round the neck to the wrists of the same person, and from a band round the waist to rings fastened on the ankles.

The believers throughout the country amounted at this time to thousands; and there were, notwithstanding the orders to the soldiers, seven houses in the capital in which those within reach met regularly for worship, besides a faithful church of sixty-eight members, who once every month united in commemorating the dying love of Christ their Lord.

After the death of Rainiharo, one of the ministers who had placed Ranavalona on the throne, and who had been a powerful and cruel persecutor of the Christians, his son, an intelligent, energetic man, who had attached himself to the prince, was appointed to his father's office. At the same time the prince was nominally associated with his mother in the official acts of the government, and was made secretary of state, as well as one of the officers of the palace. On him also now devolved the duty of authorizing the publication of the orders of the queen. The government were anxious to resume friendly relations with England, which had been for some years interrupted, and to welcome back the exiles who had sought safety in Mauritius.

Connected with the more prominent position which the prince now held, accounts reached Mauritius that the queen was anxious to see her son established on the throne during her lifetime, and that arrangements were in progress for her abdication in his favour at no distant period. These accounts were sent early in 1853 to the London Missionary Society; and in order to obtain more reliable information, before preparing to resume their mission, I was solicited to visit the country, accompanied by Mr. Cameron, in order to ascertain the actual state of the people. Embarking in March of that year, I was joined by Mr. Cameron at the Cape, and on reaching Mauritius soon afterwards, we found from the Malagasy Christians there, that there had been neither persecution nor change in the government, though the friendship and influence of the prince were highly favourable to the Christians.

On reaching Madagascar we were cordially welcomed by the authorities, who received with evident relief and satisfaction the report we were able to make of the friendly feelings of the English towards Madagascar. The vessel in which we sailed had been sent with a letter from the merchants at Mauritius to the queen, respecting the opening of the ports of Madagascar to foreign trade. We wrote to the queen asking permission to visit the capital, and in less than three weeks received a courteous reply, stating that they had very much business on hand, and could not receive us, and that we had better return, lest we should take the fever through delay.

We obtained information respecting the general state of the people, though we saw but few of the Christians, and had scarcely an opportunity of conversing much with more than one, to whom reference has already been made, nor could we meet without danger to him. We learned that the Christians were increasing, and that all felt greatly the want of books, which we were unable to supply. Some came long distances for them, and almost wept when they found that we had none to give. Mr. Cameron received an affecting letter from Prince Ramonja, expressing his earnest desire for copies of the Scriptures and other books. He also stated that the Prince Royal sometimes had Christians to read and pray in his house in the court of the palace, ordering the band to play at the same time in order that the queen might not hear. The government was reported to be chiefly under the guidance of Prince Ramboasalama, who, we heard, was plotting to secure the throne against his cousin, the queen's son.

Before leaving the country, I wrote at some length to the chief persons connected with those in whose welfare we were most interested. I assured them of the undiminished sympathy and affection of British Christians, of their prayers on their behalf, and of their readiness, when the Lord in His providence should open the way, to send them Christian teachers, who should assist them more fully to comprehend, and more widely to diffuse, that blessed gospel which they had found so precious, and for which they had suffered so much. I expressed my regret that we had not been able to communicate with them personally, and my hope that this favour might yet be granted. I also requested that if I could in any way further their wishes, they would write to me at Mauritius, acquainting me with their own circumstances and the prospects of the Christians. At the same time I sent, partly from myself, and partly in conjunction with Mr. Cameron, what were deemed suitable presents to some, also relief for the suffering Christians in bonds, which, though small in amount, might serve as some assurance of the sympathy excited by their circumstances among their Christian friends in England.

Mr. Cameron afterwards returned with a delegate from the Chamber of Commerce at Mauritius, and a satisfactory arrangement was then made for opening the ports of Madagascar to the commerce of foreign countries. I remained at Mauritius corresponding with the Christians at the capital, to whom I was able to promise a supply of the Scriptures by the earliest possible opportunity. In one of their letters shortly afterwards they told me that a number of them went out to a solitary place, to sing together for joy at the prospect of receiving copies of the word of God. I also wrote to the secretary of the government at the capital, informing him of my intention to visit Madagascar as soon as the season should be favourable.

Early in June of the following year I again reached Tamatave, but was detained in quarantine some time, on account of the cholera which prevailed in Mauritius at the time of my departure. So fearful were the government of that alarming disease, that all goods landed at this time were exposed to sun and wind for forty days, all the coin received was buried in the sand for an equal period, and no article whatever was allowed to be sent to the capital. This fear of infection prevented my being allowed to proceed beyond the coast, but I was cordially welcomed by the authorities at the port.

About a fortnight after my arrival, a fine, tall, noble-looking chief arrived, accompanied by a number of strangers recently come from the capital, who had brought letters from the residents there conveying much interesting intelligence. When my visitors wrote down on paper what they had to say, I could generally, by reference to the dictionary for a word or two, understand the meaning; I then wrote my reply, and when at a loss, my servant, a Malagasy Christian from Mauritius, acted as interpreter. Four or five of my visitors, when they left me, wrote on a sheet of paper, which at the time was lying on my desk, their affectionate salutations. This was the commencement of many agreeable and instructive interviews with my friend, the tall figure in the picture, and his companions.

In the course of a week or two after my arrival, another party of Christians arrived from Mahavelona, or Foule Point, a port about forty miles distant on the northern coast. At this port several of the officers of the government were Christians, and by their aid a number of persecuted disciples, and preachers from the capital, had found asylum there and succour in their distress. While waiting for happier days, they maintained constant intercourse with their brethren in Imerina, and spread the knowledge of Christianity among the people in the neighbourhood. These Christians, with a relative of the governor of the port, and a distinguished Christian from the south, were amongst my daily visitors.

I also spent a short time among the Christians at Mahavelona, and was surprised at their number and Christian attainments, as well as their activity in the use of the few means within their reach for maintaining their own spiritual life, and at their good influence on the non-Christian portions of the community. I also learned with pleasure that there were small parties of native Christians residing still farther north.

The evenings, until past midnight, I spent with the disciples, in one or other of their own houses, in answering their inquiries, assuring them of the unabated sympathy and good-will which the friends in England cherished towards them, and in reading and explaining the Scriptures, and prayer. I found that the Christians, who had means, relieved, to the utmost of their ability, the wants of their brethren and sisters in Christ who had found shelter amongst them; and I was greatly pleased with their affectionate, cheerful, and considerate conduct towards those who had suffered much, and were still in danger of discovery and capture by strangers coming unexpectedly from the capital.

My reception by the authorities, as already stated, was friendly, although the officers gave me to understand that there was no change in the treatment of the Christians by the government. When calling on the Governor, or meeting him in the house of a friend, I was sometimes agreeably surprised by a warm pressure of the hand, or other sign of recognition on the occasion from an officer in uniform, or other attendant, who, in plain native lamba, had been at our meeting for reading or prayer on the previous evening. It is customary to welcome visitors with small presents; and although I usually expressed my unwillingness to receive any, and transferred them to my host, on one occasion two or three women, apparently bereaved or mourners, were seen approaching. My tall friend told me they were fugitives who had suffered much, and were bringing me a present, which he begged of me not to refuse. They entered, and, on being seated, said they had brought me a present, at the same time holding out a little matting basket containing three or four eggs, adding, that though the gift was small, I should find no one to whom my coming would give greater joy than it had given to them. I said I was glad if my presence amongst them, as the messenger of friends from England, had afforded them any consolation amidst their heavy trials. To do so was one of my objects in coming; and it was the feeling with which the gift was offered, rather than its intrinsic value, which made it acceptable.

I was deeply affected by the accounts given by these, and others, of the sufferings they had personally endured, as well as of their loss of dearest friends in the past persecutions, and I was glad to aid them in providing for present wants, and cheered them with hopes of ultimate deliverance. With some I was in after years associated at the capital, others I never saw again. I left them gratified not only with their patience and stedfastness, but with the evidence I had gained of the extent to which the gospel had become known in the less frequented parts of the country.

The letters I received at Tamatave, from the Christians at the capital, furnished many subjects for instructive conversation relating to the persecuted believers, in many of whose trials they had personally shared. Some of them could speak a little English, and this helped us to understand each other. Andriambelo and other preachers were among those who were with me most of the time; and although evidently in great want, I was deeply impressed with the gentleness of the demeanour of the first-named preacher, his varied intelligence, great activity, and unremitting endeavours to strengthen the faith of his brethren, as well as to urge upon all to whom he could safely speak the claims of the gospel, and the blessings attending its reception. Sincerity and earnest devotedness to Christ appeared to be the distinguishing features of his character, and these secured for him great respect from all his associates.

I was told that spies were employed to take down the names of persons suspected of Christianity who might visit me by day; but on three or four evenings every week a number of Christians, sometimes nearly twenty, came to my house between nine and ten o'clock, having appointed some of their number to watch at the gate in order to prevent surprise. Sometimes they inquired about the privileges and the proceedings of Christians in England. More frequently their questions related to the word of God, or their own course in times of difficulty. We always associated the reading and explanation of the Scriptures with prayer, and sometimes singing; and though they bent their heads down, and only sang their native hymns in an undertone or whisper to English tunes, I was at times alarmed lest some unfriendly passer by should hear.

Some of my companions were officers who had been deprived of their rank after the severe persecution of 1849, and had been sent to labour as convicts at Mantasoa, a place near the forest, as already mentioned. This enforced labour was unusually severe. The back, shoulders, and arms of some of those who were with me still showed the marks of the wounds and bruises received while they wrought at this work. Notwithstanding this degradation and severe suffering, I never heard an expression of vindictive feeling towards those who had afflicted them, or a desire for revenge, but of thankfulness that God had supported them through their trials, and of sympathy with those whose sufferings had been severer than their own.

I found that among those at Tamatave, and at Foule Point, as well as at the capital, the great want was the word of God. I had sent from Mauritius a few copies, and I had brought a number of New Testaments, bound together or in separate portions, as well as copies of the Psalms and other religious books; but as the officers of the Custom House had strict orders to seize all books which there was any attempt to introduce into the country, my great difficulty was to get them on shore from the ship, as the captain was unfriendly. I could only conceal them tied under my dress; and in this way, and in my pockets, I managed to take eighteen Testaments and other books at a time. But my heart sometimes beat a little quicker when the bow of the boat touched the shore, and I had to jump down on the beach amidst three or four Custom House officers, lest a copy should get loose and fall on the ground before them. I generally spoke to them and passed on, breathing a little more freely when I had entered my house, locked my door, and deposited my treasures in the innermost room. By this means I was able, during my successive visits to Tamatave, to introduce about one thousand five hundred copies of portions of the Scriptures, and other books, among the famishing Christians, some of whom had only a few chapters in manuscript, or three or four leaves of a printed book, soiled, and torn, and mended, until the original was the smallest part left.

From the information I received respecting the state of the Christians in other parts of the country, as well as from those at Tamatave, I could but rejoice in the conclusion, to which all the evidence tended, that although in some instances the knowledge of the disciples might be very limited, and although in other instances there had been defection in maintaining the moral purity which the gospel requires, such instances were exceptional, and comparatively rare; while the great body of the Christians strove, by watchfulness and prayer, to sustain a conscience void of offence toward God and toward men.

At the time of my visit, these Christians had been seventeen or eighteen years without foreign teachers, or any experienced counsellor or guide, surrounded by many adversaries and peculiar difficulties. Their extreme and constant danger, as well as the absence of all earthly encouragement and help, seemed to have bound them together in a holy brotherhood of love, strong and lasting. While I heard of nothing to disturb the affection, the benevolent consideration and sacred fellowship which they shared together, I was surprised and delighted to find that their organization, for purposes of mutual edification and the spiritual benefit of others, had been according to the plain and simple model propounded in the Holy Scriptures, which so far as their means permitted and their necessities required had been adopted; and whatever distinctive form their ecclesiastical polity, if such a term be applicable, may in any future age assume, all that can be said of the Martyr Church of Madagascar in its earlier years is, that it has been built by its own members—guided, we trust, by God's Spirit—upon the few solid and imperishable principles set forth in the New Testament.

I left Madagascar in September, and before returning to England I visited the stations of the London Missionary Society in South Africa; and previously to my departure from the Cape of Good Hope, in 1855, I received a letter, addressed to Mr. Cameron and myself, stating that as the cholera had ceased in Mauritius, there was no impediment to our visiting the capital of Madagascar. A second letter to the same effect reaching me in London, in 1856, I sailed for that island, in compliance with the wishes of the directors of the society, in March of that year, and after a long detention at Ceylon reached Madagascar on the 12th of July.

Letters from the Prince Royal, and from Prince Ramonja, had been sent to Tamatave, expressing their pleasure at the prospect of seeing me, and urging me not to delay my journey. Orders had been also received by the authorities at Tamatave to provide bearers for myself and my luggage. I was, however, somewhat delayed by the arrival of messengers sent from the capital to express the condolence of the sovereign with the family of the late M. Delastelle, a French trader who had recently died. The mode of estimating the worth of the deceased appeared to me unusual, when the officer, in addressing the family, said the queen would rather have given two thousand, three thousand, or even five thousand dollars, than that he should have died. I was, however, afterwards told that this is a usual mode of expressing the sense of loss by death. The most objectionable part of the proceeding was the distribution of a number of oxen for slaughter, and the gift of several barrels of arrack, in consequence of which a large part of the population gave themselves up to drunkenness and riot throughout the night.

Soon after noon on the 8th of August, I set out on my journey, in a covered palanquin, accompanied by the bearers whom the queen had appointed to carry my luggage. The Governor sent an officer in charge of the natives, and the society of Christian officers from Mahavelona, travelling to the capital at the same time, made the journey instructive and pleasant.

I had already become acquainted with the coast in the neighbourhood of Tamatave; but the country inland exhibited not only new, rich, and charming scenery, but made me acquainted with a number of most rare and beautiful plants, the existence of many of which had, by a French botanist, been previously made known in Europe, but of which no living plant had been seen there. Such plants were abundant;

amongst them the *Angræcum sesquipedale* and the *Ouvirandra fenestralis*, or lace-leaf plant; the latter grew in the shallow waters which I frequently passed. Living specimens of both these rare and remarkable plants, as well as others, I was able to bring to England; and to deposit the *Ouvirandra* at Kew, as also in the Edinburgh and Dublin public gardens. The *Angræcum* now finds a place in most orchidaceous collections.

I halted at one place where crocodiles' eggs were dried for food, and saw several of the celebrated places on the road. At the residence of Prince

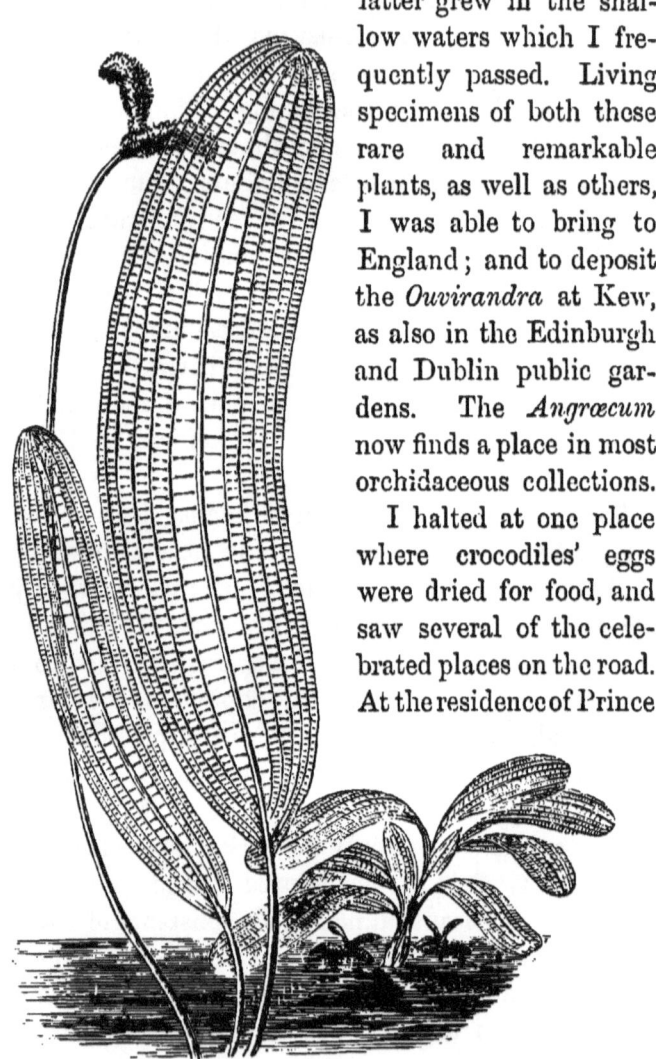

Ramonja, in the province of Ankay, I was most hospitably entertained. Letters of cheerful greeting from the Christians reached me during my journey. I had the pleasure of spending a night sometimes with a Christian traveller, or with a number of the leading Christians and preachers from the capital, grave and dignified men, who were the bearers of messages and presents, and of receiving the hospitality of Christian residents in places through which I passed. I also visited in the night, in a lonely place, a preacher and his wife and family, all under sentence of death and slavery, but living in concealment. I had passed through the eastern portion of Imerina, and halted for the night, according to instructions from the capital, at the small village of Ambohipo.

Soon after sunrise on the morning of the 25th of August, three young officers arrived, having been sent by the queen to conduct me to the capital, about five miles distant. I was glad that they spoke English sufficiently well to enable us to understand each other. They were the three young nobles who afterwards compiled and published an English and Malagasy vocabulary, which proved useful among their countrymen.

On descending to the level ground below the house in which I had slept, I found a palanquin and bearers which the officers informed me the prince had sent for my accommodation. The officers led the way on horseback, accompanied by some who travelled with us; and my own friends, several of whom were Christians, followed; my former bearers, and empty palanquin, with the bearers of my packages closing the line. Thus we passed through comparatively level country until we reached the foot of the long oval hill on which the city stands, and ascending a height of two or three hundred feet, entered the narrow streets or pathways leading through the higher parts of the town to the pleasant and comfortable dwelling, on the western side of the mountain, which had been provided for my use. The officers having with great kindness installed me in my new abode, departed to inform the queen of my arrival.

The house, occupying an airy situation, was clean, and sufficiently furnished for all my requirements, and I could not but feel grateful for my safety and health during the journey, as well as for the welcome accommodation provided for my sojourn in this, to me, deeply interesting city. Two Christian officers, with the wife of one of them, who had been my travelling companions from the coast, occupied, at my request, the house next to my own, and relieved me from all anxiety about providing for the wants of my household.

I received an early visit from the prince, accompanied by an officer whom I had known when he was a youth, being one of those sent to England for education. The prince, then in his twenty-sixth year, was frank and open in his demeanour, and easy in his manners. After a most cordial welcome, he asked a number of questions respecting the political state of Europe, the English and French alliance, and, more especially, whether there was any truth in the report of a French invasion of Madagascar. I told him I had seen something of the kind in the newspapers, but did not think it likely that France would send troops against his country. I then asked if there was any truth in a statement which I had seen in the English newspapers, to the effect that he had become a Roman Catholic, and had written to the Pope to ask that Catholic missionaries might be sent to Madagascar. He assured me it was not true, though a Roman Catholic priest was at the capital, and had tried to persuade him to adopt his creed, but that he had no wish to become a Catholic. We conversed a long time on religion, a subject on which the prince manifested great earnestness, speaking most favourably of the Christians. It was late in the evening before he left. Two companies of Christians entered as soon as the prince had departed, bearing affecting salutations and welcome from many others who could not come.

In the evening of the following day I received a visit from Prince Ramonja, and a relative, also a Christian. The meeting affected me much. After we had exchanged greetings on his entrance, he knelt down by his chair, and in simple terms, but with much earnestness and feeling, thanked God for His goodness in bringing us together. He then prayed for the Christians who had sent me, and implored blessings on the believers in Madagascar. He afterwards conversed with earnestness, but with gentleness of manner, about the friends of whom he had heard in England, of the afflictions and sufferings of the Christians in his own country, of God's great goodness throughout their long season of trial, and of their continued increase, both in the city and the country.

On the following day a number of high officers, wearing silk lambas over their gold-embroidered uniforms, some with heavy gold chains round their necks, and large bracelets of the same metal, came to my house, having been sent by the queen to inquire what was the object of my visit to Antananarivo. I replied that it was, as I had stated in my letter, a visit, not for purposes of commerce, but of friendship only, to her Majesty and the government, to talk about things for the good of the kingdom. I also stated that I was the bearer of a message of friendship from England to the government of Madagascar. That as there had been reports of ships coming from England to attack Madagascar, the Earl of Clarendon, who had been sent to Paris by her Majesty Queen Victoria to assist in arranging for the peace of Europe after the war with Russia, had ordered a letter to be written to me authorizing the statements I had made. I then read the letter to the officers, two of whom, understanding English, interpreted it to the rest. I also delivered a letter, from his Excellency the Governor of Mauritius, for the queen, and said I had some presents for her Majesty, which I should be happy to deliver as soon as my packages arrived. The officers expressed themselves pleased with my communications, and soon afterwards rose to depart. The rustling of their stiff silk lambas, and the jingling of their large loose gold bracelets, produced, as they shook hands with me on leaving, a somewhat novel effect.

On the following day an officer from the palace came to say that the queen and the government were satisfied with the object of my visit, and highly gratified with the communications of which I was the bearer. Presents of welcome, consisting of one or two oxen, sheep and goats, poultry, rice, and eggs, were sent by the queen, the prince and princess, some of the nobles and others, which I directed my Christian friends to dispose of as most suitable. The three officers who had conducted me into the city came the next day to say, that if there were any places in the neighbourhood that I wished to see, they were appointed by the queen to accompany me at any time that I might choose.

I had expected that the Christians would rejoice in my coming, but had scarcely supposed that my presence in the capital would be so generally welcome as it appeared to be, and I endeavoured to make the best arrangements possible for encouraging and aiding the Christians, while gathering information respecting them.

CHAPTER VIII.

Favourable effect of message of friendship from England—Visits to remarkable places—Interview with the commander-in-chief—The queen's hospitality—Deeply affecting recitals of sufferings of the Christians—Hopes inspired by the results of persecution in other countries—Conferences and prayer with the leaders of the Christians—Social life among the disciples—The prevalence of prayer—Times and places of united worship—Christians from Vonizongo—Conversation with the young—Visit of Mr. Lambert to the capital, and his statements to the Christians—Places where the martyrs suffered—Farewell visit from the prince and princess—Last night with the Christians—Departure from Madagascar and return to England—Review of the progress and state of Christianity in the country—Return of Mr. Lambert to the capital—The last persecution—Numbers implicated—Barbarity of the executions—Illness and death of the queen—Notice of her character and reign.

SOME account of the general aspect of the country, of its natural productions, especially of the rare and beautiful plants which adorn its surface, of its aquatic vegetation, of the ferns which adorn its woody dells, the sombre shade of its primeval forests, its trees of graceful form and strange uses, has been already given; as well as notices of the manners and customs of the people, the fondness of the court for pageantry and show on public occasions, together with the hospitality exercised at the capital. These have already been made public,* and would be out of place in a simple narrative of the introduction of Christianity to the country, of the sufferings which its reception brought upon the people, and of its subsequent marvellous progress amongst them.

Reference to the government and its proceedings are only reverted to here so far as they relate to the condition of the people, and the progress of the gospel. Suspicious as the Malagasy were of all foreigners, prior to the first friendly visits of the English, and instructed as they have since been as to the extent to which other countries have become subject to English rule, it is not surprising that they should have felt uneasy and alarmed by reports of England's aggressive intentions towards their country, which included the fitting out of a fleet to attack Madagascar; and we found they were actually building a fort to resist such attacks at the time of our arrival in the country.

Political considerations arising out of the false accusation of the Christians, as teaching sedition to the people and seducing them from the gods of their own country to the service of the God of the English, preparatory to the transfer of their allegiance from one sovereign to the other, had greatly strengthened the aversion of the government to the Christian faith and their determination to destroy it. At the time of my arrival there were recently circulated reports of the unfriendly intentions of the English towards Madagascar, which caused me to regard as most

* "Three Visits to Madagascar," and "Madagascar Revisited."

timely, and indirectly favourable to the Christians, the declaration of the Earl of Clarendon, that the British Government desired the prosperity of Madagascar and had no wish whatever to interfere with its internal affairs. I had no doubt that, to the arrival of this welcome intelligence at the time of my visit, I was chiefly indebted for the friendliness manifested towards me, as an Englishman, by the government, although I had previously been acquainted with some of its members in my own country.

The attentions of the government, though unexpected, were not unwelcome, as I hoped they might favour the objects of my visit, and I perceived that they were gratifying and encouraging to the Christians. I accompanied the prince and a number of young officers to different parts of the city. On one occasion we went to visit some bridges he had erected over broad, shallow streams about two miles from the capital; also to the country palace Isoaierana, built by Radama, on a grassy plain to the west of the city. As we returned, the prince, pointing to the granite rocks at the summit of the southern end of the mountain on which the city stands, told me that was *Ambohipotsy*, the spot on which the first martyrs had suffered. As some of the officers in attendance on the prince were heathen, I made no inquiries about the place, though I gazed repeatedly at the spot with feelings of reverence, as well as with strong and peculiar interest.

I was afterwards invited to accompany the prince

and princess, with their attendants and a number of officers, to a pleasantly situated country seat, called Mahazoarivo, the grounds of which were planted with rare and valuable trees from different parts of the island. Vines were also here under culture, and the pieces of ornamental water were stocked with several kinds of the water-fowl of the country. In the front court of the large palace I was among the spectators of a large public ball; and was invited to a bull fight, which latter entertainment I begged to decline.

One evening I received a visit from a friend of the prince and the Christians, the commander-in-chief, successor in office to his father, who had been one of the most sanguinary persecutors of the Christians. He spoke favourably both of them and of the prince, and after expressing the pleasure which the assurance of the friendship of England afforded to the government he departed, accompanied by his two attendants, herculean men, one of whom was my daily visitor and sincere friend, but who died a martyr's death in the next persecution. The other was, when I afterwards resided in the capital, and is still, a faithful and successful preacher in one of the city churches.

During my stay I was invited, by the order of the queen, to a public dinner, where I met the French consul, and a French Catholic priest wearing a dress coat and embroidered silk waistcoat. I was seated beside the judge who had examined and condemned the Christians at Analakely in the fearful persecution in 1849, a sort of Malagasy Judge Jefferies of that bloody assize, whose name struck terror into the minds of the Christians of Madagascar. And yet, in a letter received during the present year (1869), the Rev. William Cousins, the English pastor of the church at Amparibe, informed me that this same man had become a believer in Christ, and was one of a class who had been four months under regular instruction, preparatory to a declaration of his faith in the Redeemer by publicly receiving Christian baptism.

It was reported that Ramboasalama placed spies in the daytime about the premises which I occupied, so that few of the Christians visited me except those who, as well as heathens, came in considerable numbers asking for medicine; and as there was no medical practitioner at the capital, and many afflicted persons, I was thankful to give such plain, simple medicines as I possessed to many of the applicants, especially to the sick Christians, who were sometimes brought to me from a distance in palanquins under the darkness of night.

I was happy to devote the greater portion of every evening to conversation and social worship with the Christians. Sometimes those who came consisted almost entirely of the widows, orphans, and other relatives of those who had died for Christ; and deeply affecting were the recitals of their remembrance of the stedfastness, faith, patience, and suffering, as well as of the tenderness and affection, of those who, to save life, had fled to the mountains or forests, wandering in unfrequented parts, or hiding from their pursuers in caverns of the earth. Some had thus parted never to meet again in this world. Some had fled to distant provinces, and others were concealed in pits dug in the floor of their dwelling-houses, or in adjacent plantations of their friends, whose own lives became thereby endangered. Some of those who visited me were strong and cheerful under their trials, others comparatively silent; and others were unable to restrain the tears which probably afforded relief to hearts burdened with the sorrows which they still had to bear. I never once heard a syllable of regret uttered that they had become followers of Christ at such a cost, nor a word of anger or hate towards their persecutors. At times I heard an expression of belief that God saw it best that they should be thus afflicted, and that it would be overruled for good to themselves, and, they hoped, to their countrymen. Sometimes they would say, "If those who persecute us did but know the blessedness of the love of Christ, they would love Him too, and save instead of destroying those who believe in His name."

I endeavoured to console them, and to strengthen their hope and trust by adverting to the sympathy and love of the Saviour, who was afflicted in all the afflictions of His people, who knew every pang they felt, who did not willingly suffer them to be afflicted, and who would never forsake them. I said that if they did not see how all things worked together for their good in this world, they would probably know hereafter that their present sufferings had been part of the process by which the kingdom of Christ was to be established in Madagascar, and by which their own spirits were to be made meet for everlasting blessedness.

They were deeply affected on my telling them that when the Christians in England heard of their afflictions, they prayed to God for them in their families and in their places of worship; as also when some of them observed that there was no persecution in England, and I remarked that though there was no persecution in the present day, our forefathers in past times had suffered in chains, had died in prison, and had been burned alive at the stake, for their regard to the word of God and their faith in Jesus Christ. The past sufferings of the Christians of England seemed to make their bond of union with themselves, now passing through the ordeal of fire and bloodshed, more close than it had appeared before; and I do not exaggerate in stating, that the assurance of the sympathy and prayers of the Christians in the land from which they had received the knowledge of Christ, was one of the most welcome and cheering communications I was able to make.

I necessarily met many undiscovered Christians in association with others during the daytime, but any recognition on the part of either of us would have been dangerous to them, for reports had been circulated, by unfriendly foreigners, that my real object in going to Madagascar was to encourage the Christians not to give up praying, but to continue to disobey the law of the queen, and that my visit would cause more of the queen's subjects to be put to death. But though I could seldom speak to them in the day, I arranged to occupy as many evenings as possible with the preachers and leaders of the Christians, with whom I spent some of the most instructive and impressive hours of my life. I sometimes felt a solemn awe come over my spirit as I conversed with men with whom the Spirit of God was so often present.

The human victims sacrificed, the numbers consigned to chains and slavery, together with at least two thousand sentenced to lesser penalties, had for the time appeased the government; while the greater circumspection of the Christians themselves rendered their discovery more difficult. The powerful friends they had found in the princes of the royal family and the new commander-in-chief of the army, also favoured their security. Prince Ramboasalama was the recognised head of the heathen party. He possessed the advantages of wealth, and was besides an energetic and unscrupulous man. The queen's order to the soldiers to seek and arrest the Christians, still read at parade every fortnight, rendered the utmost caution necessary in all our intercourse, on my part as well as on theirs.

I had so managed as to send a few books to them from Mauritius, and I had a small supply with me, which were received with the liveliest gratitude. It was also my privilege, acting on behalf of my friends in England, to relieve, in a slight degree, the wants of the most necessitous and distressed. Besides the information I was able to give them respecting the deep interest felt by numbers in England, and the prayers offered on their behalf, I assured them that if by the Holy Spirit's aid they remained faithful to their own profession and to their divine Lord, the Christians in England believed that their present trials would, as had been found in other countries, issue ultimately in their own deliverance, and in the triumph of the gospel in Madagascar.

Sometimes they expressed their own views and feelings in reference to their sufferings, more frequently they were silent. On one occasion, when I had been speaking on the sympathies and hopes cherished in England respecting them, one or two answered, "We feel too much, our hearts are too full to speak;" then one proposed that we should pray, and all knelt down, while in simple but earnest language he poured forth the emotions of their hearts in supplication and thanksgiving to God. More than once, prayer seemed to be the most natural and satisfactory manner in which to express their thoughts and feelings on our first meeting, and we never parted without prayer.

I presented a number of inquiries to them, in writing, respecting their proceedings in relation to meetings for worship, the administration of the ordinances, and the instructions of the word of God which they found most effectual in bringing the heathen to Christ, and building up the converts in faith and holiness. I inquired also as to the social life of the Christians when living together or among the heathen; and to all these inquiries I received truly satisfactory answers. They said that when all living in one house were Christians, they united in prayer once a day; that secret daily prayer was universal; and that as many as could, with safety, attended their weekly assemblies for nightly worship; that one of the first endeavours of an uneducated Christian was to learn to read, and that the children of all Christian parents were taught to read, and many to write. I could obtain no list of the names or numbers of the Christians. They said they had never ventured to make out any list, either of places of worship or of the names of the Christians, lest in the event of their own impeachment and capture, or on a forcible entrance being made into their houses to search for books, it should be discovered and bring trouble on them all.

There were five or six houses in which they occasionally assembled, and probably about three thousand Christians; but they could not speak with precision of their numbers, as many more were said to be favourable to the gospel than were personally known to those with whom I conversed. They generally mentioned to me their arrangements for meeting, and many came to my house on the Saturday who stated that they were going to a distance for their weekly worship. On my asking if I could safely attend one of their meetings, they replied it would give them all great pleasure, but it could not be done safely, as some sick person, or servant of one of the officers, might come to my house for medicine, and my absence would excite suspicion, lead to inquiry as to the cause, and might involve others in trouble.

Several members from Christian families in the country sometimes joined our evening meetings, whose simple and almost timid conversation, together with their accounts of some who had found shelter amongst them, as well as of other Christian families in the surrounding country, were highly encouraging. Besides these I was repeatedly visited by one or two preachers, and by several Christians from Vonizongo, a district of Ankova forty miles north of the capital. These were intelligent men, and their knowledge of the Scriptures was remarkable. They were poor, and had evidently suffered much, but were firm in their faith in Christ, and hopeful for the future. A considerable number of martyrs, who had died rather than deny their Saviour, had belonged to this district. Nine had been thrown over the precipice, and three had been burned alive; but none had witnessed a nobler confession before their judges, or had more faithfully and triumphantly glorified the Lord Jesus in their death, than these Vonizongo Christians. The children of some of those who died for Christ fled to distant parts of the country, where, though they suffered much, they have been faithful witnesses for their Saviour, and messengers of mercy to the people. Two or three New Testaments, all I was able to give them to carry home, were received with unspeakable joy.

I had also opportunities of conversing with a

number of young men connected with some of the higher classes, whom I found, whether favourable to Christianity or not, eager to hear about other countries different from their own, and apparently thirsting after knowledge, and ripe for instruction. The little acquaintance they had with English I urged them to increase by earnest effort, endeavouring to kindle their enthusiasm by reference to the advantages which the opening of their country to the commerce of other nations would place within their reach, and alluding to their possible influence on the future of their country.

I have already noticed the presence of a French priest at the capital. He had recently arrived in company with Mr. Lambert, a French merchant from Mauritius, and had been left, as I was told, with the French consul as Mr. Lambert's mercantile clerk, or as teacher of mathematics to Mr. Labord's son. I heard, while there, that M. Lambert had expressed great indignation at the oppressive conduct of the native government, and had shown much sympathy with the Christians, giving money to be distributed amongst the most destitute; and that the Christians had been told of the advantages that would result to them, as well as to other portions of the community, from their being taken under French protection. They were told that religion in France was entirely free to all, and that under the protection of that country the queen would not be allowed to persecute her people. With Tahiti so fresh in my memory, these rumours, had they been nothing else, could not

P

be welcome to me, and in answer to the questions of my friends I said it was kind in M. Lambert to help them in their distress, but that in the course of nature their sufferings must soon terminate; and should God raise the prince to the throne, their religious liberty would be safe, and the country their own. I therefore exhorted them to continue, so long as God should allow them to be persecuted, to bear their affliction as they had hitherto so nobly done, to give their enemies no cause to question the loyalty which they had maintained so long, and neither to listen to any proposals nor become parties to any attempt to depose the queen by force, or to place the country under the protection of the French.

From the time of my arrival I had been anxious to see the places where the martyrs had suffered. The prince had pointed out to me the first place erected for Christian worship at Ambatonakanga, afterwards, and at the time of my visit, used as a prison. He had also directed my attention to Ambohipotsy, where the first martyrs suffered. A Christian friend had conducted me, in the early morning, to a spot whence I could obtain a view of the Tarpeian rock from which the Christians were hurled. Ambohizanahary, where Paul the diviner and his companions were put to death, was visible from my residence; and I had also seen Faravohitra, where the nobles were burned. I found a melancholy satisfaction in gazing on places which, for generations to come, will be associated with the love and constancy even unto death, of which the early members of the Malagasy church there gave such all-convincing evidence.

In the message of permission for my visit to the capital, a month had been specified as the period of its duration; and though, as already stated, I had been treated with kindness and hospitality, it was evident that my prolonged residence in the country, under existing circumstances, would not have been agreeable to those in authority, and might have been prejudicial to the interests of those whom I most wished to serve. I therefore prepared for my departure at the appointed time, with feelings of thankfulness for having seen and learned so much, and not without hope that my visit might eventually prove of service to my friends.

A day or two before the time fixed for my departure, the prince informed me that the princess his wife, and a friend, would come and spend with me the last evening of my stay in the capital. Between six and seven o'clock on the evening specified, the prince and princess, accompanied by her adopted daughter, the child of the first Radama's sister, arrived, attended by an escort. After a slight refreshment the evening passed pleasantly and rapidly away. The princess said that the queen and the members of the court were pleased with my visit, and hoped that nothing would occur to interrupt the friendly intercourse between England and Madagascar. Speaking of the frequent rumours of hostile intentions against them, she said, "Why cannot we be allowed to live in peace in our own country? We don't interfere with others, we are neither invaders nor usurpers. We inhabit the country of our ancestors." She made many inquiries about the Queen of England, but the conversation chiefly related to education, and the advantages which it would give to Madagascar. At ten o'clock, the hour at which all persons are expected to be in their own houses, the palanquins were ordered, and with many expressions of good-will my visitors departed, the prince's band playing the English "God save the Queen" as they left the premises.

A number of Christian friends who had been waiting then entered my house, and others continued to come until midnight. They had many of them questions to ask, which I endeavoured to answer. To two of them, who had obtained from an English physician some knowledge of medicine, I gave all the medicines I had left, and divided amongst them my remaining Malagasy books. I likewise gave them a few useful articles, and confided to them some others to be sold, requesting that the proceeds, together with some money which I left, might be distributed amongst the afflicted and destitute. We then commended each other to God, and it was drawing towards dawn when they left.

On the morning of the 26th of September I finished my packing. Several of my friends, and others to whom I had given medicines, brought small presents, as expressions, they said, of their sense of my kindness. Others came to take leave. During the forenoon I called on some of the sick, and went to take a farewell look at the rock from whence the Christians had been thrown, and the spot where others were burned—places of deepest interest to me, and which I did not then expect to see again. The queen sent bearers, and I was informed that eight officers would accompany me, in order that there might be no delay in the fever districts.

About one o'clock the prince and one of the nobles arrived. The courtyard in front of my house was crowded with people. After a grave conversation with the prince and his companion we rose to depart, when the prince, with evident emotion, took me by the hand, led me out of the house and through the crowd to my palanquin, and then entered his own. Thus I commenced my homeward journey, receiving the recognition of friends as I passed through the narrow streets to the open plain, where other nobles were waiting. The prince's band preceded us as we continued our journey. The afternoon was fine, and there had not been a shower of rain while I was in the capital. We conversed as we travelled on to Ambohipo, where, as the officers who had the arrangement of the journey proposed to proceed farther, the prince took leave of me with evident feeling, as did also his attendants; having commended me to the protection of God, he accompanied me back to my palanquin, telling the leader of the band to go with me to the next halting-place. The prince and his companions then entered their palanquins, his attendants mounted their horses, and they turned towards the capital, while I continued my journey to Betafo, where I found my packages had already arrived.

The Christian friends who had kindly accompanied me on my first day's travel returned the next morning to the city, and I proceeded towards the coast. On my way I passed a surgeon and three French priests,—one of them travelling as the surgeon's assistant; another was the Abbé Jouen, the principal of the Jesuits' College at Réunion, afterwards *Préfct Apostolique de Madagascar*. These travellers were accompanied by a French gentleman with whom I was acquainted, and who had kindly brought me letters from Mauritius and England.

Though the season was late I reached the coast in safety, but had to wait some time for a ship. In reviewing the weeks I had spent at Antananarivo, I was deeply impressed with the power and goodness of God, as manifested in the marvellous progress of the gospel among the people, as well as with the numbers and position of the Christians; and while there was much in their circumstances and in their afflictions to be deplored, there was also much to demand the liveliest gratitude, as promising a happier future. All the reports of the progress and effects of the gospel which had been sent to England and circulated amongst our churches, had, by personal inquiry and observation on the spot, been more than verified. A more correct acquaintance with the standing and influence of the Christians had been obtained, as well as of the relative position and power of their enemies and their friends; and although grounds of apprehension, arising from the hostility of the leader of the heathen and the probable attempts of the French on the country, still existed, there was nothing to diminish trust in divine Providence for still greater results, or to justify doubt of the final triumph of the gospel in Madagascar.

The last members of the earliest mission left Madagascar in 1836. Twenty years had now elapsed since these brethren had been forced away. The newly gathered church of Christ, strong only in reliance on the truth of God's word and the faith and love of Christ implanted by the divine Spirit in the hearts of its members, but weak in the immaturity and inexperience of its earliest childhood, had sustained, throughout these twenty years, the combined assaults of an idolatry and a despotism as blindly fanatical and as recklessly cruel as had ever afflicted mankind. This comparatively feeble church had, during that period, not only maintained its ground unbroken in the conflict, but had gained a more advanced position, and was, by increasing power and numbers, drawn from every rank of native society, gathering strength for future triumphs for Christ its Lord.

What the moral state of the people was when the gospel was first brought amongst them, has been described in the earlier chapters of this volume. And not less remarkable than the outward progress of Christianity, has been the influence of the word of God and the grace of the Lord Jesus over the hearts and conduct of its members, whose lives and characters had become so changed that even the judges, before whom they were arraigned, declared that no charge could be sustained against the Christians, except on the ground of their religion.

Doubtless there were some to whom this testimony would be too favourable; but they were few—fewer in all probability than they have been since. One of the earliest causes of bitter hostility against the followers of the new religion, was their forsaking and resisting the vices and immoralities of the general population. That was what they were charged with, when accused of changing the customs of the people which idolatry sanctioned and authority commended. The whole fabric of social life was elevated and purified amongst the Christian families, who were, in this respect, witnesses for God, as well as in their faith and their worship; and I considered it a privilege to have been permitted to see, even for a few weeks, such evidences of this divine and wonderful work.

Having been detained some weeks at Tamatave, waiting for a ship, I finally left Madagascar on the 17th of November for Mauritius, where I obtained a passage home in the *England*, and reached my native land in March, 1857.

Little change in the circumstances of the Christians took place after my departure until the return of M. Lambert, who reached Antananarivo about two months after my arrival in England. That gentleman, on leaving Madagascar in 1856, had proceeded to France and to England, to solicit from the Emperor and the English minister the aid of troops to dethrone the queen of Madagascar, as a means of delivering her people from the miseries of her rule. Having failed to obtain troops, he returned to the island, and, associating himself with several other foreigners, proposed, with the assistance of the prince and his friends, to deprive the queen of power, and instal the prince in her place. But the prince and his friends soon withdrew from the project, and the former endeavoured to persuade the French to relinquish the attempt. They, however, thought the plan might succeed; but about a month after the first movements, the queen became acquainted with the intentions of the conspirators, as well as that the French had assisted the Christians. M. Lambert and his companions were consequently, at a few hours' notice, sent under a guard to the coast, and put on board the first ship sailing from the port.

A month before the foreigners were sent out of the country, Ratsimandisa, an inferior chief, who had been educated by the first missionaries, and had been associated with the Christians as one of themselves, treacherously made out a list of seventy names of the Christians, charging them with being implicated in the treasonable plot. This list he carried to one of the officers of the queen, who, previous to laying it before the sovereign, gave it to the prince. As soon as he had read the list, the prince tore it in pieces, and ordered information to be immediately given to the Christians of their impending danger.

Whether the Christians were reported as being concerned in the conspiracy is not stated. I made every inquiry; some said a few might have known of it, but none took any part therein, and that the great body of them certainly knew nothing about it. In the meantime it became known to the queen that numbers were in the habit of meeting for worship, and that they were encouraged by the French.

The inhabitants were immediately ordered to assemble to attend a kabary, and the portentous firing of cannon on the 3rd of July, 1857, announced that a message from the queen would be delivered. Thousands assembled, and the avenues to the place were guarded by troops. The bearer of the royal message announced that the queen had heard that there were many Christians in and around the capital. These were ordered within fifteen days to accuse themselves, on pain of death. But few reported themselves. Soldiers were then sent out to search for Christians, and a few were captured, and tortured in order to extort the names of their companions. The queen was greatly enraged. Additional troops were sent in pursuit of the Christians, and the inhabitants of the villages, in which they might be harboured, were threatened with death if they concealed or succoured them, but promised rewards if they captured or reported them.

Six Christians were concealed at a village two or three miles from the capital, and the soldiers, having searched the house in which they were hidden, in a pit covered over with straw, were leaving the building, when some one within was heard to cough. The soldiers renewed their search, discovered the Christians, and bound them prisoners. The officer then ordered the inhabitants of the village to be also bound and taken to the capital, for having afforded shelter and concealment to their friends.

The queen was highly incensed against these villagers, as well as the Christians, and declared that every village should be searched, all the pits examined, and even the swamps or rivers dragged with nets, rather than the Christians should remain in the land. So great was the terror of the people, that the inhabitants of whole villages fled. A number of soldiers were sent to arrest Christians at the mountainous village of Ambohitrabiby, ten miles from Antananarivo; but when the troops arrived the houses alone remained, not a single inhabitant was in the place.

During this season of extreme distress and danger the Prince Ramonja and the commander-in-chief, especially the former, were deeply moved on behalf of the Christians, and, whenever it was possible, aided their escape, which a number of them effected. They also furnished houses for their shelter, with the means of subsistence. Maternal instinct on the part of the queen, the only one restraining element in her cruel nature, not only protected the prince, but enabled him, during this period, to save many lives.

One of the disciples, when told by the officer who discovered him that he must take him prisoner, asked, "What is my crime? I am not a traitor. I am not a murderer. I have wronged no one." The officer replied, "It is not for any of these things that I must take you, but for praying." To this the Christian leader replied, "If that is what I am charged with, it is true. I have done that. I do not refuse to go with you."

This was the charge on which most, if not all, were arrested, and it included reading the Scriptures and singing hymns, or the several acts of Christian worship. I heard of no instance in which any one, when accused, denied the charge, or refused to meet the consequences. More than two hundred suffered different kinds of punishment, most of them severe. The greater number of those who suffered death were men of mark, distinguished among the Christians for their position, piety, devotedness, ability and usefulness. Fourteen were stoned to death at Fiadana, more than a mile distant from Ambohipotsy, as were also others afterwards. Fifty-seven, if not a larger number, were chained together by the neck with heavy iron fetters, and banished to distant parts, where more than half of them died a lingering, agonizing death in their chains.* Fifty took the poison, of which eight died. Sixteen, amongst a large number reduced to slavery, were redeemed, at heavy cost to their friends; and six devoted, leading

* An iron ring was passed through an aperture at one end of a heavy iron bar, nearly three feet long, and the ring was then riveted on the neck of the Christian; a heavy iron ring was also riveted on each ankle. A second ring was passed through an aperture at the other end of the bar and riveted on the neck of another Christian, and in this manner seven or more were chained together. The fetters which I brought home, and which had been worn four and a half years by one Christian, weighed fifty-six pounds.

CONSOLATION TO A CHRISTIAN IN FETTERS.

P. 220.

men among the Christians, who had been condemned to death, escaped, and remained in concealment for four years and six months, often suffering from want of food.

The barbarous, brutalizing mode of inflicting death by stoning was a new kind of punishment, devised, it is supposed, as the most terrific that could be adopted, in the hope of its being successful where other methods had failed. The heads of those stoned at Fiadana were severed from their bodies, in some instances shortening the suffering by terminating life; the heads were then fixed on poles. Those whose friendly eyes had watched, as near as safety would allow, the last moments of the departed, guided afterwards the footsteps of friends, who repaired to the spot during the hours of the night, to drive off the hungry dogs, and to bear away the bruised and mangled remains of the martyrs who had that day sealed their faith with their blood. These remains, regarded with hallowed affection, were received by loving hands, and finally consigned in secret to the resting-places of their ancestors.

The wholesale slaughter of 1857, less than twelve months after my departure from the capital, although the one most deeply felt by the Christians, in consequence of the number and the character of those put to death, was, by the merciful providence of God, the last which the Martyr Church of Madagascar was called to sustain. Only one other attempt was made, and that proved disastrous to its authors alone.

In June, 1860, the governor of Mananjara, a port

on the southern coast, accused two high officers (one of them Ratefe, an eminent Christian whom I had known at Tamatave, and afterwards corresponded with from the capital), and thirty soldiers, of violating the laws of the queen by meeting together for worship. The accusers and the accused were summoned to the capital, and the queen ordered the test of the tangena to be employed vicariously, as was occasionally done in other cases, to discover the innocence or guilt of the accused. The result of the ordeal declared the accused to be innocent, and, according to a practice sometimes followed amongst the people, the accuser was sentenced to the punishment which would have been inflicted on the accused had they been found guilty. The man who brought the charge was, in this instance, put to death, and this was the last accusation preferred against the Christians in Madagascar.

The first who died on account of their connection with Christianity suffered in 1835, soon after the departure of the early missionaries. The last who laid down their lives for Christ suffered in 1857. But notwithstanding the fearful destruction of life during this protracted period, two-thirds of the duration of a generation, the faith of the Christians was stronger, and their love of the Saviour not less, than when the first martyrs died for the name of the Lord Jesus. But far more remarkable is the fact that during all these years of oppression and suffering, the number and the influence of the Christians had continued steadily to increase.

After the expulsion of the French, little intercourse was allowed even at the ports, and no foreigner was allowed to advance beyond the coast into the country. It was some time before the Christians ventured to write, and communications from them during this period were few. In one of their letters which reached England, the writer, in speaking of the native Christians, states, "And in respect to those who are in concealment and those who are in bonds, it is Rakoto and Ramonja who have taken on themselves the charge of concealing and protecting them, and giving them their daily bread. And those of their companions who have any property, give for this according to their ability; and those of their brethren who are in distress or want, though not in bonds or concealment, are looked after and cared for by these two princes, sometimes receiving from them clothes, rice, and even money. We know that such liberality presses hard at times upon their means, but they cannot abandon their own afflicted brethren, *for they are to them as their own flesh.*"

Some idea of their circumstances after the last persecution may be derived from a letter addressed to me by a Christian at the capital in 1861, in which, after expressing gratitude to the God and Father of our Lord Jesus Christ for preserving their lives, he continues:—" Pray, dear sir, that the blessing of Jesus Christ may be with us, and with you, and that we may be helped to endure the affliction that is so severe. May we have love and courage during our lifetime upon earth (Rom. v. 8—11), and may the

God of peace quickly subdue the work of Satan, and advance the knowledge of the people respecting Jesus Christ (2 Cor. ix. 10; x. 45).

"The distress of the people here is increasing daily, for they are in darkness, and have no knowledge. The country is not tranquil. There is much war with the enemy, so that they are hated and hating one another. Therefore we say, pray to God that light may spread among us, the people of Madagascar. Let us ask the God of mercy that darkness may be scattered from the land; and perhaps while we both are alive we shall see your face, and shake hands with you, dear sir; and even though we be not permitted to see one another in this life, may God help us to meet in the great salvation that was accomplished by our Lord Jesus Christ, to increase our gratitude and praise (Luke xxiii. 43; 1 Cor. xv. 52, 57).

"With respect to the royal prince, indeed, dear sir, it causes us to rejoice and bless God that he supports and makes the people of God strong to bear the affliction and trouble in Madagascar. Yes, what he has done he has done by the help of God, and we therefore bless the Most High on that account (Matt. xvi. 17); and not towards the Christians alone does he show kindness, but to the people in general, when he can."

So long as the strength of the queen allowed her to attend to proceedings amongst the people, Ramboasalama's friends were ready to enforce her orders against the Christians, and but little improvement

ILLNESS AND ALARM OF THE QUEEN. 225

in their condition was allowed. She was said to have been very cruel in her treatment of her people generally. But now, as her strength began to fail, her severity against the Christians was relaxed. Some of the sentences against them were only partially executed, and a number sold into slavery obtained their freedom. In this altered state of things the minds of the people became susceptible to alarming impressions, and the queen especially was disturbed by strange apprehensions. Fires were said to be seen on the land and voices heard in the sky, the meaning of which the diviners could not explain, though some said these were signs foreshadowing death. From this time the queen prayed earnestly to the idols and the other objects of her trust, for she was afraid. She afterwards became ill, and a month later made a journey to a healthy place; but returned weak and wasted. Again the queen went out for a charm or medicine, but her disease increased. The skill of the diviners, the succour of the idols, the medicines or charms ordered by the sikidy at whatever distance or cost they were to be obtained, all failed to revive or stay the failing life.

The prince was counselled not to leave the palace. The princess his wife, and other members of the royal family, were also collected within its precincts. The high military officers assembled at the house of the commander-in-chief. The judges ordered the people to circulate no idle rumours in the capital, and the commander-in-chief augmented the troops in the court of the palace to five hundred.

Q

On the 16th of July the queen died. After fourteen days had been spent in the observance of the usual ceremonies, the body was taken with great pomp to Ambohimanga, and on the 30th of July was buried there, in the course of the night. The heads of the people, according to long usage on such occasions, were ordered to be shaved; amusements and the use of gay clothing were discontinued; but few other ceremonies of national mourning were observed.

Ranavalona was the wife given to Radama by his father, with the expression of his will that a child of his, of whom she should be the mother, should be his successor. But she was neither the wife of his choice nor the mother of his children, her only child having been born twelve months after his death. During Radama's life she occupied no conspicuous position, and exercised no commanding influence. After his death she continued to encourage Mr. Cameron's lectures on chemistry to the young men, and promoted the secular instruction given by the missionaries. As she had ascended the throne with the public assurance that she would not change what Radama had done, she gave permission for the converts to Christianity to be baptized, as had been done before. She also gave the people permission to attend the preaching and worship of the missionaries; and, on their application, sent men, as Radama had done, to work at the press and to transcribe writing.

The assistance in printing was continued for some time, but the Christian privileges were withdrawn almost as soon as granted, and it was only in furtherance of secular advantages that any encouragement was given. Whatever different elements of her own character might have been developed in another station of life, or with different associates, it is useless now to imagine. It has been said, even of this queen of Madagascar, that she was not incapable of acts of personal kindness. But her position as a queen called into exercise her fiercest passions and indomitable will, fostered and intensified by the superstitions of her country, by which she was declared to be the visible god, invested with absolute rule and resistless power.

By the overruling providence of the supreme Disposer of the world and the love of Christ Jesus in the hearts of the Christians of Madagascar, Ranavalona, by her fierce and unrelaxed persecution, pursued through the greater part of her protracted reign, became the instrument of testing, purifying, and strengthening in her country that divinely implanted faith which the chief energies of her life were employed to destroy.

CHAPTER IX.

The end of the persecutions—Radama II. proclaimed king—Proclamation of religious liberty—The exiles and Christians in fetters recalled—The claims of the idols disregarded—The use of the tangena and sorcery abolished—The king's orders for the administration of justice—His treatment of the conquered races—His want of better counsellors—Increase of intemperance in the country—Return of French traders and priests—Voyage to Mauritius—First movement towards the erection of the memorial churches—Letter to the king on the subject—Arrival in Madagascar—Journey to the capital—Interview with the king and queen—Visits from the widows and children of the martyrs—Prince Ramonja and the prime minister—Visit to Ambohipotsy and Ampamarinana—First Sunday in the capital—Deliverance from dread of slavery.

PERSECUTION on account of religion had now ended in Madagascar; freedom and security were in prospect; and not more welcome to weary and suffering watchers through the night could be the breaking up of darkness and the dawn of day, than were the events which we now have to record in that land.

We have seen that on the night before the queen's decease, the commander-in-chief left the Prince Royal in the Silver Palace, with a guard of five hundred men. It has also been stated that there was a powerful claimant who intended to dispute the right to the throne with the prince. Ramboasalama had declared himself ready to acknowledge the rightful heir; but the collecting by himself and his friends of their retainers under arms, did not inspire confidence in his sincerity. The prime minister of the late queen and the chief judge of the kingdom favoured this prince; but during the night before the queen's death, the commander-in-chief not only surrounded the royal palace with troops, but also the palaces of the rival prince and his adherents; and when, early next morning, the appointed signal announced to the commander-in-chief that the queen had ceased to breathe, he placed additional troops around those palaces, with orders that they should allow no one to leave. He then gathered his own soldiers in and around the court of the royal palace, so that when the queen's death was publicly announced, Ramboasalama and his friends, instead of being able to proceed and claim the throne, found that the troops and populace were shouting for Radama and throwing up their caps for joy, while they themselves were prisoners.

The members of the royal family then proceeded to Andohalo, where Ramboasalama, Ramonja, the Princess Rabodo wife of Radama, and all the members of the royal family took the oath of allegiance to the Prince Royal, who was proclaimed king, with the title of Radama II.

When the people heard the proclamation, they shouted *Hiobe!* (the Malagasy cheer), and the shouting spread from the city to the suburbs, and the people came out in their holiday attire, for they said Radama was the king they desired. At four o'clock in the afternoon the officers, judges, and heads of the people, followed by the troops, proceeded to the court of the palace, while Radama came out on the verandah, wearing the crown and scarlet lamba. The commander-in-chief then declared that Radama was lord of the kingdom, and the troops presented arms, while all the people shouted their acknowledgment and benediction. The young king's appearance affected the people, for he seemed, they said, as if he had been weeping for his mother. The queen and the commander-in-chief then did obeisance at the feet of the king; and when he had asked their confidence, and assured the people of his protection, he re-entered the palace, and the people retired.

The king's humane and generous disposition, as well as his conduct towards natives and foreigners, led all parties to expect great and favourable changes. These expectations were in some instances realized, but in others painfully disappointed. One of his earliest proclamations gave to every man liberty to follow such religious worship as he judged best, whether heathen or Christian, Mahomedan, Catholic, or Protestant, and every man was declared free to teach or preach his own religion. At the same time, every man, whatever might be his religion, or if he had no religion, was required to obey the laws of the country. This proclamation relieved the heathen from all fear of the king's enforcing Christianity upon them. The Mahomedans comprised only a few Arab traders at some of the ports;

and the Christians were well content to be protected and free. The only Catholics were the French, and perhaps some of their dependents.

The condition of the banished ones also received the early attention of the king and his chief minister, who sent promptly and recalled all who were in exile or concealment on account of their religion. Messengers were also sent to bring to their homes the bruised, emaciated, feeble, and dying Christians who had been banished in heavy fetters. The king restored, as far as practicable, the lands and other property of those whose possessions had been forfeited for refusing to worship the idols of the country.

A Christian widow who had survived the torture of fetters in the last persecution, whose husband had been stoned to death, and whose property had been divided as spoil amongst the officers by whom the Christians were condemned, came one day while I was with the king to complain that her plot of land—her only means of support—had been appropriated by a rich and powerful chief, who refused to restore it. The king listened patiently, inquired if it was so, and when the widow's statement was confirmed, told her not to grieve, and said her land should be restored to her. He then sent to the chief to ask why the land had not been restored; and directed the officer to say that it was no crime to pray to God, but a thing to be rewarded rather than punished, and that it was suffering enough to the woman that her husband had been killed; at the same time ordering the chief to restore the land, or to give another piece equally valuable. The widow came to me about a fortnight afterwards to say that God had caused her to obtain a good piece of land, adding that she "blessed God that Radama was king." The king also set at liberty those who, for the same cause, had been sold into slavery. He welcomed the banished exiles on their return, and encouraged the Christians by giving them buildings for public worship; one at Ambatonakanga, where the first Christian temple in Madagascar had been erected, and another at Analakely, where the government workshops had formerly been situated, in which many of the Christians had been employed. These and other favours not only cheered the Christians, but deterred others from annoying them, who, while desirous of pleasing the king, regarded with disapproval the increase of the adherents to what they termed the faith of the foreigners.

Radama had long lost all faith in the idols. On one occasion, when the priests had been boasting of their power, and that nothing could harm them, the king sent some Christians to set fire to the house of Ramahavaly, one of the national idols, and watched with his companions, from the front of his dwelling, the ascending flames of the burning idol-house. He never afterwards put any faith in the representations of the priests or the power of the idols; that occurrence also greatly weakened their hold upon the young men of the period.

No idols were retained in the king's palace, and

he required neither the attendance nor official services of the priests. Although leaving the people who believed in them free to employ the priests and to present offerings, he declined to afford them the sanction of his own example, either by gifts or homage. When the priests on one occasion reminded him of the benefit his ancestors had derived from the idols, and said the present of a bullock would secure the favour of the god, he replied, that he doubted whether the god would derive any benefit from the gift, adding, " If the god wants an ox, let him come and ask me for one."

The king also prohibited the use of the tangena, or poison, not only as a means of discovering the guilt or the innocence of any one accused, but for every other purpose. He also abolished the practice of sorcery, or the calculating of destinies, by which so many infants had been destroyed, and ordered that in trials before the judges the innocence or guilt of parties accused should only be decided according to evidence, publicly brought forward at the trial.

Radama had been accustomed, when only prince royal, personally to superintend the public works in which he and his friends engaged, such as improving the roads in the capital, or building bridges over some of the adjacent rivers; and he now made himself still more accessible to the people, endeavouring to secure right and justice to those who, after personal inquiries, he had reason to believe had suffered the wrong of which they complained.

The king's treatment of the Sakalava chiefs, and

others taken in war and held in slavery, whom he sent home to their own country with presents and with the bones of their countrymen who had died in Imerina, bound the hearts of those races to him by the strongest ties; and had his conduct in other respects been as wise and as considerate as it was in his treatment of these conquered people, he might have attached to himself and have reigned over a community co-extensive with the entire country, united by affection and confidence to their sovereign. These acts of Radama after he had become king— viewed in association with his conduct and disposition towards the people before his mother's death— were sufficient to produce the enthusiasm with which so many at that time regarded him, and to strengthen the confidence and hope which his accession to the throne had inspired.

What the young king now most wanted to enable him to realize the advantages of his elevation, so as to prove a blessing to his people, was a more just sense of the responsibilities of his high position, more true and disinterested friends in his foreign associates, and more able native counsellors. Only three of the ministers of the late reign were retained among his own advisers, and the one whom he most trusted was probably, in regard to character, judgment, and principle, the least worthy of his confidence. In the rest of the offices of government, including the highest judicial post, the king placed young men connected with different families or parties from those who had long held the highest offices, or had been associated with the government; many of these young men had been the companions of his own early years. The secular enactments of the king were so opposed to the views of his prime minister, who had been the commander of the forces, and the chief instrument of placing him on the throne, that the latter seldom took any part in the business of the government.

The king was told of the advantages of free trade, and ordered the ports to be opened to the ships of all nations, abolishing at the same time all custom-house duties. The first evil resulting from this was the inundation of the land with ardent spirits, sixty thousand gallons of rum from Mauritius having been imported in one week. Retail houses for the sale of intoxicating drink were opened in all the chief villages, especially in the main thoroughfares of traffic, and a vast amount of intemperance, with its attendant miseries, ensued. This act also created great dissatisfaction among a large number of officers whose salaries, having previously been paid out of the custom-house dues, ceased with their abolition.

Among the first foreigners who proceeded to the capital, after the opening of the ports, were the French consul and M. Lambert, with some Catholic priests. Others soon followed. The benevolent and cheerful disposition of the young king made him fond of the company of foreigners, whose convivialities conduced to the more frequent indulgence in those habits which his best friends deplored; while his impulsive nature, unrestrained passions, and love of pleasure seemed to be strengthened by the means of indulgence now at his command, rather than restrained by a sense of the obligations with which his position was associated. Unhappily for him, the companions who, as political adherents, exercised the greatest influence over him, seldom expressed dissatisfaction with his personal conduct; while others sought the accomplishment of their own purposes by encouraging those excesses into which he was too easily led.

Among the earliest acts of his reign, the king had sent information of the opening of the ports to the governors of Mauritius and Réunion, inviting the merchants to resume trade with the country, and also assuring exiles of a welcome to their homes, if they chose to return. On receipt of this intelligence, Sir William Stevenson, Governor of Mauritius, sent a mission, headed by Colonel Middleton, to the capital, with congratulations and presents to the king. The embassy was welcome, not only to the king and his government, but to the great body of the people, who rejoiced in the reception of these official communications of friendship from the English. Colonel Middleton and his companions returned gratified with their reception, and with the apparent prospects of the country. Mr. J. J. Le Brun, accompanied by a Malagasy Christian, also visited the Christians at the capital, and received from the king assurances of his earnest desire for the return of missionaries, and the extension of the gospel among the people.

At the same time information of the accession of the king, and of his desire that the missionaries should resume their labours, was sent by the Christians in the capital to the London Missionary Society, also messages expressing the wish of the king that I should return to Madagascar; in consequence of this the society invited me to comply with the wish, so far as to go out again and arrange for re-establishing the mission which, as soon as practicable, they were anxious to send to this important field, to which divine Providence had now opened the way.

The intelligence I had personally received expressed the wish of the native Christians that I should proceed to their assistance, and towards the close of November, 1861, I sailed again for Mauritius on my way to Madagascar. On reaching Port Louis at the end of the year, I was gratified by the report of the embassy sent by the governor, and the tidings received by Mr. Le Brun. I also found letters from the Christians, and an invitation from the king, urging me to proceed to the capital without delay. The season was at that time unfavourable for entering Madagascar, but I was able to send letters occasionally, as well as to collect information respecting the actual state of the people. I heard that Roman Catholic priests were already at Tamatave, and also at the capital, but that the whole body of the Christians were anxious for their former teachers, or for others sent from England.

It had occurred to me, when reflecting on the

places where the martyrs had suffered, that it would be a means of great benefit to the Christians of this generation, in which the martyrs had died, and perhaps of greater value to succeeding generations, if these spots could be consecrated to the service of the true God, by the erection on them of substantial stone churches for His worship; and that the buildings might also be memorials of the constancy and faith of the men and women who, in these places, had yielded up their lives rather than deny that divine Saviour who had redeemed them by His own precious blood. These sites were also eligible in position; and as I heard that the foreigners at the capital were purchasing land in different places, it appeared to me that it might be too late to secure them when I should arrive, as they might then have been previously disposed of.

I therefore wrote to the king, congratulating him on his accession to the throne, and informing him that I was only waiting at Mauritius for the healthy season, to set out for the capital; adding also that if agreeable to him, I wished him not to allow the places where the Christians had been put to death to be sold or built upon until I should arrive, as I might, when I had seen them, think it well to write to the friends in England on the subject, as they might wish to build on these spots churches for the worship of God, and so perpetuate among the Christians in Madagascar the memory of the faith and hope of their fellow-believers, who had died on account of their love to Jesus Christ.

This letter I sent, with a few Malagasy books for the Christians, by a trusty Malagasy catechist then sailing from Mauritius, directing him to proceed to the capital and give the letter to the proper officer to lay it before the king, and to say that he would wait to bring back any letter the king might have to send. In due time the messenger returned with a letter from Radama, stating that he and the officers of the government approved of my proposal, that the pieces of ground were vacant, and should neither be sold nor built upon until I came. This communication—which was the first movement towards the building of the memorial churches, a work which has already produced a far more important effect upon the minds of the people than I ever expected to live to see—being thus successful, greatly encouraged me. I had only seen the places from a distance, and did not feel justified in taking any further steps until I had personally examined them.

As early as it was safe to attempt to travel through the fever districts of Madagascar, I prepared for the voyage, and the owners of the *Jessie Byrne* having generously given me a passage, I embarked on the 17th of May, 1862; two young Malagasy officers, a German naturalist, several traders, and a number of exiles, one of whom on a former visit I had seen in chains, being my companions. On entering the harbour of Tamatave, on the morning of the fifth day from Mauritius, the flag of Radama, floating over the battery, was the first symbol which greeted us of the great change in the state of the country.

A boat from the shore brought off several Christians to welcome me, who said that messengers from the king were waiting to conduct me to the capital. When I landed towards evening a crowd had gathered on the beach, and when I stepped on shore an officer came forward and handed me a letter from the king, of which he was the bearer. Another officer bade me welcome on behalf of the governor and of the local authorities, saying that accommodation had been duly provided for me.

In the meantime the Christians gathered round, and with cordial greetings walked with me to the house of a friend who had been among the first to welcome me on shore. It was strange to be thus walking and talking publicly through the village with men to whom on former occasions I could only speak by stealth, within closed doors and under the darkness of night, while friends kept watch at the gate to prevent surprise, sudden seizure, and perhaps death. Many friends joined the family with whom I was a guest, delighting to tell of the marvellous change which had taken place, as well as of the growing feeling in favour of the gospel.

The next day I met the Christians in a house which the king had given them as a place of worship. There were about sixty persons present. The portions of Scripture read, the expression of their own feelings in connection with our meeting, their standing up and singing aloud with cheerful voice, a part of worship which I had before only heard offered in an undertone or whisper, as well as their simple, fervent and appropriate prayers, were to me deeply impressive. There were exiles present who had fled from persecution, and at the close of the meeting they sang, with indications of the most joyous feeling, the native jubilee hymn relating to the captive and the exile's return. The assembly seemed unwilling to separate; and when I remembered our meetings, not far from the same spot, in former days, I was not surprised at their strong and grateful feelings.

On Sunday I attended worship at the native church, where about a hundred were present. There were a large number of foreign traders and seamen on shore. Spirituous liquors had been largely imported, and intemperance and immorality appeared to be greatly increasing among the people.

On the 31st of May I took leave of my kind host, and set out for the capital. The number of travellers on the road seemed increased since my last visit, as well as the drovers with herds of cattle, of which 10,000 are exported to Mauritius annually. The meeting and conversing with Christian brethren, and the receipt of frequent letters from the capital on the way, were truly cheering. The only drawbacks were the drunkenness and quarrelling of the natives in the houses for retailing rum, and the humiliating spectacle sometimes seen of a whole village intoxicated before twelve o'clock in the day.

As we advanced towards Ambatomanga, in the province of Imerina, a large company of men were waiting by the road-side. When we approached they all rose and commenced singing a hymn. I alighted, and as soon as we had exchanged greetings, they informed me that they had been sent by the Christians in the capital to meet and bid me welcome. When I had thanked them we resumed our journey, the company singing as they walked—a mode of greeting which I had received from the Christians in South Africa. Towards evening we entered the picturesque village of Ambatomanga, and halted at the house appointed for my lodging. With some of the Christians I had been previously acquainted, but all expressed their pleasure at our arrival. The presence of the mother of one of our company, who had fled for his life, and the relative of another who had been sold as a child into slavery, added to the general gladness. A large number attended our evening worship, and my companions had so much to tell that it was late before they left for the night.

The next day was Sunday, and a number of the people of the village attended our worship. Andriambelo, one of the friends from the capital, who, when I had last seen him, was an exile flying from place to place with his life in danger, preached an excellent discourse to a numerous assembly. We had just closed the evening service when the king's secretary and others arrived, informing me that they had been sent by the king and queen to conduct me to the capital. Our congregation was considerably augmented by the new comers, and one of the preachers proposed that our worship should be continued, as no one seemed disposed to leave. Another simple discourse, followed with prayer, closed the services of this deeply affecting and most interesting day.

Although the officers who had come to welcome me joined in our Sabbath services, it was not until the next morning that they delivered the letter from the king, of which they were the bearers, expressing his pleasure on my arrival. Our party, though large when we set out for the capital, was now considerably augmented by our meeting on the road officers sent with letters of welcome, and messengers with the one universal request that if I had any Bibles I would promise one of them to the applicant, or writer of the letter. I knew they were Christians who made this request, and gladly promised copies, adding that a larger supply, with the expected missionaries, would soon arrive.

The inland mountain city of a thousand towns, as the name Antananarivo implies, had long been visible before we reached the small village of Ambohipo. Here we halted for a time, and on reaching the base of the mountain commenced the ascent to the city. Passing through the ancient stone gateway of Ankadibevava (the great mouth of the ditch), we crossed the summit of the hill and descended on the western side, halting at the edge of a wide hollow, or ravine, in the yard of the house appropriated for my residence. Here the officers gave me possession, and then went to inform the king of my arrival.

For some hours the Christians came in one continued stream to bid me welcome. Among them

Ramaka, an energetic man of middle age, who had been zealous for God during the time of the persecution; he had been subjected to the tangena, and had passed some years in prison bound so tightly that his flesh had been deeply cut by the cords. Later in the evening a number of the native preachers came, expressing their wish that we should unite in acknowledging the divine goodness in allowing us to meet under circumstances so full of enjoyment and of promise.

The next morning I received a number of welcomes and presents, the latter in abundance. The animals, including several oxen, sheep and pigs, besides poultry, I gave to the Christians to take care of, in case I might want them; the superabundance of other edibles I was glad to distribute among the poor. I only had occasion to apply for one of the oxen afterwards, which I gave to the workmen on the day when we laid the foundation-stone of the first memorial church.

Soon after noon an officer came to conduct me to the palace, where the king and queen received, with evident satisfaction, the communications which I was able to make, relative to the friendship of the English Government, and the intention of the London Missionary Society to send religious teachers to Madagascar. I then delivered the letters which the Governor of Mauritius had confided to my care, one of them being the copy of a letter from Queen Victoria, to the reading of which, by the secretary, the sovereigns and officers listened with profound attention. The king said the assurance of the continued friendship of England was exceedingly welcome and encouraging. The elder of the officers who had accompanied me from Mauritius, and the exiles who had returned, were then allowed to enter and present their hasina, or expression of loyalty to the sovereign.

During the remainder of this day my house was literally thronged with visitors; amongst others four of the widows of those who had suffered martyrdom since my former visit came, with their children, to see me. The husbands of some of them had been stoned to death, others had died in the heavy fetters in which they had been banished to different parts of the country. They said that from forty to sixty had suffered this punishment. With some of these men and their families I had held frequent intercourse in 1856. Other survivors of that last cruel persecution also came. The details which these women, or rather their companions, gave of the capture, condemnation, torture, and suffering of the departed was most harrowing, as they described the cruel manner in which they were stoned to death, or in which the massive irons were riveted on their persons, or the hunger and sickness they endured before released from their misery by death.

There was an indescribable appearance of shrinking from the contemplation of such suffering, especially on the part of the women, whose manner was generally subdued and silent; but, at the same time, there was an irrepressible sense of the intensity of that suffering in the expression of their countenances, which seemed in an astonishing manner to change and to indicate calmness, if not joy, so soon as they spoke of the stedfastness of the sufferers, or made any allusion to their present condition.

Afterwards the widow of another noble-hearted man, who had suffered death in the same persecution, came, attended by an interesting young woman whom she called her daughter, and a Christian slave who had shared in their sufferings, and was regarded almost as a child; companionship in suffering for Christ, as well as fidelity in the hour of trial, having, as in more than one instance I had occasion to observe, supplanted the tie between owner and slave by closer and holier bonds, superior to any merely social or earthly relationship. Many were the instances they recited of the perils and sufferings of the departed, before the death which the proto-martyr Stephen died brought them relief.

I had received a number of valuable communications from the deceased husband of this widow; and when I showed the survivors his signature to the last letter I received from him, written not long before he suffered, they were deeply affected. They remained with us to family worship, and I have seldom noticed more tenderness of feeling in singing than they evinced on that occasion. My own deep interest in this aged widow was not diminished when I afterwards heard that she had desired to secure the mangled body of her martyred husband for burial, and had, through the efforts of her friends, obtained the head, which had been carefully preserved in a box in her own room until it could be safely buried among the graves of his family. We almost shudder at a state of society in which so ghastly an object could alleviate distress or be cherished as a treasure, and yet I met with few more sensible, benevolent, useful and considerate Christians than this honoured martyr's widow.

Having been informed that Prince Ramonja, the friend of the Christians during their season of persecution, and a partaker of their sufferings, was seriously ill and wished to see me, I visited him on the following day. He appeared feeble and suffering, but expressed his gratitude for the altered circumstances of the Christians. He seemed glad to hear that a doctor was coming with the expected missionaries. His son returned with me to join the Christians, a number of whom now began to meet for worship at my house every evening, where also four of them slept every night in the outer room to insure my safety.

Early the following morning a message came from the prime minister, in consequence of which I went to his residence. To his inquiries about the objects for which the missionaries were coming, I replied that schoolmasters and printers would also come; that their objects were educational and religious; that the missionaries would not be allowed to engage in trade, but would teach the people to fear God and honour the king, would obey the laws and promote the welfare of all classes, both for this life and the life to come. He said he knew that this was the chief object of the missionaries; that the true Christians were always to be trusted; that he esteemed them very highly, had protected many in his own house in times of persecution, and would continue to afford them all the protection in his power. With regard to persecution, he said he had strongly advised the king against allowing anything of the kind, and that on this subject the king's opinion exactly coincided with his own.

When formerly in the capital I had only been able to look from a distance at the spots where the martyrs suffered. I now took an early opportunity, being in the neighbourhood of Ambohipotsy, of visiting the place where the first martyrs were put to death. It is situated on the northern declivity of the hill, a rugged and dreary region, long used as a place for public executions. Parts of the rude earthworks, or fortifications, by which this end of the city was defended, still remain near a path leading past some stone quarries to the cultivated plain below. The most perfect of these is part of a ditch, about four or more feet in width, and somewhat more in depth. A little beyond an ancient, unhewn stone pillar, where the path crosses the ditch, the first martyrs suffered death in 1836-7. A number of human bones lying near the spot were pointed out to me as marking the place where the Christians suffered, and that possibly some might be the bones of martyrs.

My companions, some of whom had witnessed the executions, said that a number of Christians had been put to death here. A few rude, low mounds, marking the spots where by special indulgence the friends of a criminal had been allowed to bury the body, were visible. The lower end of a cross, on which a renowned Sakalava warrior taken in battle had been crucified, was still standing near the fosse.*

In the early part of one memorable day I had visited the upper portion of the Tarpeian rock of Antananarivo. It is a precipitous part of the western side of the massive hill on which the city is built. A narrow path runs north and south along the western edge, which, for about two yards from the outer extremity of the path, is bevelled or rounded off, forming a sort of projecting curve. From this the rock bends inwards for a depth of about fifty feet, where it rests upon a lower stratum. This, which projects still further out, is then bevelled or rounded off, curving slightly inwards for a second depth of about fifty feet. Below this, broken masses of rock are heaped up for about the same depth, so that, viewed in profile, the precipice exhibits two successive rounded ledges of rock, with a mass of broken fragments of stone at the base, the whole at least a hundred and fifty or sixty feet below the upper edge.

On reaching the ground below I was struck with

---

* I visited the same place a short time afterwards with Mr. and Mrs. Toy. Mr. Toy has gathered a congregation that now meets for worship in the memorial church erected on the high ground a little to the north of the hollow or fosse. On this occasion I took a photograph of the spot where the first martyrs suffered.

the appalling aspect of the place. Large blocks and rugged fragments of granite of different sizes lay confusedly heaped up at the base of the precipice, and must have fearfully broken and mangled the bodies falling from the upper edge. An involuntary shudder passed over me as I looked up from ledge to ledge, or gazed on the masses of granite lying at the foot of the precipice; but it appeared to me more fearfully appalling to look down from the upper edge, than upwards from the rocks below. And this was the place at which thirteen men and women were hurled down the rock of death—their only crime being their refusal to abjure the name of Christ, and to swear by the idols of the country.

One of the high officers of the palace, as he told me in conversation afterwards, had said to his companions on that day, "Let us go and see how these Christians behave. They are said not to be afraid to die." And when I asked what effect the executions produced on his mind, he said he could not describe it. "We were near," he said, "and saw all that took place; but the Christians were not afraid, and did not recant."

On the first Sunday that I spent in the capital, I went to Analakely. I was told about seven o'clock that the chapel had been full ever since daybreak, and that in about an hour the first congregation would leave the place, and another would assemble. The son of Ramonja with a number of young chiefs accompanied me at the appointed time, and as we approached the long, low-roofed building, open on the side towards us, in which the Christians were assembled, we perceived they were at prayer, and stopped. The young chiefs took off their hats and remained standing until the prayer was concluded, when we entered.

On the side of the building opposite the entrance there was a raised space covered with matting, on which was a small table and a chair, which I was requested to occupy. On my right hand the house was filled to the farthest extremity with Christian women, some grey with years, others young persons and children, many of them well dressed, and all decent and becoming both in appearance and demeanour. Around me were the preachers and a number of officers, and on my left was one densely packed crowd of men; while along the open front were half as many outside as there were within.

When I looked round on that large assembly, as they stood up and poured forth their loud and joyous hymns of praise, and recalled the time when we could only meet a few together in secret and in comparative silence; and when I further contrasted the air of joyous freedom and conscious security beaming in almost every countenance, with the sorrow occasioned by some mournful loss, or the trembling anxiety of those who were themselves, at that former period, proscribed and had their lives given them for a prey, I was filled with wonder and delight. I was not surprised now that in the letters I received from some of them, when describing their present state, they had said, " We are like them that dream."

After the hymn was concluded and the 91st Psalm had been read, I offered our thanksgivings to the Most High, and then spoke to the people of His mercy to those who had departed, and to those who could now call upon His name without fear or trouble. One of the native preachers then read, prayed, and delivered a short but encouraging discourse, and the service closed. Joy seemed beaming on every countenance, and amid many friendly greetings the people separated. There appeared to me to be not less than a thousand persons present, probably more.

The places of worship at Ambatonakanga and Amparibe, in the same neighbourhood, were, when I visited them, equally crowded; and the assemblies gathered seemed to experience the same devout and joyous feelings. The building at Amparibe was large, and at the first service I attended there were at least one thousand persons present. The house at Ambatonakanga was smaller, and the attendants fewer in number. Besides these three principal places of worship, smaller numbers were accustomed to meet for worship in other parts of the city.

I have already mentioned the early recall, by the king, of the survivors of those who had been banished for undiscovered crimes of the past, which had been acknowledged according to the order and in reliance on the clemency of the queen. The restoration of such fugitives as having been sentenced to death had escaped, and had remained for years exiles and wanderers, was not delayed. They were brought on their return first into the house of the commander-in-chief, who spoke kindly and encouragingly to them, and told them they might go to their homes in safety, for now Radama was king, and no injury would come to them.

As they passed through the streets their countrymen crowded to look at them. The report of their return greatly astonished the people, then assembled in great numbers at the capital. Most of the Christians knew that they were living, but others supposed they had long since been dead. Numbers came to see them, saying, "We thought you had long ago been buried or eaten by the dogs, and when we heard you were here, we could scarcely believe it was you. It is like coming again from the dead." And some said, " Great is the power of God."

Messengers had been sent for the survivors of those Christians who had been bound in heavy fetters; and on my arrival I found some of them—feeble, wasted, bedridden sufferers; yet to them and to their friends this return was indeed a jubilee, but a jubilee kept with tears, and with touching memories of the absent ones. To some it was like coming to their Christian home and friends to die; to others it was to live and to rejoice in the free course of the gospel in their country.

The suffering connected with these fetters did not always end with the recall of the wearer and their removal from his person. One instance of this may suffice. An excellent Christian woman in middle life, a worshipper at Analakely, who often visited my house, when I was about to leave Madagascar gave me the fetters which her husband, a soldier, had, on account of his faith, worn four years and a half on his person, in banishment in the province of the Antsianaka. His wife had accompanied him on his agonizing journey as far as the soldiers would allow her to go, and then returned home. During his long months of suffering, she borrowed money to send him a little clothing and bedding, with such other comforts as she could procure. On his liberation by the proclamation of Radama he went to the north, where he had been previously a soldier. After I had left Madagascar, the officer who had lent the money required it, and, as the poor woman had no means of paying, it was expected that the lender would sell the debt for what it would fetch, when the purchaser, if no other prospect of obtaining the money presented itself, would have the debtor appraised and sold for what she would fetch if bought for a slave. This calamity threatened Razafy, who had given me the fetters.

Mr. Cameron informed me of the danger of this Christian woman being sold under the circumstances as a slave, and asked if something could not be done to save her. I wrote by the next mail requesting him to pay the money immediately, and I would be responsible. I had no difficulty in obtaining even a larger sum than was ultimately required. The distressed woman had herself been working hard in making silk lambas or scarfs towards discharging the debt. Mr. Cameron wrote in reply to say that my letter did not arrive a day too soon; that Razafy had been appraised, but that he sent by two of the Christian ministers the sum of money owing to the creditor, who gave her a discharge in full. In a letter which she wrote to me soon afterwards she expressed her sense of God's great goodness. How few amongst us can understand one simple item of her gratitude!—" I can sleep at nights now."

CHAPTER X.

Teaching English—The king not a Christian—Early commencement of Sabbath services—Conversations with the Christians—Influences favouring the reception of the gospel—Family religion—Parental attention to the young—The mother's good influence—Statistics of the progressive increase of the Christians during the successive persecutions—Astonishing results—Influence of character—Arrival of foreign embassies—Visits to the places where the martyrs suffered—Present to the English embassy—Notice of a converted warrior priest—Introduction of the gospel to Betsileo—Description of the idols—Satisfactory conversation with the Bishop of Mauritius respecting Church of England missionaries—Views of the Society for the Propagation of the Gospel respecting Madagascar—Principles on which Scriptures were distributed among the people.

I HAD scarcely been a week at the capital when several young officers, who had been learning English under a native teacher, came to read with me in order to improve their pronunciation, and as some nobles of high rank, including the prime minister, applied to me to teach their sons English, I appropriated two hours daily to this duty. The sister of the minister directed her messenger to ask what she was to pay for the instruction of her sons. I replied I was glad she wished to have them taught, that I did not go to Madagascar to obtain money, but to help them to become intelligent and earnest in seeking the blessings of this life, as well as of that which is to come. I soon had a class of twelve sons of the highest chiefs, who by their earnestness and attention encouraged my efforts.

The queen afterwards sent to me an interesting boy, the grandson of the first Radama's sister, whom she had adopted, and two others of whom she was the guardian; and in consequence of the more frequent intercourse with the English, for which the new regulations had opened the way, many were now anxious to secure the advantages which a knowledge of our language would afford. The king also, having heard that I was teaching the sons of the nobles, sent his secretary to ask me to go and read English with him as often as I could conveniently. I therefore went to his residence, and finding that he had made some progress and seemed earnest in his desire both to read and to speak English, I agreed to go to him for one hour every afternoon, which I continued to do until within a short time of his death.

At the time of my arrival Radama was employed in erecting a stone house for a school, and as soon as the building was finished, he sent word by his secretary that he wished me to hold religious worship in the large room every Sunday afternoon for himself and the officers, or any others who might choose to attend.

I knew that the services which the king had rendered to the Christians, as well as the help he had afforded them when all other influence was against them, had been of unspeakable value; and I did not wonder that the believers themselves should regard him and speak of him as a Christian.

Nor did I much wonder, considering their circumstances and his conduct towards them, that they should have written of Radama to their friends in England as being a Christian; but I had too much reason to believe that, whatever he might become, he was not a Christian at the time; and notwithstanding all my efforts to serve him, I did not leave him in doubt about my own opinion on that subject. On one occasion, when the members of the British embassy, including the Bishop of Mauritius, referred, in the presence of the king and queen, to his abolishing so many evil usages, of his having saved so many lives, and having proved such a friend to the Christians, the king looked at me as if he wished me to speak. I said, before the queen and all his own officers as well as the foreign visitors, that he had undoubtedly done much to promote the welfare of his people, for which they were grateful, but, I added, "there is one great thing wanting—the one thing needful. He has not yet become a Christian himself." The king looked gravely towards me, and said with some emphasis, "He [Mr. Ellis] knows what is in my heart. He knows that I desire to understand and serve God; I desire—I pray to God to enlighten my mind—to teach me what I ought to know."

For the first few Sundays that I went to the king's house his secretary interpreted my address, sentence by sentence, as I proceeded; afterwards I undertook the whole in the native language. Sometimes many officers were present, and the numbers amounted to fifty or sixty persons during great part of the time that the services were continued; and only on one occasion, when some foreigners had fixed that time for the transaction of business connected with the coronation, was the king absent. No one behaved with greater propriety, or paid more attention to the service, than the king did on every occasion. Some of the officers who attended, I had reasons to believe, were Christians; others, I was told afterwards, became such.

Until the influx of foreigners which the coronation brought to the capital, the attendance of the king and his companions at my readings and Sunday services was marked by strict propriety; but after that period I was often depressed by evidences of the evil influences to which he appeared to be surrendering himself. A large French piano was placed in the schoolroom, and music, singing and dancing were substituted for the lessons. I had selected the Bible as the book which the king and I should read together, and he always came to the room in which we met as soon as I arrived. I could not, however, conceal from myself that his habits were changing, and I learned that music and dancing were often followed by feasting and drinking, and that the host, in these revels, was always the first to lose self-command under the influence of the latter.

I spoke very plainly, but earnestly and kindly, to

the king of this degrading vice, and of the consequences, both to soul and body, of his becoming the slave of those habits which I feared were gaining mastery over him. He acknowledged the truth of my remarks, and promised to exercise watchfulness for the future; but only to be overcome again. I sincerely pitied him, and so long as he was willing to attend to what I said, I did not think it right to leave him. Considering how he had been brought up, the lightness and pliancy of his natural character, his passion for music, and his love of gaiety and pleasure of every kind—considering also how much good he had been the instrument of securing for others, I not only felt deep compassion for the king on account of the many influences operating against him, but hoped to the last that the Holy Spirit might change his heart, and that he might become a partaker of those spiritual blessings which he had been the means of preserving so many to enjoy in this world, and to hope for in the next.

My instructions to the young nobles were continued daily until the time of the coronation, when Mr. Toy, one of the recently arrived missionaries, kindly relieved me. My daily reading and conversation with the king, and my service at the school-room, were also continued until near the time of Radama's death. Much of my time was spent in conversation with intelligent men in the capital or from the country, whether Christians or not. It was so long since an Englishman had resided amongst them, that most of those who came to the city favoured me with a visit. These interviews were sources of much information to me, and afforded opportunities for bringing subjects under the notice of my visitors which were sometimes profitably remembered long afterwards.

But my chief attention was given to the Christians. Besides the congregation at Analakely, with whom I had spent my first Sabbath, there were two other important places of worship, Ambatonakanga and Amparibe, and I attended the chief forenoon service every Sunday in rotation at each of these three places.

Like the inhabitants of all warm climates, the Malagasy are early risers, and I was surprised, on the morning of the first Sabbath which I spent at the capital, to hear that the members of the Christian families in the immediate neighbourhood of my own residence—men, women, and children, all dressed in their clean Sunday attire—had left their homes in the early morning before it was light and proceeded to their Sabbath worship, which at that time commenced at daybreak, if not before.

Prince Ramonja's son, who had undertaken to guide me to the place of worship on the first Sunday which I spent amongst them, reached my house before eight o'clock, and said that by the time we should arrive at the place of meeting, three quarters of a mile distant, the first congregation would have left, and the second would be gathered. I afterwards inquired of several their reasons for meeting so early then, when there was no danger in their being seen, and when the whole day was appropriated to social and public worship. They said it was not from any fear of discovery that they now assembled so early; but they had been so long—twenty-five years—accustomed only to feel at ease and safe in their Sabbath worship under the shelter of darkness, that it still seemed most natural to them; and also that they liked the cool, calm, early dawn better than the later portions of the day for their Sabbath services.

At first I generally reached the places at which their worship was held about eight o'clock; they had themselves held an earlier service, with perhaps an address, before my arrival. After singing, reading the Scriptures and praying, I delivered a discourse or address on some passage of Scripture, followed by singing and prayer. One or more addresses or discourses were afterwards delivered by accredited preachers, with the same accompaniments; after which the benediction closed the service, usually between ten and eleven o'clock, when the congregation dispersed and I returned home to breakfast and to rest awhile, preparatory to the engagements of the afternoon.

So far as regards a clear and distinct presentation of what the preacher intended to say, the native addresses were vastly superior to anything which I could give them; but as both preachers and people expressed their desire that I should not only be present, but should preside at the services in which I took a part, since it made their meetings more like what they used to be when the earlier missionaries were with them, and as they had the courtesy to say they understood what I said, and wished me to take part with them, I could not refuse to do so. They also remarked that I sometimes presented the same truth in a different form, and accompanied by other illustrations, than they were accustomed to. Thus encouraged, I gave as much attention as possible to this part of my work, and secured the best available assistance in the acquisition of their language, in order that my services, so long as I remained amongst them, might become increasingly useful. These services were often a means of spiritual refreshment to my own soul, as well as a cause of astonishment and gratitude such as I had never before felt.

Besides my familiarity with their position and circumstances ever since the preparation of the "History of Madagascar" in 1838, my correspondence with some of the Christians after the return of Mr. Freeman, who left the country in 1835, and my personal intercourse with a number who afterwards fell in the maintenance of their faith, had produced strong and lasting impressions on my own mind; and when I remembered the circumstances in which I had first known some who were now unfettered and faithful ministers, and my eye glanced from some of these men, perhaps seated beside me, to the congregation before us, where there were generally some of the earliest converts—some who on their own persons had worn the fetters, or who had drunk the poison, or borne the yoke of slavery for Christ,—and when, further, I saw also the widows and orphans of those who had died in the flames, or among the rugged granite rocks, or by the executioner's spear, I felt, indeed, my spirit stirred by the evidences of God's wondrous grace and power, in a manner never elsewhere experienced by me before or since.

The habits of the Malagasy do not favour evening meetings. The family usually meet for their most important meal after dark, by the light of lamps or fires. The whole family is then gathered together, and, except on extraordinary occasions, it is not customary for the members of respectable families to leave home after dark. Nor is it either pleasant or safe to do so; the rough, undressed stones which cover the roads or pathways which, after a fashion, may be said to be paved, are with difficulty traversed by shoeless feet, while total darkness on nights when there is no moon follows within half an hour after sunset, and continues to within half an hour of break of day. None either of the broad or narrow intricate and winding paths are lighted; and, as a rule, the families remain at home after the evening meal. Where houses are within the same enclosure, or are near, their inhabitants meet in the evening. When Christianity was proscribed, the darkness favoured the meetings of the Christians without detection; but since freedom of worship has been allowed, they have, as a general rule, ceased to meet for worship in the evening.

From the time of my arrival, Christians inhabiting houses in the near neighbourhood were accustomed to come to my residence for the purpose of evening worship. Frequently on Sabbath evenings more than one of the native ministers met with us, and such evenings were always welcome and encouraging. Occasionally I invited a number of the ministers and others to spend the evening of a week day with me, for the purpose of conference on matters affecting the progress of the gospel, or for general information. In our early meetings my inquiries chiefly related to the circumstances and proceedings of the Christians during the *mazina*, or darkness, as they frequently designated the supremacy of heathenism; and as to what they thought must chiefly be ascribed the astonishing increase in their numbers which had taken place during that long and suffering period. In general they replied promptly that it could only be ascribed to the influence of the Holy Spirit on their hearts. But on being asked further they would add that other causes combined in producing the change, such as preaching, praying, reading the Scriptures, or the conversation of Christians; or an indescribable feeling of interest in the Christians, or sympathy with them in the injustice and cruelty which they suffered, impressed some with a feeling that there must be something important connected with Christianity. The patient and most uncommon conduct of the Christians under such trials—not cursing their persecutors, but praying for them; not seeking to be revenged, but to convert—affected the minds of many.

They said that various were the thoughts and

considerations which first suggested the idea of a personal adoption of Christianity, sometimes long nursed in secret, occasionally mentioned between intimate friends, and finally avowed by speaking to some Christian or uniting in prayer with some in concealment, or praying themselves to God to teach them and bring them to acquaintance with those who could explain more fully to them the way of salvation.

After persecution ceased and the Christians were more generally inmates of the families to which they belonged, the preachers were of opinion that the spirit, conduct, and character of those in the family who were sincere believers, most frequently brought other members of the same family to Christ; and this was one reason why the gospel seemed to be received and avowed more generally by families than by individuals. There were some families in which there might for a long time be only one Christian, but very few in which there remained very long only one heathen or unconverted member.

Parental discipline, or training of children, appeared to be a thing unknown among the heathen, and simply as *discipline* it was but little practised among the Christians. But a habit of taking them to the house of God from their earliest years, training them to the most respectful attention during seasons of family prayer, urging a reverential regard for the Bible, as well as an affectionate and kind inculcation of its great truths, were, I believe, universally practised among the Christians.

Few more affecting spectacles have ever come under my observation than a Malagasy family after the reading of the Scriptures; the father and mother kneeling by the seats they had occupied, and the children, down to the youngest able to walk, bending their foreheads to the ground on the matted floor, while the father offered up their united thanksgivings and petitions to the great Parent of all. As a rule the mothers appear fond of their children, and much of the religious principle and feeling which exist among the younger members of Christian families is to be ascribed, under God, to the affectionate teaching and prayers of the Christian mothers.

I early sought information from the preachers as to the actual amount of the increase which had been made to their numbers during the years of persecution. They had generally stated, in most of their communications, that their numbers were augmenting; and now, as persecution had ceased, I was anxious to learn what was the state of the church, in regard to numbers, as compared with its position at the time when Christianity was forbidden in the country. On one occasion, very soon after my arrival, they told me that they thought there were about five thousand Christians in the capital, and two thousand more in the suburbs, without reference to the believers scattered over the outlying parts of the country. Of these, about nine hundred had been admitted to the communion at the capital. I did not obtain any specific number of the communicants in the suburbs; they probably amounted to two or three hundred.

In 1835-6, when the early missionaries were driven from the country, it is supposed, from the nature of the buildings in which their meetings were held, these being chiefly ordinary dwellings, that the two congregations reported up to that date could not have amounted to more than from one to two thousand. Two hundred had applied for admission to Christian communion.

In 1856, twenty years after, when I visited them, while persecution remained in unbroken power upon them, although they could give no information as to the number of communicants, since they only met in small companies and in out-of-the-way places, and although they had not attempted to make any lists of the disciples, they supposed them to amount then to about three thousand.

In 1861 persecution ceased, and liberty of worship and teaching was restored; and as soon as they became settled in their new position, the leading men amongst the Christians endeavoured to form an approximate estimate of their numbers. The stern, determined repression of Christianity had continued throughout twenty-six years. Persecution in a chronic form marked all these years, and seldom, if ever, did one year pass without some of the Christians suffering. Besides the persecution of 1845, in which the influence of the prince with his mother saved more than twenty of the Christians from the consequences of the accusations brought against them, the Christians had endured four general and severe persecutions.

In February, 1835, when the missionaries were forbidden to teach or preach Christianity at any time or in any form, and death was threatened to any native who should read the Bible, pray to God, receive baptism or join the communion of the Christians,—in this persecution, although no life was taken, two thousand five hundred suffered different punishments. In July, 1845, the capture of Raintisheva and other fugitives attempting to escape from the country brought severe persecution, when large numbers suffered. In February, 1849, four nobles were burned alive, thirteen were hurled down the precipice, and two or three thousand punished; and in July, 1857, when the names of seventy Christians were carried to the government by Ratsimandisa, who had been a pupil of the missionaries and associated with the Christians, thirteen were stoned to death, and more than fifty fastened together in heavy fetters, under which half the number died. These were the several persecutions which had fallen on the church in Madagascar during Queen Ranavalona's reign.

In these four great persecutions, besides those who suffered at other times, more than 10,000 persons were sentenced to different kinds of penalties; and what had been the result? After death had been threatened, in the name of all that was powerful and dreaded in heaven and on earth, to every one who should avow the hated faith—after encouraging informers, after scouring the country with troops, and recommending vigilance in Christian hunting as a test of loyalty and a means of promotion; after employing divination, and invoking the gods of the country against the defenceless Christians, what had been the result? The Christians had increased in the land from one thousand, when the persecution commenced, to seven thousand when it ended; the communicants, from about two hundred, had increased to a thousand. Such, by God's divine grace and power, was the blessed fruit of six-and-twenty years of persecution!

During these years the Christians had been destitute of all human guidance and all human aid. No European teacher or preacher had gone in and out amongst them. God had been their helper, and the Holy Spirit, who, as the Christians said, was the best teacher, had been with them; and these were the marvellous results.

Equally valid and extensive were the collateral evidences of this divine work as seen in the altered lives and elevated characters of many among the Christians. This was known and recognised by all; while not a few were selected by their heathen rulers to fill positions of responsibility or trust, in consequence of their integrity of character. The character of the Christians had also its effect in disposing others to regard their creed with less aversion, and so preparing the way for its wider extension. Thus notwithstanding some causes of regret amongst the Christians, there was far more to enkindle gratitude and to inspire hope.

Invitations to the king's coronation, which was to

take place in the month of August, had been sent to the Governors of Mauritius and Réunion, as well as directions to the governors or representatives of several provinces of Madagascar to proceed to the capital; but, as it was found that the native chiefs and their retainers could not come from the remote provinces in time, the ceremony was delayed until September. The change, however, was not made until it was too late to inform the foreign visitors who had been invited.

The French embassy, under Captain Dupré, arrived at the end of July, and the English embassy, with General Johnstone, accompanied by the Bishop of Mauritius, reached the capital about a week afterwards. An account of the valuable presents sent by the sovereigns represented by these embassies to the King and Queen of Madagascar, and of the ceremonies connected with the coronation, having been already published,* it is not necessary to refer to the embassies here, except so far as their presence and influence might be supposed to affect the interests of Christianity among the people.

The arrival of Commodore Dupré brought the first mission of peace from France to Madagascar, and, as an earnest of the future, it was peculiarly welcome. M. Lambert was also in the capital, and it was only in reference to his proceedings with the king that any apprehensions were felt. With the several members of the English embassy I had been previously acquainted, and was happy to share their

* "Madagascar Revisited."

society during their stay. The Bishop of Mauritius, as well as General Johnstone and Colonel Anson, accompanied me to the school and to the public assemblies of the Christians on the Lord's day, and manifested an interest in the welfare of the Christians and the progress of the gospel, which was most welcome and encouraging to the people. They also visited the places where the martyrs had suffered; and as we met at these spots a number of Christians who had been spectators of their last moments on earth, or were in some cases closely related to the departed, their information and remarks rendered these visits instructive and deeply impressive. It appeared to these friends that the several places would be admirable sites for the churches which it was proposed to build.

The people were prepared to meet with friends in the English, and anxious to show, according to the usage of the country, their sense of the kindness of the distinguished visitors, the Christians, with the assistance of their wealthier neighbours, prepared a present for these friends, and towards evening on the 15th of August they came to ask me to go with them to the general's quarters. On reaching the court in front of the house I found a number of them assembled, and a fine fat ox standing near the door, which they intended as a present. I explained their object to the general, and when, accompanied by the Bishop and Colonel Anson, he reached the verandah, Rainimarosandy, a portly Christian officer, advanced a little in front of his companions, and in a brief and sensible speech expressed, on behalf of the Christians of the capital, the great satisfaction which the visit of the general and his companions from England, the country of their earliest friends, had afforded them. He said they felt, after the kindness shown them, that they were regarded as friends, and were bound by new ties to their Christian friends in England; and that, following the custom of their own country, they had brought a present of an ox, of which they begged his acceptance, as an expression of their gladness on seeing amongst them the friends of the Christians and the friends of Radama.

The general, with much kindly feeling, returned an appropriate acknowledgment, to which the bishop added the expression of his satisfaction at meeting with them as Christian friends. I interpreted their addresses, and the parties separated with much apparent pleasure.

As the time for the coronation drew near, the influx of strangers in various and, in some respects, antiquated costumes greatly increased. I gazed on many of these strangers with peculiar interest, believing that the time would soon come when the glad tidings of salvation would be conveyed to their distant abodes. I was visited by some of them who had friends amongst the Christians. One of these was from the remote south, the neighbourhood of Fort Dauphin, a most energetic man, formerly a distinguished priest, who had been wounded in battle while carrying on his shoulder the idol of which he was the keeper, and which was regarded as the palladium of safety to his party. This event had given a shock to his faith in the idol, from which it never recovered; having also met with some of the Christians, on a former occasion when he visited the capital, and having heard the gospel preached, all his lingering doubts were removed, and he destroyed the idol, which he had brought with him, consigning it to a place of concealment from which he felt sure it would never emerge to be again an object of religious veneration or trust. He was a strongly built, vigorous man, scarcely past middle age and, though a priest, had been reputed one of the best spearmen in the country; and in times of disturbance or apprehension was considered by friends and enemies alike as a host in himself—an ally to be trusted, a foe to be feared. He was highly esteemed by the Christians, and respected by the authorities at the capital. I saw him frequently, both during his present visit and when he afterwards came to the capital.

I was also much gratified with the energy, intelligence, and apparent interest in the claims of Christianity manifested by a chief from the neighbourhood of Itasy, the large lake by the foot of the lofty Ankaratra, one of the highest mountains of Madagascar, forty or fifty miles from the capital. But my greatest interest was excited by the visitors from the Betsileo country, a large province joining Ankova to the south, where, at Fianarantsoa, the chief military post of the Hovas, Christian officers and men connected with the garrison there, had not only maintained their faith in Christ, but had been the means of converting some of their comrades; and had besides been honoured as the instruments, in the hand of God, of bringing some of the people of the country to a knowledge of Jesus Christ, and to believe and trust in Him for salvation. These converts were welcomed by the Christians as brethren, and were to me cheering as the appearance of the early stars of morning, ushering in the dawn of a brighter day over the regions of superstition, ignorance and vice from whence they came.

In the pageants and ceremonies of the coronation, which took place on the 23rd of September, there was no official recognition of the idols; no priest walked in the royal procession, no idols were borne near the sovereign's person, as had been the case before, and was afterwards. But in the apportioning of the ground to the different parties who were expected to be present, spaces were marked off, near the gallery occupied by the court and the embassies, for the missionaries and the Protestants, for the priests and the Catholics, for the idols and their keepers, or their priests; and in passing along a narrow part of the road, I unexpectedly found myself in the very midst of the idols and their bearers.

These idols or objects of worship had very little to recommend them in their form or appearance. They were about thirteen in number, carried on tall slender rods or poles. They were chiefly composed of dirty pieces of silver chain, small silver balls, pieces of coral, silver ornaments representing crocodiles' teeth, with strips of scarlet cloth, and in one instance something which looked like a red woollen cap resembling a cap of liberty. Others were tied up in small baskets or bags, and were probably only charms or emblems of the idols. This I had no means of knowing. Yet such were the objects of worship, or their representatives, on which the safety and welfare of the nation were supposed to depend, and for refusing to worship which many of the most intelligent and worthy among the people had been subjected to banishment, slavery, torture, and death.

The postponement of the coronation requiring the visitors to remain a longer time in the capital than had been expected, and finding that no arrangement could be made for its taking place earlier, the Bishop of Mauritius and one or two of the English embassy returned to Mauritius. The bishop had taken an early opportunity after his arrival of explaining to me the object of his visit, expressing his gratification with what he had seen of Christianity amongst the people at Tamatave and along the route from thence, and inquiring very particularly into the state of the Christians and the progress of the gospel in the capital. We conferred together on the best manner of extending Christianity in Madagascar. The governor, he said, had appointed him to come, and he had done so very cheerfully, that he might see for himself the state of the people, the various openings for usefulness, and in what part of the country he could co-operate with us in forwarding the evangelization of the island. His lordship added that he did not wish to interfere with our line of operations; but, supposing we considered ourselves equal to the Christian culture of the capital and central provinces, asked whether there was not some part of the coast which they could occupy.

I answered that it had been suggested to me at Mauritius that missionaries of the Church Missionary Society should occupy Madagascar, and I had always replied that the understanding between the London and the Church Missionary Societies, viz., not to interfere with each other's spheres of labour, had hitherto proved so advantageous, that I did not think it likely it would be disregarded in relation to Madagascar, and that I had written to England suggesting that missionaries of the Church Missionary Society should occupy some parts of the field.

His lordship then asked if we considered ourselves able to occupy the capital and central parts of the island. I answered that we certainly did; and when I pointed out the positions we proposed to occupy with the missionaries then on their way and the native assistants available, and when the bishop had observed that he should prefer occupying stations on the north and east coast, I answered that I should rejoice in his doing so, adding, " Had you proposed to come here I should have felt differently." I then adverted to the regret I should feel at seeing the missionaries diverted from their great work of recommending Christ to the heathen, and the inquiring people perplexed by the presentation of the religious differences existing in our own country. The bishop observed, "It must come some time." I said, "Most likely it will be so, but I hope not now. I can conceive of nothing more likely to unsettle the minds of the people about Christianity itself than the introduction of another form of Protestantism, for which there is no need; there is room enough for us both to labour without disturbing the minds of the people, or interfering with each other's work. In the north you will find the best climate, in the south the most people."

His lordship replied, "I should deem another missionary establishment here undesirable, and injurious rather than otherwise;" he then said, "My mind is greatly relieved by this communication. I see my way clearly. I shall most likely go to England to propose to the Church Missionary Society, and other friends, to send out a good mission to the north and the east coast, and we shall thus take part in the great work opened before the Church in the providence of God." He said they might work from the coast until they should meet us working from the centre, or we might extend our labours to the south.

This arrangement has ever since been honourably adhered to. The Society for the Propagation of the Gospel have a mission on the eastern coast, the Church Missionary Society one on the same coast, further to the south, and their missionaries are encouraged by the success of their labours. Although the former society does not feel itself bound by the arrangement of the Bishop of Mauritius with regard to not sending missionaries to the capital, the fact that the inhabitants of the capital and central provinces are well provided with Christian teachers, by the increased number of the agents of the London Missionary Society now occupying different posts of duty in and around the capital, may induce a change of opinion.

So large a proportion of the people in this part of the country having now entirely renounced idolatry, and become brethren and sisters in Christ,—having also endured for five-and-twenty years the most fierce and sanguinary persecution which the Church in modern times has witnessed, and having manifested, throughout that long and fearful ordeal, a degree of stedfastness and constancy of love to Christ their divine Lord which has called forth the admiration of their brethren in every part of the Christian world, and demonstrated to believers and unbelievers alike throughout Christendom that what the gospel was in the first ages of the Church, that it is still—"the power of God unto salvation unto every one that believeth,"—it is most earnestly to be hoped that the missionaries of the London Society and their numerous faithful fellow-labourers should be left to pursue, without interruption, those labours which the great Head of the Church has been pleased to crown with such remarkable success, and in which they have now been engaged for fifty years.

At the same time other races, inhabiting distant parts of this large island, are awakening to a perception, faint though it may be, of the importance of Christianity, but remain altogether unprovided for; isolated portions of the country alone having been reached by native evangelists. And although the work will be more difficult in many respects than that part in which the labour was commenced fifty years ago, the very success which has attended the missions existing in the island will be useful to other missionaries, as all pioneering work is, and may be expected to accelerate the growth and ripening of the harvest unto Christ, the great Lord of missions, which other parts of this important country may be expected to yield.

I have already adverted to my early visits to the places in which the martyrs suffered. Being confirmed in my opinion of their eligibility for the purposes contemplated, and having been assured by the king that they should be appropriated to that sacred use, I wrote to the directors of the London Missionary Society, stating that one great want at that moment was places of public worship.

I said the proposal for building memorial churches in the situations specified had pleased the king, and had greatly encouraged the Christians, adding that three at least of these buildings should be of stone; and that, so far as I could judge, the cost of them would not be less than £10,000. "The Christians here," I stated in my letter, "will do all they can, although twenty-six years of spoliation and suffering have greatly reduced their means. Labour for building the churches can be obtained here or at Mauritius, but help will be required from England. The present state of feeling in relation to Madagascar favours the attempt to achieve this important work now, rather than at any future time. May the Lord put it into the hearts of His people to enable us to effect it.

"Will England give to Madagascar these memorial churches, and thus associate the conflicts and triumphs of the infant church with the remembrance of the source from which, through divine mercy, Madagascar received the blessings of salvation, and thus perpetuate the feelings of sympathy and love which bind the Christians of Madagascar to their brethren in England?"

The directors of the Society stated that they felt the appeal to be irresistible, and that they had no choice but to submit this important case to the kind and generous consideration of their constituents, and to the Christian public in general; which they did with their own earnest recommendation. The result was most encouraging. Before the next annual meeting of the Society the fund for the erection of memorial churches in Madagascar exceeded £6,500, and ultimately reached the truly munificent sum of £13,000.

I had taken with me to Madagascar a few copies of the Scriptures, but the knowledge that I had some in my possession brought upon me such an extraordinary number of applicants, from remote as well as adjacent places, that I was exceedingly distressed on account of the many to whom I could not give a copy of the smallest portion of the inspired volume. Very few of the early Christians or their descendants possessed a Bible; a large number of Christian families were without even a Testament; a greater portion had a copy of the Psalms or of the Gospels bound separately; some few had both these; others had copies of even smaller portions of the word of God. Many Christian families, several preachers of the gospel, and sometimes the inhabitants of a whole village in which there was a Christian congregation, or in which Christian worship was regularly held, were all without a single copy of the New Testament. The visit of an itinerant teacher or preacher, with a copy of the New Testament, caused unusual joy in such villages. A number of Christians, during the time of persecution, had committed portions of the Scriptures to memory, which they recited at their meetings, and taught to others.

It appeared equally marvellous to me that, during the years in which no public religious teaching and no reading of the Scriptures had been allowed, the Christians should have maintained their own spiritual life in the strength and energy in which it had existed, and that, under circumstances so unfavourable, their faith should have spread so extensively in the country.

As soon as I had received intelligence of the arrival of the expected missionaries in the country, I informed the leaders of the Christians; and when, in reply to their inquiries, I told them that I expected a supply of the Scriptures, they rejoiced greatly. A number of them requested me to write down their names and the names of their friends, together with the number of books which they wished to obtain.

I said that, excepting copies of parts of the Old Testament, there would be a sufficiency for the supply of the wants of all, as there were 10,000 copies of the New Testament, besides other books.

Firmly believing that on every ground it was better that those who were able should pay a reasonable sum towards defraying the cost of the books, than that all should receive them gratuitously, and knowing the extreme difficulty and dissatisfaction that would be caused at any subsequent period by requiring ever so small a payment from those who had been accustomed to receive them as gifts, I told them that the books would be given to those who were able to read and too poor to pay for them, but that other persons would be required to pay a small sum towards the expense of production and transport of the books,—about fourpence or sixpence for a bound copy of the New Testament, and double that sum for parts of the Old Testament bound together; which money would be sent to England to those who had provided the paper, and paid for the printing of the books.

Some of those present observed that in former times both the rich and the poor had received these books from the missionaries gratuitously. This led me to repeat what I had before stated, that the help of their friends in England was now given under somewhat different circumstances from those under which it had been afforded when the missionaries first came to Madagascar. Then the missionaries found them heathen; they were Christians now. They came then to persuade them to become Christians, but now to help them to act like Christians, by providing for the nurture of their own spiritual life, and for making the gospel known to their heathen countrymen; that their faith would only become living and strong as Christianity was prized and sustained amongst themselves, and not left to depend on foreign support.

Two or three rich men recommended me to follow the conduct of the Catholic priests, who gave books to the people. I said it was generous of the priests to do so; but as I did not think it was right, or that the books could in such case be so highly prized or so carefully preserved, as they would be if those who were able paid a small sum for them, I could not adopt their advice. The same parties urged that the people would deem it as sacrilege to sell the Bible for money, because they regarded it with reverence, as being something sacred. I replied that there was danger of our mixing superstitious feelings with our estimate of the Bible. That in regard to its origin and teaching it was the most sacred and precious treasure the Christian could possess. It was the means whereby God instructed us concerning Himself, His love, His power, and His willingness to save mankind; and that the knowledge of these things was a benefit and a privilege which no gold could purchase, and which was given freely. That the wisdom and love of God taught in the Bible were divine and sacred; but the paper and other material parts of the Bible were the same as those used in making other books, and had all been purchased with money. Therefore, while it would be unkind and wrong to withhold the Scriptures from the poor because they were unable to pay for them, it was right that those who had money should return a small portion of the cost to those who had paid for making the books and sending them across the sea.

Other of the Christians said they were thankful that their friends in England had bought the paper, and had the Bibles printed and sent out, and that they would very cheerfully repay what was required to help their friends to prepare more books for themselves and others, and even proposed themselves to pay a larger sum than I had mentioned.*

* Our discussion about the books was reported to the prime minister the same evening, and such was the desire of his people for them, that early in the morning one of his aides-de-camp came to say the minister would send his own slaves to Tamatave for one box of books and another of school materials for the use of his own people, and would pay for them when they arrived, if I would write to the person in whose charge they were, to deliver them; this I did while the messenger waited.

From a Photograph. Washerman. Bearer. Water-carrier. Bellows-blower. Market-boy. Cook.

MY KITCHEN.

arrival of the wives of the missionaries, as indicating intended residence amongst them, and not a visit.

I had secured the dwelling-houses on the premises formerly occupied by Mr. Griffiths for the temporary accommodation of the newly arrived missionaries, hoping they would be more suitably accommodated before the ground was needed for the training school. The greatest difficulty arose from there being only one kitchen, and that, as usual, separate from the dwelling-house. It was larger, however, than my own kitchen, which, though not very promising in appearance, seldom gave me cause to complain of the cooking. It was, however, much crowded by its inmates, among whom was generally a little boy brightening up the charcoal fire with a piston in a wooden cylinder, the usual Malagasy bellows.

The next Sunday, being the first Sunday in the month, I went, accompanied by the missionaries, to Amparibe. The house was filled with people, and the native minister was concluding the usual morning service when we entered. The members of the three churches in the capital had arranged that their first public association with the newly arrived missionaries should be a united communion. They desired thus to express their sense of the divine mercy, by partaking together of the symbols of the one great manifestation of the dying love of Christ in the sacrifice offered on the cross, and, in the celebration of this ordinance, to unite with them in renewing their solemn consecration of themselves to God.

When the non-communicating members of the ordinary congregation had retired, the members of the other two churches entered, and the communicants, amounting to between seven and eight hundred, sat down—the men on one side, and the women on the other. After singing and reading, the elements were distributed by one of the native ministers of the church and myself, an address was given by a native pastor from one of the other churches, and the minister of the third church closed the services with prayer.

The greater portion of the assembly were neatly attired, chiefly in native clothing; and when I looked on the calm, cheerful countenances of many in that assembly, seated on the matting before me, and remembered the deeply interesting events in the history of not a few with whom I was acquainted, and reflected that forty years before there was not a single native believer in Christ in Madagascar, I could not but regard with renewed wonder and admiration the goodness of God and the power of the gospel.

The missionaries appeared gratified with the service; and, after making every necessary abatement, it was indeed a soul-moving spectacle which thus greeted them on entering the field of their future labours. The communicants had all been admitted to Christian fellowship by native pastors. They knew of the love of God to sinful men, and of the great salvation completed on the cross; and they followed, so far as they understood it, the teaching of God's holy word;

and, notwithstanding all deficiencies among the converts, such evidence of the fidelity of these native ministers could not but encourage the abler and better trained servants of Christ, who now came to take part in the work, to believe that they would find efficient fellow-workers in conveying the blessings of the gospel to the surrounding regions of heathenism.

The coronation of the king and queen, which was attended by many foreigners and vast multitudes of people, took place on the 23rd of September, and has been elsewhere described.* A somewhat strange accompaniment had preceded the ceremony,—a kind of pseudo-coronation, enacted by some Catholic priests, who went to the palace to see the crown which had been presented by the Emperor, and which they then sprinkled with holy water. They afterwards published the following account of their proceedings:—

"La messe terminée, j'ai récité sur la couronne royale les prières indiquées par l'Eglise; puis, après l'avoir aspergée de l'eau sainte, et invoqué sur elle toutes les bénédictions d'en haut, je l'ai prise entre mes mains, et, m'approachant de Radama, je la lui ai posée solennellement sur la tête, en prononçant ces paroles: 'Sire, c'est au nom de Dieu que je vous couronne. Régnez longtemps pour la gloire de votre nom et pour le bonheur de votre peuple.'

"Il était près de 8 heures quand cette cérémonie s'est terminée n'ayant en guère pour témoin que Dieu et ses anges," &c., &c.—"*Relation d'un Voyage à*

* "Madagascar Revisited."

Tananario, à l'Époque du Couronnement de Radama II," par le T. R. P. Jouen, Préfet Apostolique de Madagascar.

The king, referring afterwards to the circumstance, said that the queen and himself were unprepared for any such proceeding, and were greatly surprised at the conduct of the priests.

Many Christians from Vonizongo, the Betsileo, and other distant parts, came to me the day after the coronation to ask for books to take to their homes; and on the following morning the members of the English embassy departed. The influence of the English chiefs had been most honourable and encouraging to the Christians, as well as a source of much gratification to myself. They had seen much of the effects of Christianity among the people, and expressed themselves gratified by the conduct of the native Christians. The General promised—and gave me—the first encouragement in connection with the memorial churches, by the generous donation of £100 towards their erection, beside £5 to distribute amongst the Christian poor. Captain, afterwards Lieutenant Colonel Anson also collected £60 in furtherance of the same object.

Next to Antananarivo, the most interesting place in the province is Ambohimanga, a romantic-looking village crowning the summit of a granite hill, five hundred feet above the undulating plain from which it rises, and which is green and fertile with plantations and cultivated fields of rice. The mountain is clothed to its summit with slender and graceful trees of rich and varied foliage, often festooned with creepers, and altogether so attractive that the native bards have sometimes described the queen as resembling—

> "The woods of Ambohimanga
> Bending down in their growth."

It was the birthplace of the founder of the present dynasty, and contains, besides the tombs of the sovereign rulers, the house of Fantaka, one of the national idols. No foreigner was allowed to enter its gates, nor even a native, who was not a resident, without a pass from the authorities. Yet even here there were Christians. They worshipped in the house of a Christian family; and in the month of November, 1863, they sought my assistance to obtain for them a piece of ground on which to build a chapel and a school. This the king cheerfully gave them. They then asked me to go and preach to them, which, having obtained the king's approval, I consented to do.

The king sent instructions to the prime minister to inform the authorities of the place that he had granted the ground specified to the Christians, and to request the authorities to deliver it to them; also to state that in about ten days I should go there to preach to the Christians with his entire approbation. The day before I went, the king sent a judge, one of the high officers of the government, to tell the authorities that I should be there on the following day, and that, as I went with his full approbation, he had no doubt they would receive me courteously, as his friend.

Early on Sunday morning, the 16th of November, I set out, accompanied by a friend of the commander-in-chief, a native preacher and some Christians. On the outskirts of the city we overtook the chief officer of the palace, himself a Christian, and by eight o'clock halted at the gate of Ambohimanga. There we found the officer in command with a few soldiers, drawn up outside the gate, and the judge sent by the king waiting for us. The officer of the palace then stated that a friend of the king's, a foreigner, and some Christians had come to visit them and the Christians in the city, and that by his Majesty's wish he had accompanied me. To this the chief replied that what pleased the king was pleasing to them, and that they were glad to see any one who was his friend.

After the usual salutations between my companions and the officers, the latter bade me welcome; then, giving the order to march, the drum beat, the officers and soldiers advanced, and we passed through the gate, the guard of honour with their music leading the way, the messenger from the king and I following next, and the Christians bringing up the rear.

As soon as we had all passed through the gate, the Christians began to sing, and thus we proceeded along the well-paved and gradually ascending road up the side of the hill, until we reached an open space, some considerable distance below the higher parts, where the buildings belonging to the sovereign are situated. Here we halted beneath the shade of a large spreading tree; leaving our friends with the authorities, who held a kabary, a Christian officer led the native preacher and myself to the house in which the Christians of the place and the friends from adjacent villages, to the number of about two hundred, were assembled. They occupied a newly matted room, where a few chairs and a table stood near a window, outside of which a number of heathen were gathered.

After praise and prayer to the true God, Andriambelo, the native preacher, delivered a short but exceedingly appropriate address to the Christians within and the heathen without, from 1 Pet. ii. 17: "Honour all men, love the brotherhood, fear God, honour the king." From these words, in a few brief, clear, and pointed sentences, he exhibited the fear of God in the heart as the foundation of all that is true in religion, and their love towards each other as the tie that binds Christians together; that respect was due to their fellow-men; and that loyalty to their sovereign was inculcated by the Christian law, as well as the fear of God.

On the conclusion of the first service we were conducted, through crowds of children and wondering heathen, to the house of a Christian officer, the son of the priest of the heathen temple, where those from the capital took breakfast with us. On returning again to the house of worship, we found it so crowded that some of the company had to come out before we could enter. After singing and prayer a native minister, born in the place, gave a short address. I then read and briefly expounded the parable of the "Prodigal Son," as illustrating the loving character of God, the Father of all mankind, and the welcome of affection and joy which awaits every returning child. At the close of the service we sang the national anthem, which is a prayer for the king; and I then told the company, that as we wished to visit another village on our return, we could not remain longer with them.

On leaving the house we thanked the chief officers for the present of rice and poultry which they offered us in token of their hospitality, and asked them to give it to the Christians, as we could not remain. We then walked together under the grateful shade of umbrageous trees, down the side of the hill opposite to that by which we had entered the city, and on reaching the plain below the officers took friendly leave of us.*

* Such having been the actual course pursued on this occasion, I was somewhat surprised on receiving, nearly nine months afterwards, from home, a copy of an official report from Madagascar, which was sent to me for "explanation." In this accusation it was stated that, before making the above visit, I had obtained from the king "armed followers," and had gone to "preach there by force;" and that I had afterwards induced the king to degrade "all the officers who, in the first instance, resisted," &c., &c. The facts above stated afforded ample explanation. There were two or three accounts of the same event. I heard it was stated that I had "preached at the point of the bayonet, on the tomb of the late queen." And I read in a newspaper that I had gone with Radama to Ambohimanga, to pray at the tomb of his mother for the repose of her soul.

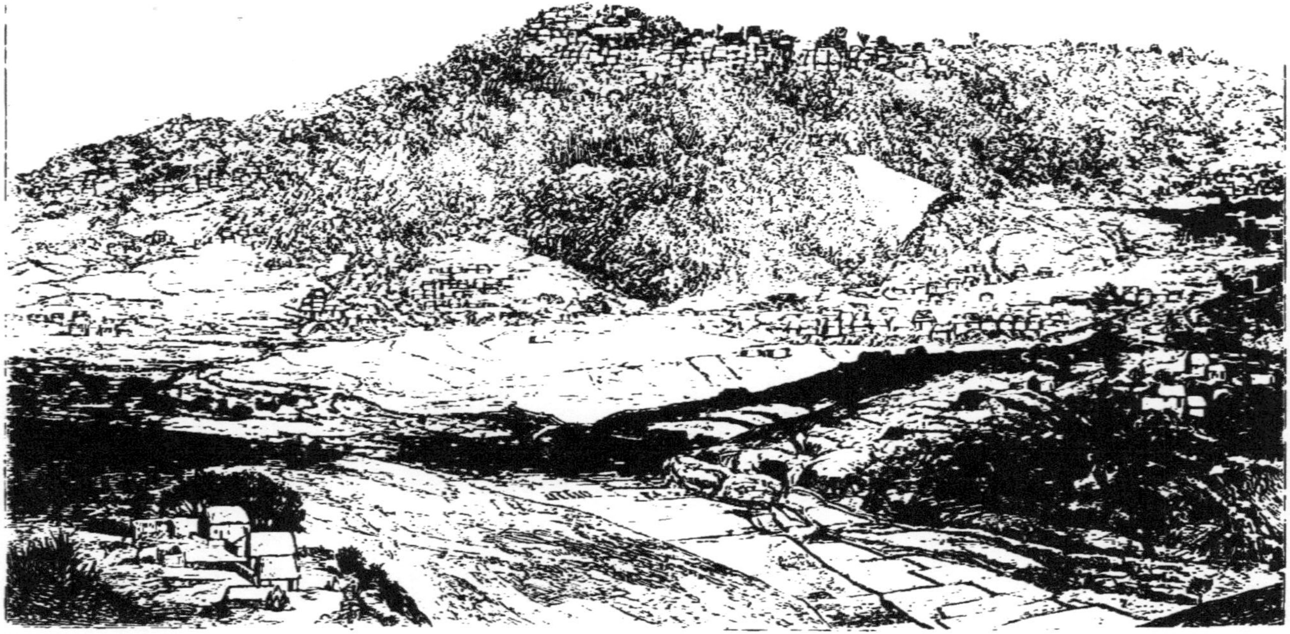

From Photograph by REV. W. ELLIS.

AMBOHIMANGA, FROM THE NORTH-WEST.

THE SACRED CITY OF AMBOHIMANGA. 295

I had subsequently an opportunity of making further observations on this ancient, sacred, and historically celebrated place. The great charm of Ambohimanga is its position, standing out like a bold promontory, overlooking a wide range of country. 'On the eastern summit of the hill on which the city is built, tombs and other important structures are seen, while houses of a respectable class stretch along the upper part to the west. Lower down and outside the city, in different directions, two or three houses grouped together here and there, with gardens and a few trees, forming rural homesteads with their orchards and other accompaniments; or a cottage or two standing under a clump of trees of richest foliage, with deep perpendicular precipices on one side, and the level land of the cultivated plain stretching far away on the other, present altogether bits of landscape scenery that would make perfect gems of pictures.

For two or three weeks after my first visit, a native preacher was sent to Ambohimanga from our congregation; then the authorities took possession of the house, threw out of the window the table, seats, matting, &c., placed a sentry at the door, and forbade the worship of the Christians there. The latter complained to the king, who removed the officers from their posts, and appointed others. One reason assigned for the proceedings of the officers was that the usual amount of rain had not fallen, and that the failure of the rice crops and consequent starvation of the people were feared, on account of the offence given to the idols by the worship of the Christians in the sacred city.

The death of more than one officer of high rank about this time made us acquainted with the inconsolable grief occasioned by death among the heathen, and also presented some strange scenes in connection with the last hours of those whose relatives comprehended both Christians and heathens. Among these was an officer of the government, whom I found dangerously ill on my return from Ambohimanga. I visited him daily during the progress of his disease, and spoke to him and prayed with him when I had reason to suppose that he was conscious of what I said, which indeed was but seldom. The scene in his sick room was often deeply affecting. The members of his family were untiring in their kind attentions. In the room with him I often found one of the Catholic priests, while in the room adjoining, his sister, the wife of a judge, who was not a Christian, would be employing the sikidy or divination for his recovery.

I spoke consolingly to the wife and family, some of whom were Christians. I had prayed with them the last time before I left, and in a few hours received a message to say that the spirit had departed. The king, with two of his ministers, was present when I went to the house later in the day, and I took occasion to speak of the danger of delaying preparation for the great change common to us all, as the deceased, who was not unacquainted with Christianity, had said, the last time I conversed with him while he was sensible, that he *hoped to* become a Christian.

The next day, when I paid a visit of condolence to the family of Rahaniraka, I found them exhausted with fatigue. The king's band was playing in the yard to divert the minds of the survivors from the grief of their loss, and the house was crowded with mourners. The wife of the commander-in-chief, the sister of the prime minister, and other women of distinction were employed in decorating the bier and hearse, and numbers of cattle were being slaughtered. At seven o'clock next morning the funeral procession passed my house on its way to the village of Inosy, in the north, where the interment took place.

Before the close of the year I was much encouraged by a welcome letter from my old and valued friend, Dr. Livingstone, who had passed along the west coast of Madagascar to Mohillo, one of the Comoro Islands. He had found that a cousin of the king of Madagascar was queen of the island, her father having escaped from the massacre of the chief part of his family, on the death of the first Radama. This letter, the last I received from Dr. Livingstone, is given at length in "Madagascar Revisited." I brought his statements about slavery before the king, who sent instructions to the western ports to prevent the importation of slaves into the country.

I have already mentioned the religious organizations which the leaders of the Christians had introduced among the believers during the time of persecution. It was now unequal to their necessities in the altered state of the church, since perfect religious liberty had been established, and the avowal of Christianity was no longer an impediment to their temporal prosperity. The Christians sought advice from the missionaries, and we drew up a simple statement of the chief principles on which their churches should be organized; mainly with a view to the maintenance of the law of Christ, as contained in the New Testament in relation to His church, the watchful care over the purity of that church, and its employment as the legitimate and appointed agency for the conversion of the heathen.

The men who had acted as leaders of the small companies which were scattered over the face of the country during the persecution, were now joint pastors and teachers in the three large congregations in the capital. We recommended that the communicants in each church should select at least two of them to be their pastors; to preside over their public religious proceedings, the appointment of deacons and the admission of members. We informed them that we had not come to assume the government of the churches, but to give them the advantage of our knowledge and experience in promoting the welfare of the church in Madagascar.

We further stated that if, when their churches were organized, they wished us to associate ourselves with the native pastors, we were willing to do so, but that the maintenance of the church in its order and purity, and its extension in the country, was the work which the Lord had devolved on them, and in which we would do our best to aid them.

Upon this plan the churches in the capital were then organized. Mr. Cousins was solicited to take the oversight of the church at Amparibe, in association with Andriambelo and another native preacher. I was asked to help the church at Ambatonakanga. Mr. Toy became the pastor of the church which he himself had gathered in the northern part of the capital. He is still pastor of the same, which now worships in the beautiful memorial church erected at Ambohipotsy, where the congregation, then consisting of only thirteen persons, first met on the Sabbath afternoon in his own house. A temporary chapel, capable of holding six hundred persons, was built for their use at Ambohipotsy, and opened for public worship in the presence of the king, the widow of Ramboasalama, and other persons of distinction, in February, 1863. This congregation now sometimes numbers more than fifteen hundred, with seven hundred communicants. Some slight changes or additions have since been made in the organization of the churches; others will be indicated by growth and experience, which the elasticity of the system will enable them without difficulty to introduce.

The commencement of the new year had been celebrated by the great national bathing festival of the people; the Christians had been accustomed, even in the times of persecution, to celebrate Christmas day with extra service, and with such means of rejoicing as their circumstances admitted. On Christmas day, 1863, the king and queen, having on their way been to the Catholic chapel, came voluntarily in state' to the worship of the Christians at Ambatonakanga. This act prevented the heathen from continuing to report that, although the king favoured the Christians, the queen was averse to their creed and practice; and showed that she was, in this respect, favourable to the Christians.

A week or two afterwards the king invited about sixty of the chief ministers and leading Christians to a breakfast at his house, after which he expressed his pleasure at the success of their work, and his readiness to assist them. Statements were on this occasion made respecting the great need of public worship in the central and southern sections of the city, all the existing chapels being in the northern suburb; and those present were recommended to obtain sites and erect places of worship in the populous but neglected parts of the capital. The king encouraged the proposal, and several who were present promised to assist in the work. In less than six months two chapels, and subsequently a third, were opened, and congregations gathered in these important centres of influence.

Having learned, in the month of March, that the directors of the Society approved of the proposal to build the memorial churches, and that the supporters of the Society were so favourable to the object that there was reason to believe the sum required would be furnished, I applied to the king for written titles for the ground. Radama having, with the consent of his ministers, duly executed these deeds, I lost no time, in company with some of the missionaries, and with the government officers, in fixing the boundaries of the land, and arranging for the payment for any buildings or fences occupying the ground. I also engaged some of the most experienced quarrymen to provide stones for the foundation and commencement of the walls of at least one of the buildings. The Christians engaged to help, and undertook to level the ground, which was accomplished at Ambohipotsy by the end of March.

Going down to Ambatonakanga early one morning in the beginning of April, I was delighted to find nearly the whole congregation at work, masters and slaves digging down the hillocks and levelling the ground which had then been obtained, women and children carrying the earth, stones and rubbish in baskets on their heads, while the preachers were superintending and encouraging them, and singing for joy. I gave them a piece of silver to send to the market to buy cooked manioc for the workmen, when they should rest in the middle of the day. I did not wonder at their joy. The spot had probably been to some of them a place of bondage, on account of their faith in that Saviour for whose worship it was now to be a sanctuary.

In the mean time the church was extending its influence to new and important portions of the population. By the middle of April, the Christians on the eastern side of the city had finished their large chapel, just outside the ancient eastern stone gateway, called Ankadibevava. This building, though a hundred feet long and proportionally wide, was filled on the day of opening, when the king and a number of officers attended. The house, somewhat larger than at first required, was not substantially built; but we rejoiced in the means of increased usefulness which it afforded. It was the only place of worship on the eastern side of the capital, which is two miles from north to south. The ground, which is most eligible as being near the chief eastern entrance to the city, was given by one of the people; and, with a little assistance from the missionaries, a few of the nobles, and some of their fellow-Christians, the building was erected by the people themselves. A stronger church was subsequently built on the same spot, and a third, larger and more substantial, is now in course of erection.

One of the ministers, one of the deacons, and about thirty of the communicants, removed from Ambatonakanga as soon as this building was completed, for the purpose of forming the nucleus of a church and congregation connected with the place; and on the first communion Sunday, fifty-eight persons commemorated the dying love of Christ in the newly erected church; on which occasion ten adults received the rite of baptism. In connection with few of the churches of the capital has the progress of the gospel been more encouraging than at Ankadibevava. Although the attendance on the means of religious instruction scarcely diminished in any of the former places of worship, or in the schools connected with them, the services associated with the newly erected buildings drew within their influence many of the residents of the localities which they occupied.

There had been for some time considerable uneasiness among the different political parties in the capital, and greater activity among the agencies connected with the superstitions of the country. It first reached the capital in the form of rumours, from villages at a distance, of the prevalence of a sort of sickness, which rendered the subjects of it, at certain seasons, unconscious of what was passing around them, but accessible to communications from the spirit world. It was said that at times they saw visions, and heard voices from invisible beings delivering messages from the ancestors of the present dynasty. These voices were said to deplore the apostasy of the king from the gods and the customs of his ancestors, and to forewarn of fearful calamities, unless the king should put a stop to the worship of the God of the foreigners.

This was the general burden of all the communications, whether it was reported that the ancestors of the king were coming to tell him what to do in order to preserve the kingdom, or whether it was to denounce some fearful supernatural visitation of avenging calamity. This was followed by a number of persons, chiefly young women from the country, who, seized by some inexplicable disease, were said to be unable to remain in one position, or in the same place, and who, first singly, then in large numbers, and sometimes attended by their friends, came into the capital, running and dancing along the streets or the suburbs, and making their way notwithstanding the sentries who, with crossed bayonets, stood on each side of the gate, into the courtyard of the king's house.

From the beginning the pretended messages from the ancestors of the reigning family had all been brought as if sent to the king. Radama repeated to me the messages, and sometimes I was reading with him when the messengers came from the villages around. At first I treated the whole as a delusion on the part of these sight-seers and dancers, or as a symptom of disease; but to my surprise, as well as grief, I found that the pretended revelations of the will of his ancestors was seriously affecting the mind of the king. He lost his natural cheerfulness, and became absent and silent. When he one day said to me that his ancestors were coming in great pomp, with cannon and all the outward insignia of power, I quietly asked, "Where do you think they obtained the cannon? There are none in the spirit world, and your ancestors were all dead before any were brought to the country." But he only half smiled, and then, turning away, spoke on some other subject.

At other times I spoke very earnestly to the king on this subject, which seemed to have taken possession of his mind. My own life, I believe, was on one occasion in jeopardy, from a number of the priests with the dancers bursting open the door and rushing into the room where I was sitting with the king, the French consul, and some of Radama's officers. The mad dancers wheeled round the room, while the priests or idol-keepers, with menacing looks and gestures, seemed bent on evil towards me. I stood up when they burst into the room. The king did the same, taking hold of my hand and leaning his shoulder against mine, while he ordered them out of the place. His attendants at length succeeded in clearing the room and fastening the doors and windows, with the exception of one small glass door, through which I saw the women dancing and the men, with large stones in their hands, gathered around it outside. Though it was three o'clock when I went to the palace, it was long after dark before I left to return home.

I was afterwards informed that the heathen party had arranged to attack me on that day, as they said that my presence with the king was the great hindrance to their success with him. I was also warned that they intended to employ sorcery against me, and for nine successive nights small baskets containing what I was told were death warrants, or intimations of evil, were laid at my door. I did not fear their sorceries, but as incendiarism was sometimes employed to favour the objects of the evil-disposed, I was glad when two soldiers were sent every night to keep guard over the premises which I occupied.

From this time the king's mind became more dark and unsettled, and it was said that he had intimated his purpose to issue an edict authorizing those who

x

quarrelled to settle their dispute by force of arms. My own impression is that his mind had already given way. The prime minister and a large number of his adherents more than once besought the king to forbear issuing such an order, but he refused to accede to their wishes; on this they left him and proceeded to deliberate on the course they should pursue.

There were other causes of dissatisfaction of older date and deeper root than this obnoxious edict, especially regarding the conduct of the counsellors by whom the king had surrounded himself; and it was evident to most, except Radama himself, that a change was impending, though few perhaps expected so tragical a one as that which followed. I never afterwards saw any dancers or sick persons running about the streets.

When I returned from the palace on the afternoon of the day on which the nobles held their last conference with the king, I found two officers from the prime minister waiting with a message, to the effect that I was not to remain in my own house that night, but repair to a place mentioned, where farther directions, if necessary, would be sent to me. I passed that night at Dr. Davidson's, and, on looking out the next morning, saw the plain of Andohalo filled with troops under arms, and heard that thirteen of the king's ministers were prisoners. Some of them had already been put to death, and others were seized and killed during the day. A number of the king's advisers, who remained with him, were surrendered to the nobles, on condition that they should be banished in chains for life; but they were all put to death on the day they were delivered up. Thirty-one had been sentenced to death, twenty-nine were actually slain. Some were irreproachable Christians, others unprincipled profligates, neither Christian nor heathen, but gross materialists.

Whether the conspirators included the death of the king in their original plan, or feared a reaction against themselves if he survived, is not known; but shortly after cock-crow on the 12th of May two officers, with a number of men, forced an entrance into the room in which he had slept, and, disregarding alike the efforts and entreaties of the queen to save his life, removed her from the apartment; they then seized the king, he exclaiming, "I have never shed blood!" then, casting the mantle over his head, they tightened the sash round his throat until he sank a lifeless corpse on the floor,—murdered by the authority which had been chiefly instrumental in placing him on the throne, and which then held the power wrested from his hands. The body of Radama was carried forth at night to the royal village of Ilafy for interment.

God had raised up this young prince at a most critical period of the early history of the Martyr Church of Madagascar. He gave him influence with his mother which no other human being ever exercised, filled his soul with a horror against the destruction of human life in any form, and warmed his heart with sincere and disinterested sympathy towards all suffering from injustice and cruelty. Radama had been honoured by the Christians' God, to lighten in their favour the heavy iron rule under which they had been so long bowed down, and to inspire hopes of a better future. He had saved many persons' lives, denounced persecution, established perfect religious liberty, and, while guaranteeing unfettered religious action, had afforded complete legal protection to Christians and heathens. His own imperfect acquaintance with the theory of Christianity, his destitution of the principles of religious life in his own soul, the unrenewed state of his heart, and the course of his life, disordered and confused as it had latterly become, not only by bad influences, but by many conflicting forces, which he wanted thoughtfulness and stability of character to meet—all these had disqualified him for anything closer than a mere external association with the outward progress of Christianity in the country. But while the Christians deplored the disastrous effects of his own destitution of the power of religion, they justly felt grateful for the many benefits which, during the brief number of his days, he was instrumental in bestowing upon his country.

Within a few hours after forcibly separating queen Rabodo from her husband, the conspirators offered her the then vacant throne, which she accepted; and her reign, while continuing to the Christians the liberty and the privileges which Radama had bestowed, inaugurated the first germs of approximation to constitutional government ever known in Madagascar.

The conditions on which the new queen received the crown were, that the power over life and death should not be vested in the sovereign alone, and that the word of the sovereign alone should not be binding on the people; but that the agreement of certain representatives of the nobles and the people should be necessary to the putting any one to death, and the enacting of any law which the people should be obliged to obey. It was also stipulated that perfect religious liberty should be guaranteed to all classes and creeds.

About noon on the day of the king's death, the firing of cannon called the people to Andohalo, where a number of officers soon afterwards arrived. The chief officer announced to the eager multitude that during the night Radama had put an end to his own existence, and that his widow, under the title of Rasoherina, was now queen; he further announced the conditions on which the crown had been received.

At the first audience she gave to the missionaries, the queen stated that the liberties and privileges of the Christians would be preserved in their full extent, and they were at the same time assured that the objects of the mission were approved. The queen herself was not a Christian, but was publicly regarded as the head of the heathen and the patron of the idols; yet she faithfully preserved inviolate the liberty of worship and teaching to the missionaries and their converts.

Though many of the Christians were almost

stunned and bewildered by the shock of this sudden change, it operated favourably on them as a whole, by causing many to feel the insecurity of earthly things; and it thus induced greater spirituality of mind, and increased earnestness and attention to the requirements of the gospel. The churches were well attended, and considerable numbers were added to their fellowship, frequently as many as twenty at one time.

The missionaries justly considered that the capital had the first claim on their attention and efforts, but they did not confine themselves to this important position. Congregations were reviving in the villages around, many of which had contained one or more of the schools established by the first missionaries. Some of these had been visited by the native teachers, and by the missionaries recently arrived. Mr. Toy had extended his care to the villages in the south. Mr. W. Cousins had gone to the north. Mr. Toy soon afterwards formed a small class of young men in his church, to whom he gave special instruction with a view to their becoming preachers among the surrounding villages. Messrs. William and George Cousins, and Mr. Hartley, also trained classes of young men for the same important work. In order to excite deeper Christian sympathy in our congregations on behalf of their countrymen, we arranged with the ministers and churches of the capital to commence a monthly missionary prayer meeting.

This meeting we proposed should be held in

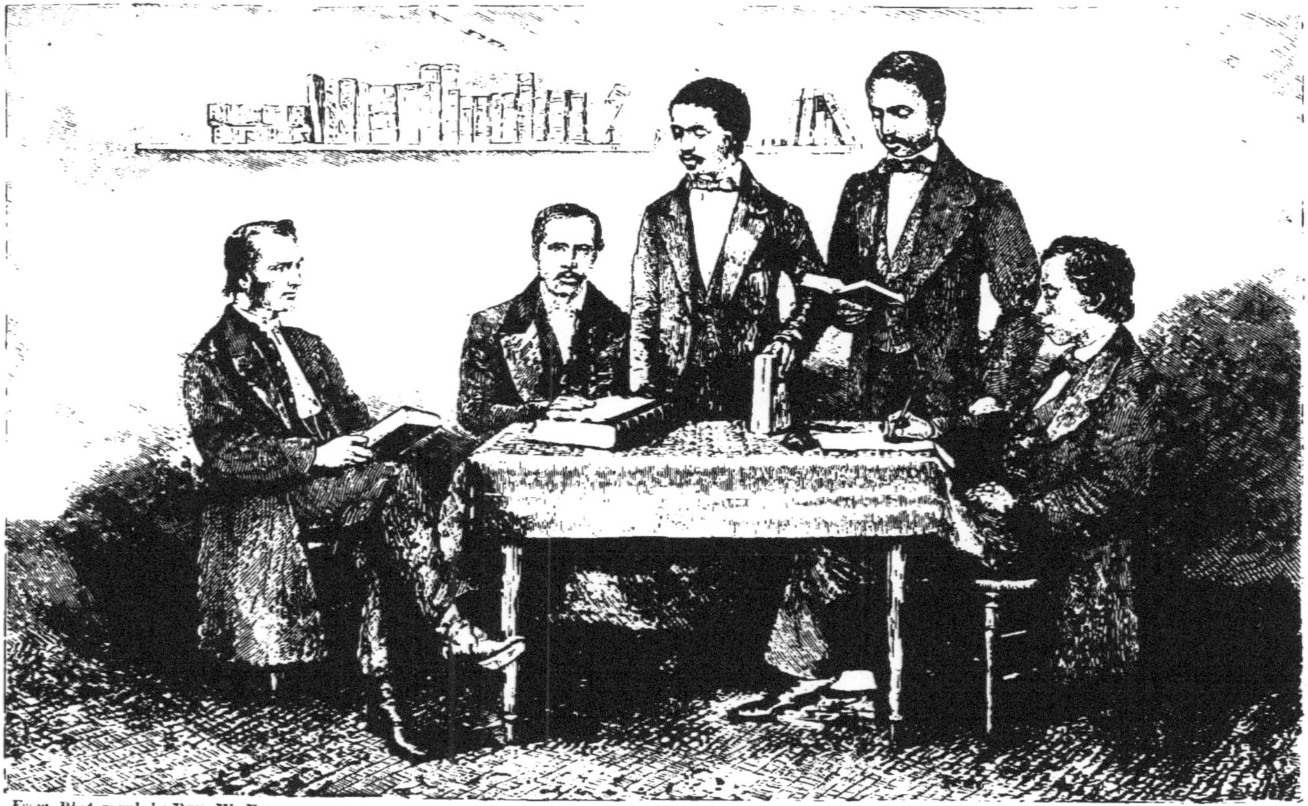

From Photograph by Rev. W. Ellis.

REV. R. TOY AND HIS CLASS OF NATIVE PREACHERS.

P. 310.

rotation at the largest places of worship in the capital, the services at each place to be arranged by the ministers of the congregation. Some of our people suggested that such a public gathering of Christians would be premature, and might alarm the government. The heathen had always pretended to be scandalized, as well as offended, by large meetings of Christians, which they called kabaries in favour of the foreigners.

Perfect liberty for prayer and teaching had been publicly guaranteed by the queen and the government, but so deeply had the long-continued and abject submission to authority become ingrained in the very nature of many of the people, that amongst the teachers even some did not venture to attend the prayer meeting, without first inquiring from the authorities whether or not it was approved. We had previously ascertained that some of the Christians connected with the government intended to be present.

These monthly missionary prayer meetings commenced at Analakely on the first Monday of August, 1863, and long before the appointed time many more people had arrived than could gain admittance within the building, so that we removed the pulpit to a large doorway, in order that both those within and those without might unite in the service. There were at least three thousand persons present. All seemed gratified, and when they dispersed, as the sun was approaching the horizon, many expressed their regret that they had not met at an earlier hour.

Nor was it at Antananarivo alone that these encouraging tokens of the divine blessing were manifested. The change in the government brought many persons from distant parts of the country to the capital, and amongst those from the west, and from Fort Dauphin, the extreme south, came Christian men, whose conversation, spirit, and conduct gave satisfactory evidence of their faith. They encouraged us also by the accounts they brought of other Christians in these remote parts. One individual received into communion with us had, as an officer, been most active in arresting some who had died for Christ.

But more remarkable still was the case of the inhabitants of a village to the north, Amparafaravato, the whole population of which had been votaries of the idol or idols kept in the village. But the gospel had penetrated even here. A number of these villagers had become Christians, and appropriating one of their houses for Christian worship, had abandoned the idols and met together in the house thus set apart for the worship of the true God. Some of these now came to Ambatonakanga, attended our worship, and applied for admission to fellowship with us. Those who knew them having testified to their Christian character, they were baptized and afterwards received to the church.

Fears were entertained by some lest these proceedings should displease the queen; but when her Majesty was informed of what had taken place, she said, "If any of the people of the villages are Christians and wish to leave, they may do so. It is nothing" (meaning there is no blame). "Let those who wish go, and those who wish stay; for there is no impediment to the following of the idols, or to uniting with the Christians." On this word of the queen, some of these Christians had come and united themselves with our church and congregation. This speech of the queen had been delivered publicly; it was now repeated before the officers of the government and others who were present, inspiring confidence while it gave encouragement.

The dispensary which Dr. Davidson had opened as soon as practicable after his arrival, had been for some time in successful operation. The assistance rendered to the sick, and the skill with which the doctor had treated a large proportion of the multitudes who daily sought his help, had deeply impressed the inhabitants of the capital and the suburbs, not only with the benevolent aims of the mission; which, while seeking chiefly to lead the morally diseased to the great Physician of souls, did not leave, as beneath its notice, those afflicted with bodily infirmity and disease to suffer without help. The cure in some cases and relief in others from long and, in their circumstances, hopeless suffering, which so many had now experienced, was regarded with great satisfaction by all residing within reach of the dispensary. But the fame of the cures effected spread far beyond those who had experienced these benefits; and of the vast number of strangers who thronged the capital at this period, few returned to their native homes without a visit to the dispensary, to witness the benefits bestowed upon others, or to seek relief for themselves.

Writing about this time, Dr. Davidson observes:—
" In addition to the usefulness of the dispensary in alleviating a certain amount of physical suffering, it undoubtedly exercises a powerful influence for good as an auxiliary to the Protestant mission. It is a standing testimony to the beneficence of our divine religion, and is calculated to impress upon the people a more just appreciation of the value of human life than has hitherto, unfortunately, prevailed. It has, to no inconsiderable extent, disarmed the prejudices and conciliated the affections of the people. Its influence in this respect has been felt among all classes, from the sovereign downwards. It has done more; it has brought the gospel to a large class who could not possibly be reached by any other agency whatever. Many have listened to the gospel for the first time in the medical missionary dispensary, where they had resorted for the cure of their bodily ailments, whose enmity or indifference would have prevented them seeking or even submitting to counsel or instruction from any other source. During the past year, a year of revolutions, above three thousand patients have been prescribed for, out of tens of thousands who have applied."

CHAPTER XII.

Coronation of Rasoherina—Rumours respecting Radama—First public recognition of the Christians—Religious services at Ambohimanga during the queen's visit—Christian procession to the palace on Christmas day—Review of the events of the year—Opening of the central school—Visit to Vonizongo—Employment of native preachers—The Christians in Betsileo—Instance of the power of the gospel—Chapel at Ambohitantely—Historical statistics of Ilafy—Visit to the Martyrs' Home—Chapels opened in the capital—Return of a captured slave to her home—Christians at Imerinamandrosa—Scene of the martyrs' suffering.

RABODO had been crowned by Radama as queen consort; but as she had now been proclaimed sovereign, under the title of Rasoherina, and had received the homage and allegiance of the distant races who acknowledged the Hova rule, it was necessary that she should be publicly recognised as such by the representatives of the people gathered in the capital.

The queen had restored the idols and the priests to the position which they occupied in the palace during the reign of Ranavalona, and the public official movements of the government were regulated by divination. The diviners had declared that Sunday was a day favourable to the queen and her family, and the coronation—or official and public announcement of the sovereignty of the queen—was, much to the regret of the Christians, fixed for the last Sunday in August. It took place, according to the direction of the diviners, at Andohalo, the place of public meeting within the city. The place was smaller and the numbers fewer than at the late coronation, though the native officers were as gorgeously attired as then. The chief difference consisted in the prominence of the priests and the idols. One of the national idols was placed in the palanquin with the queen, as she was borne through the city, while priests mingled with the officers in attendance; and when her Majesty ascended the platform, a priest followed bearing the idol, which was fixed at the right hand, the priest standing on the platform immediately behind the sovereign.

The queen, as already stated, was regarded as the head of the heathen party; but when, in the course of a very judicious and conciliatory address, she declared that every one was at liberty to worship God in the way he thought best, and to teach his religion to others under equal protection and with equal security, so long as the laws of the kingdom were obeyed, it was felt by many that the presence and position of the idols, as well as the priests, was but the form without the power—the lifeless corpse, without the vital energy which had once made idolatry so fearful a scourge in Madagascar.

It is only due to the memory of Rasoherina to say that, by identifying herself with the adherents of the idols, she quieted the apprehensions and calmed the spirits of those who were alarmed and impatient at the numbers and the power which Christianity was drawing to itself; and that, except in allowing the diviners to fix so many pageants and public amusements as well as other proceedings for the Sunday, which greatly interfered with the due observance of that day by a large number of Christian officers and others, there was little cause for complaint. The queen faithfully and carefully guarded the liberties and privileges of the Christians, showing them at the same time much personal good-will; and by the placing of her adopted children under their instruction, she further manifested her confidence in their integrity and general character.

At intervals after the revolution which placed the queen on the throne, the peace of the province and some of the neighbouring districts was greatly disturbed by rumours that Radama, though reported to be dead, was still living, and waiting in concealment for his friends to replace him on the throne. Whether these rumours were, as some said, originated by parties seeking to discover any who might be hostile to the recent change, or by parties having political aims of their own to accomplish, or by others bent on plunder, did not very clearly appear; but many lives were sacrificed among the tribes in the west, and sixteen were put to death at the capital.

The queen's mother died in July, but for reasons of state it was deemed undesirable that the court mourning should delay the ceremony of coronation beyond the appointed time; the decease was consequently not announced until after the coronation had taken place. The remains were then conveyed to the ancestral grave, with the pomp and ceremony suited to an event in some respects national. Among the observances on this occasion, a large number of oxen were killed and given to the several classes of persons in the capital. The heads of the Christians were invited to attend, and, in the distribution of the animals by the queen's minister, seven oxen were apportioned to the leaders of the congregations, as the gift of her Majesty to the Christians. The Christian leaders acknowledged the queen's bounty, and, attended by their servants, removed the slaughtered animals.

This gift was welcome to all as a token of recognition, but especially welcome to the poor Christian families. It was, however, chiefly prized by the more intelligent Christians, as indicating the altered light in which they were regarded by the government. Heretofore their existence among the queen's subjects had been ignored. It was now publicly recognised, for the first time, in the same manner as were other sections of the community, and tended to remove from the minds of the Christians the apprehensions which the prominence of the idols and the priests at the coronation might have awakened. It was another step in advance towards the recognition of equal rights for all.

Our second monthly prayer meeting, which certainly in warmth of feeling showed no diminution of interest among the Christians, was held on the first Monday in September at Ambatonakanga, where Mr. Cameron had formerly resided while superintending the government works, and where the bell to call the workmen together still occupied the place where he had fixed it thirty years before. The service was about to commence, when Mr. Cameron, whom the directors had invited to superintend and assist in the building of the memorial churches, arrived at the gate on his way to his residence at Analakely, having reached the capital that same afternoon. The spectacle presented at that spot, together with the object for which the multitude had come together, must have been as cheering to him as it was unexpected.

It had been first proposed to send out plans for the memorial churches from London, but the directors afterwards appointed Mr. James Sibree as architect, to prepare the plans and superintend the building; and he reached Antananarivo about a month after the arrival of Mr. Cameron.

Soon after the conclusion of the ceremonies connected with her mother's funeral, the queen and her court went for a season to Ambohimanga. A number of priests, with one of the idols, went a day or two before the queen, whose journey in its minutest details was regulated by the diviners. Ambohimanga had long been the stronghold of idolatry; and as at this time there would be a large number of priests and idol-worshippers there, we were apprehensive that the Christians, who had necessarily accompanied the queen, might be obliged to abstain from their accustomed observance of the Lord's day.

We were therefore thankful when we learned that the queen's personal officers, who were Christians, were told that they must arrange for part of their number to be in attendance, while others went to their worship, and that any Christians not on public duty were at liberty to attend Christian worship outside the gates of the city both morning and afternoon; we also heard that some of the officers in personal attendance upon the queen had been among the preachers on these occasions.

The holding of these services at the gates of this so-called "sacred city" was at the time most favourable to the Christians. They found that their confidence in the queen's word was not misplaced; and the idolaters saw that, however favourable the queen might be to them personally, she would not allow the Christians to be deprived of their privileges. It also stimulated the efforts of the believers, strengthened their hope, and confirmed their expectations of still greater triumphs of the cross in Madagascar.

Even in the dark and depressing years of persecution, the Christians had observed the return of the season when the birth of Christ is commemorated; and having received the queen's approval of their proposal to pay their respects to the sovereign on this annual Christian festival, they met first in their several places of worship at daybreak on the morning of Christmas day, concluding their morning service about eight o'clock; after which they repaired to Andohalo, the place of public assembly within the city, where the number assembled amounted to seven or eight thousand. Then, preceded by the high officers of government who were Christians, and the ministers of the churches, they walked, four abreast, in one long joyous procession to the queen's palace, singing part of the way.

When they reached the palace, the ministers and officers of the court, with the members of the royal family, were already assembled outside, and when the queen came out of the palace she was welcomed with cordial greetings by the vast assembly. The singers sang the national prayer for the queen. The hasina was tendered, and two Christian officers addressed her Majesty, one of them with much feeling and propriety. The queen gave a brief but approving reply, and by words as well as gestures assured the assembly of the satisfaction which their declaration of attachment had afforded. All appeared pleased with the singing, and surprised at the number of the Christians. The national anthem was again sung, after which the queen rose and, amid renewed expression of cordial feeling on the part of the assembly, returned to the palace.

The year thus closed, although it opened with bright prospects, had been one of great changes, of uneasiness, alarm and apparent danger to the mission; but it had closed under circumstances which stimulated to greater effort and inspired stronger hope. There had been a continued increase among the believers, and this although the supreme objects of the nation's worship and dread—the spirits of the ancestors—had sent from the invisible world denunciations against the worshippers of the true God. Though the maddened priests had threatened personal violence, and death warnings against the servants of Christ had been repeatedly given, the confidence of the Christians had never failed. Through all these attempts to intimidate, and amid all the wild, erratic movements of the idolaters; through conspiracy, revolution, and appalling shedding of blood, the destruction of one sovereign and the exaltation of another, Christianity had not only held its own, but had increased in numbers and influence, until, at the close of this eventful year, it occupied a more advanced position in the estimation of the people, and exercised greater power for good than it had ever attained before.

The mission had also been strengthened by the arrival of additional helpers in Mr. and Mrs. Pearse and Mr. Kessler. Two additional places of worship had been built, congregations gathered, and churches formed; other buildings were also in progress. The large central school had been finished, and was in working operation, with a hundred and thirty children daily attending and making satisfactory progress. In reference to these children Mr. Stagg, the schoolmaster, expressed his opinion that the youth of Madagascar might be educated up to a point equal to that attained in schools of the same class at home. The mission had always been distinguished by the efficiency of its educational efforts, and much of the success attending the missionary work has been instrumentally attained by the ability and industry with which, in early years, this part of the work had been prosecuted.

In connection with four of the chapels, schools for the children of the people attending were also in operation. Mr. Parrett had been able to print a supply of the most necessary books for teaching, and was training natives to aid in the work of the press. The missionaries in charge of the several city congregations had extended their personal labours to the adjacent villages. Mr. Toy had already under his care six villages in the south, to which he sent native preachers on the Sabbath day. Mr. Cousins had spent some time in Vonizongo, where he found three good congregations, with six hundred Christians and upwards of a hundred and twenty communicants. When it is stated that the people in this border district of Ankova had suffered severely during the long season of persecution, and had seen the face of no European teacher or preacher since the expulsion of the first missionaries, it need not be added that the visits of Mr. Cousins afforded unusual satisfaction.

The chapel at Amparibe, one of the largest in the capital, of which Mr. Cousins is the English pastor, had been so often enlarged that it became necessary to build a new one. A building with clay walls was consequently commenced, which the people themselves undertook and finished soon after his return from Vonizongo. At the opening service one thousand five hundred persons entered the building, while two or three hundred remained outside. The ordinary attendance was seldom less than fifteen hundred, and during the year then closed a hundred and eighty-two communicants were added to the church.

The new year called to new efforts and probably new trials, but it was hoped that it would be attended with continued progress. Mr. Pearse directed his attention to Analakely, where there was a congregation of a thousand persons and a hundred and eighty communicants without a European minister.

On the 14th of January, 1864, the foundation-stone of a new hospital, to be built by Mr. Cameron, was laid by the prime minister; and about a week afterwards the foundation-stone of the first memorial church, to be built from plans furnished by Mr. Sibree, was laid by the same officer at Ambatonakanga. The commencement and prosecution of these great and important works were not the only encouragements with which the new year opened. Quietly and satisfactorily the gospel continued to spread among the people, and it was the continual privilege of the missionaries to behold the evidences of the work of the Divine Spirit on the hearts of the people. No month passed for a long time in which additions were not made to the number of communicants in the churches, and few weeks passed in which messengers did not arrive from distant places with letters of salutation and applications for books.

In the month of February the Christians of Vonizongo sent messengers with a letter of inquiry respecting a course of Christian duty in special circumstances, and also asking for Testaments and Psalms. They said they were indeed many, and their books exceedingly few. A reply was sent and their need of books supplied; and though the messengers had been two days on the journey, they only rested one night in the capital, and the next day set out for home with their treasures.

A few days afterwards a Christian messenger, from a military post three hundred miles to the south-east, arrived with a letter from the Christian governor of the place, whom I had met during my former visits to Madagascar. His letter gave an encouraging account of the increase of the Christians in that neighbourhood, and asked for books. The messenger had been thirteen days on the journey, and when he came to say that he was about to return, and I pointed out to him the large package of copies of the Scriptures and other books which I had prepared, observing that I feared he would find it somewhat heavy, it was quite refreshing to witness his eye sparkle with joy, as he surveyed the package and took it up. He set out the same day on his journey of three hundred miles to his home.

Ever since the believers in Imerina had experienced Christian liberty themselves, they had regarded with deep interest the progress of Christianity in Betsileo, the inhabitants of which district are more closely allied with the Hovas than any other races in the country. The queen or chieftainess of that large province had charmed the court at Antananarivo by her noble bearing and glowing eloquence when she, with her brother and attendants, came as the representatives of the Betsileo to take the oath of allegiance to Rasoherina. Her brother Rafinana, himself a Christian and the representative of a number of his Christian countrymen, was welcomed as a brother by the believers in the capital, between whom and the Betsileo, notwithstanding the distance, cheering and fraternal communication was not unfrequent. The following is one of the satisfactory evidences, not only of the extension of the gospel, but of its power over the hearts and consciences of those who received it in the distant provinces.

An officer at Fianarantsoa lived, before his knowledge of the gospel, as other heathens lived. A number of wives, or of those who scarcely stood in the rank of wives, was allowed by law; and the custom prevailed amongst all classes. This individual had several *vady kely*, or little wives, as such individuals are called. The relation had been entered into when all were heathen, and it was not esteemed in any way disreputable. Most of these persons, including the officer, became Christians; and although no European had ever been there, and no correspondence had taken place between them and any of the missionaries on the subject, they became convinced that, for Christians, their manner of life was wrong. The chief, influenced, so far as we could ascertain, solely by the requirements of the gospel, stated that it was not right for them to live together as they had done; and it was arranged that one of the women should continue to live with him as his wife and the rest should return to their respective homes, with the suitable provision which he made for their maintenance.

Such was the decision at which these Christians at Fianarantsoa arrived amongst themselves, simply from what they deemed to be the teaching of the New Testament on this sometimes difficult question. Some of these women were connected with families at Antananarivo who had become Christians, and were members of the congregation with which I was connected. They were sent home honourably, under the care of a trustworthy Christian officer and his attendants. These men frequently visited me during their stay at the capital, and they also stated that the cause above mentioned was the only reason for the separation which had occurred. I do not recollect having met with any more striking instance of the power of the gospel on the consciences of those who had received it.

While evidence so encouraging was received from distant parts of the country, we were cheered by the new centres of Christian influence continually arising amongst us. On the last Sunday of February, Mr. Toy and I had opened a newly-constructed place of worship at Ambohitantely. It was capable of accommodating six hundred persons, and was filled on the day of opening, though I scarcely saw any present who were connected with the other congregations. This building is situated near the centre of the capital, only a few yards from the gate of the prime minister's dwelling, by whom the building has been aided, and where he himself and members of his family have at times attended.

The progress of the gospel was to us all not only a cause of joy for the time, but every month it seemed to be casting forward a light upon the future, which rendered the return of persecution less probable. For although we might witness nothing extraordinary connected with our work, we had increasingly solid grounds for encouragement and hope. Never were labourers more needed; never, perhaps, were claims more urgent than those which Madagascar presented at that time. The difficulties were great, and the influences in many respects unfriendly, but still the Christians held their ground, and continued to increase. This steady advance made all the difficulties and trials appear comparatively slight; and it had also its effect in producing a difference in the outward conduct even of those who did not connect themselves with the Christians.

Our united monthly prayer meetings still continued to be well attended, and the people, now beginning to understand their duty in providing their own places of worship, were making commendable efforts for the furtherance of this important object. We frequently had brought to us lists of native contributions towards the erection of places of worship, and in these the members of the church and congregation tried first what they could raise amongst themselves, and then came to ask assistance of their friends in the capital.

From the villages in the north we had even greater encouragement than from those in the south. Some of the missionaries had visited Ilafy, a royal village beautifully situated on the summit of a hill, sheltered by gigantic and umbrageous trees. These visits had cheered the people, and revived their Christian zeal. One of their early efforts was to provide for their own spiritual improvement, by erecting a new and enlarged place of worship. They first drew up a statement of their numbers and means, and then sought assistance from the Christians connected with the several congregations in the capital and its neighbourhood.

In the brief statement preceding the list of contributions was the following historical and statistical summary, which was sufficient to set forth the truth of their appeal. The translation is as follows:—

"What the Christians of Ilafy suffered during the time of darkness (persecution).

4 Christians were hunted, seized, and put to death.

3 Christians died in fetters.

2 Christians died from the tangena, or poison.

4 Christians took the poison, but survived.

25 Christians continued stedfast to the end of the persecution.

28 Christians at Ilafy during that time.

260 added to the Christians since the light, (liberty of teaching and worshipping) came to the land.

298—total number at the time this appeal is issued. Of these—

87 are communicants.
51 have been baptized, but are not yet communicants.
160 have not yet been baptized.
———
298 total."

This appeal was successful. They completed one of the best furnished village chapels in the country, which, when I preached at the opening service, was well filled with the residents and their visitors. Mr. Pearse, the missionary at Analakely, now exercises a friendly oversight of their spiritual affairs, and visits them frequently.

The above statement of this people is interesting and instructive, as showing probably the average number of Christians in the villages around the capital during the season of persecution, and the proportion of those who actually suffered during "the time of darkness," as they expressively call it. More than one-third of the whole were tried for their lives on account of their faith, and very nearly one-fourth were put to death because they were Christians.

If the experience of the Christians of Ilafy be regarded as setting forth that of other villages, it will assist us in understanding the severe ordeal through which, in the very commencement of their religious life, the Christian villages of Ankova had to pass. The addition to their number after the proclamation of religious freedom, which they speak of as the "coming of the light," will also serve to show the blessed results of that change within three years after it had occurred.

A notice of my visit to Ambohimanga, to assist in the recognition of the pastors and the appointment of deacons, will show the kind of duties to which we were frequently invited among the village churches connected with those in the capital. The house of worship, outside the gate of this city or village, was not capable of containing many more than sixty persons, and, when we entered, it was crowded. After the reading of the Scriptures, singing and prayer, I told the people that I did not come with any authority to enjoin laws, but as a friend, and as the minister of the church with which some of them had been connected, from which church the gospel had been brought to them, and with which they desired to be associated.

I found the communicants perfectly unanimous in their wish, viz., that two men of middle age belonging to the place and congregation should be recognised as their pastors or overseers, an office which they had filled from the time of the persecution. I then explained as simply as possible the nature and duties of the office, and asked the two individuals if they were willing, in dependence upon the Holy Spirit's assistance, to undertake the office and duties of Mpitandrina; and each having answered separately that he was willing, I implored the divine sanction and blessing upon the sacred engagement into which they had entered.

In a similar manner I explained the teachings of

the New Testament with regard to deacons, and asked how many persons they thought it desirable to appoint to assist the Mpitandrina in promoting their spiritual and temporal welfare. They said the people were thinly scattered over a wide extent of country, and that one of the preachers sometimes went a long way to preach. They therefore thought that there should be four assistants to the ministers. The individuals named having expressed their willingness to become assistants to the ministers, they were then appointed, and prayer was offered. After this I delivered a short address of instruction and encouragement to the newly selected officers and the congregation, assuring them of the interest the churches in the capital felt in their welfare, and of their readiness to render help when needed, and of their constant prayer for God's blessing to rest upon them.

The oldest pastor, though the youngest man amongst them, Rainikioto, is a very interesting Christian. He is a native of Ambohimanga, an amiable man and a good preacher, and at that time was scarcely thirty years of age. He had welcomed and entertained Andriambelo and myself on my first visit when we preached in the city. His mother was sister to one of the ministers of the late queen; his father, guardian or priest of Rafantaka, the tutelar idol of Ambohimanga, and one of the national idols of Madagascar. On his father's death the office descended to him, but being a Christian he could not hold it, and it was given to his sister.

My kind friend the prime minister had, unknown to me, sent to the authorities of this city informing them that I was going with the entire approval of the government, and that they were not to allow any of my proceedings to be interrupted.

After leaving Ambohimanga, and travelling about ten miles to the eastward, I reached Isarotrafohi, the dwelling-place of Andriamanantena, one of the distinguished leaders of the Christians, who, after having survived several severe persecutions, fell during the last and most sanguinary one. I had received in England letters from him till within a short time of his arrest and execution, and had felt deep interest in the welfare of his family. On reaching the abode of his widow and daughter, by whom I was often visited in the capital, I was received with a truly Christian and hospitable welcome. By the energy and influence of this devoted man the gospel had been conveyed to a number of villages in the neighbourhood, among the inhabitants of which his name and character were held in high esteem.

Andriamanantena was a civilian, a man of energy and of property, possessing more than one farm or small estate. The house at which I had arrived was the last which he built. It is pleasantly situated on a broad terrace, near the foot of a sloping granite mountain, crowned by the celebrated village of Ambohitrabiby, and about thirty feet above the water of a winding stream. Between the high banks on which the house and out-buildings stood there was an orchard of densely foliaged orange, citron, loquat, peach, and other fruit-trees, all of which had been planted by their late master, and some of which were laden with fruit. He had also cultivated, on the terrace above, the vine, as well as other exotic trees.*

The house and its surroundings were evidences of the enterprise and industry of its master. His widow, a woman of energy and of kindness, as well as an active and devoted servant of Christ, seemed to live but to carry forward the great work for which her husband had died, and by the quiet influence of her unobtrusive kindness, had gained the affectionate esteem of all around. She had carefully instructed her slaves, and in order to encourage them, when desirous to avow their belief in Christ as the only Saviour, she had more than once accompanied a female slave, who was wishing for guidance and instruction in her religious life, to my house.

I have said that I was hospitably welcomed after my labours and my long journey in the dust and burning sun; but even more gratifying than the generous kindness of my hostess was the quiet, thoughtful, and assiduous attention of the slaves (for all servants in the country were slaves) to their mistress. Indeed, few things in my observance of the social life of the Malagasy Christian families, have struck me more forcibly than the marked difference between the treatment of their slaves and those belonging to heathen. By the former the slaves are encouraged to attend religious meetings,

* The view of the Martyr's Home, as well as the other illustrations, are chiefly from photographs taken on the spot.

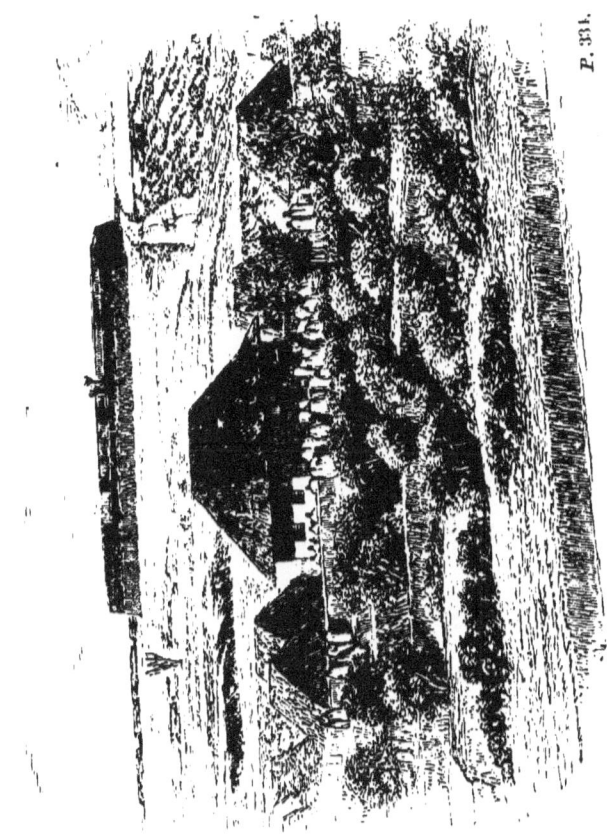

From Photograph by Rev. W. Ellis.
ISAROTRAFOHY, THE MARTYRS' HOME.

and seek the blessings of religion for themselves; and where there is reason to believe they have become sincere disciples of Christ, they are often treated with a measure of consideration and kindness, which makes their yoke very easy, and causes them to feel that all are one in Christ Jesus.

Slavery may co-exist with heathenism, but is incompatible with Christianity, which can only produce its genuine fruits when men are free; and should the Malagasy retain their country, the existence of slavery will at no distant day be one of the chief sources of their anxiety. But nothing appears so favourable to a peaceful and satisfactory change in this respect, as the influence which Christianity is silently exercising over both master and slave.

There were several congregations in the neighbourhood, the ministers of which, with the relatives of the family, were present on the occasion here described, and our conversation during the evening was deeply interesting and affecting. They narrated the perils of many of the Christians in that region who had been put to death; they described the concealment of the master of the house and his companions in the neighbouring caverns, or amongst the tall reeds of the swamps, and of the canes near the river, as well as his marvellous escapes from those who were dogging his steps for weeks together during a long series of years, until the last severe persecution in which he died.

I had always heard Andriamanantena spoken of as a superior man, and the general aspect of the place, as I looked around on the following morning, gave evidence of his judgment and taste, as well as of the industry and enterprise with which the affairs of his different estates were conducted. The circular enclosure at some distance beyond the house, with a couple of palm trees, as represented in the plate, is a kind of homestead common in Madagascar, and was the residence of the owner before the house with the orchard was built. Here he was concealed at the time when the martyrs were thrown over the precipice; and although diligent search was made for him by the emissaries of the queen, he eluded discovery, and finally escaped at that time.

Accompanied by a number of the Christians, I walked towards a sugar plantation, where, in 1846, the owner of the place, with Andriamandry, and Ratsimavandy, another distinguished Christian who was stoned to death eleven years afterwards, were concealed for more than a week, while spies and persons sent to seize them were passing to and fro in eager search. Two of these Christians escaped at that time, but the second of the above-mentioned three was taken and died under the trial by poison.

With the brother of Andriamanantena, and other Christians, I also walked for two miles up the rocky mountain to three other places, in which, during twenty years of the persecution, the husband of my hostess, and others, had at times found safety; we then descended to a village where I had arranged to meet the people, and found the place of worship nearly filled. Near one of the doors I observed a place like a cupboard, and on asking what it was, they lifted the board and showed me a passage for escape, by which, in time of danger, a person could leave without being seen by those outside. I addressed the people, for a short time, on the mercy and faithfulness of God, as their presence there under circumstances of peace and safety testified, and encouraged them to endeavour to bring all around them under the influence of the faith and love of Christ.

We had quite a large gathering at the house of my hostess in the evening. I found much to encourage me in the simple, earnest piety of many of the Christians, but heard of some things which required to be rectified. On leaving the next morning, I proceeded in a south-westerly direction across the country to a village about seven miles distant, where I had promised to meet the congregation at ten o'clock. We arrived a little before that time, and found the place of worship filled. Proceeding in a similar way to that adopted at Ambohimanga, I assisted them in appointing overseers and deacons; also in setting apart, in consequence of the number of villages connected with the place, three of their number to itinerate as evangelists in the surrounding neighbourhood.

I had visited and assisted these Christian communities in compliance with their earnest request, but chiefly because some of the Christians in these infant communities had been associated—and nominally were so still—with the church and congregation of which I was one of the ministers; and who

z

wished to regard Ambatonakanga as their parent church. The same considerations have influenced my brethren in their endeavours to cherish and assist the village churches under their care.

The western side of the city was still without any public place of worship. The Christians in that quarter had, with commendable zeal, built a temporary place of worship, in the early part of the year, near the edge of the precipice from which the martyrs had been cast; but in a great fire which, in the month of May, had consumed a large number of houses in that part of the city, it had been burnt down. The people soon afterwards commenced, with renewed energy and a little assistance, the erection of another building, on the site which had been procured for the more substantial memorial church, to be erected in the centre of the western side of the capital. It was near my own residence, which stood on the opposite side of a broad hollow, or valley, opening to the west.

By the fifteenth of August it was finished and opened for Christian worship. In and around the building, on that occasion, seven hundred persons were assembled, including some of the officers of the palace, and members of the families of others residing in the neighbourhood. On the following Sunday a number of persons, dwelling in the vicinity of the chapel, who had not previously associated with the Christians or attended any place of worship, were among the hearers, and their number continued to increase. Messrs. Hartley and Briggs

From Photograph by Rev. W. Ellis. Mr. Ellis's house. House of Prime Minister's sister. Prime Minister's house.
VIEW IN ANTANANARIVO.
V. 338.

had recently arrived at the capital; and Mr. Briggs, who, associated with native assistants, became minister of the chapel, opened a school for the boys of that part of the city, while Mrs. Briggs attended to the education of the girls, to the no small gratification of their parents.

Other means of usefulness within the city were soon afterwards provided. A number of Christians residing in the city, but worshipping at Analakely, anxious to obtain ground in one of the best parts of the city, near the daily market and the place of public assemblies, adjacent also to one of the great roads leading to the north, applied for assistance; and I was so convinced of the importance of the position, that I gave them, from my own means, a hundred dollars with which to secure the site. They built a neat chapel on the spot, which was opened for public worship on the 22nd of October. Mr. Hartley became the minister, and the congregation soon became too large for the chapel, though no diminution was witnessed in the attendance at the previously existing places of worship.

About this time, at the close of our weekly Bible class, Razafy stated that she was about to visit her native place in the Sakalava country, a month's journey to the north-west from Antananarivo. Razafy, with two brothers, when they were all quite young, had been seized and brought away as booty by the troops sent against that part of the country by the late queen, in 1849. On reaching the capital all had been sold as slaves, and had now become Christians.

She had married a Christian man, and had two children—one an infant in arms. Her brothers had returned some months before to their native place, where they found their parents still living, and longing to see Razafy and the children. Her brothers had also sent word that there were several persons in that part of the country learning to read, and also inquiring about the gospel; and she wished therefore to take with her a few spelling-books and copies of the Scriptures.

The master of Razafy gave her an excellent character; and when she called to take leave, I gave her some books, with a few words of encouragement. This incident will show the marvellous ways by which God was then spreading the knowledge of the gospel in Madagascar.

I visited frequently the villages to the north, most closely connected with Ambatonakanga, and soon after the arrival of Mr. George Cousins I repeated my visit to the "sacred city;" after preaching there to the people, I proceeded westward for about five miles to Imerinamandrosa, fifteen miles from the capital. My arrival was welcomed by the Christians, most of whom came to visit us during the evening. Some of them I had met at Tamatave in 1854; others had suffered much during the last persecution, and had lost beloved relatives. Two of those who spent the evening with us had worn the heavy fetters for four and a half years, and they now exercised great influence for good amongst the people of the place. I found there were a hundred and twenty-six Christians in this place, of whom twenty-six were communicants.

A number of Christians sentenced to wear the fetters in the last persecution had been banished for a time to a small village about two miles distant. Accompanied, amongst others, by one who had been imprisoned in fetters there, I went the next day to visit the spot where the Christians had suffered. One of these led us to a small house having only a doorway, and one or two little windows. In this place nine Christians, chained together night and day, had been confined, and my guide showed me how the heavy bars of iron were either supported by cords from the roof, or propped up by stones against the wall, when they sat or lay down on the ground. It was a deeply affecting place. My friend pointed to a slave woman, with a child in her arms, belonging to the place, and, with grateful emotion, stated how kind that slave had contrived to be to them during their sufferings. I also saw the market-place of the adjacent village of Alatsinaina, round which the heavily manacled Christians were led every market day, in order to deter the spectators from following their example.

The following day was the Sabbath. The native minister from Ambohimanga, and a number of people from a village five or six miles to the north-west, joined in the morning services, when the minister from the sacred city preached, with much affection and great earnestness, a truly instructive and impressive discourse to a large and attentive congregation. Our friends from a distance returned home for their evening services, and I preached to the people of the place in the afternoon.

A large number of Christians assembled at the house I occupied, and joined our evening worship. The statements they gave afforded joyful evidence that not a few had believed to the saving of their souls. There was with them, as there is in many village Christians, such simplicity as well as evident sincerity in their account of the progress of the gospel amongst them, and of their earnest endeavours to bring the tidings of salvation to their heathen neighbours, that I could not resist the conviction that their experimental sense of the validity and certainty of the things of which they spoke was due, in no small degree, to the patience, fortitude, and love to Christ of which the Christians, who had suffered in their immediate neighbourhood, had presented such noble examples.

CHAPTER XIII.

Bereavements of the mission—New churches and increased attendance—Introduction of public Christian marriage—Visit to Lazaina—Notice of Ranivo's family—Treaty with England—Queen Victoria's message, and Queen Rasoherina's reply—Journey to the west—Reinforcement of the mission—Departure of Mr. Ellis—Prosperous close of the year—Opening of the first memorial church—Its influence on the people—Welcome arrival of missionaries from the Friends—The queen's visit to the coast—Zealous efforts of the Christians among the heathen—Return of the queen to the capital—Results of the preaching of the gospel—Remarkable increase of the Christians at the close of the year.

THE year 1864 had not been altogether one of peace. Repeated rumours of Radama being still alive unsettled the minds of some. The disgrace and banishment of the prime minister had unsettled the minds of others, though it removed a cause of uneasiness; but the more liberal and consistent policy of his successor promised tranquillity for the present year, as well as for the future.

Heathenism, although patronized publicly by the queen, and brought more prominently before the people by the exhibition of the idols in frequent heathen processions, intended to show their reviving influence and power, was in reality only exhibiting the last struggles of a system mortally wounded, and from which the life once possessed was rapidly ebbing away.

The year had been in some respects one of affliction to the mission. Mr. Stagg, the master of the central training school, had suffered under repeated attacks of fever shortly after commencing his important work, although his death did not take place before he had seen the normal school in promising operation. His removal was justly regarded as a heavy calamity to the mission, which, for a length of time, found itself crippled in one of its most important departments of effort, for want of trained and qualified teachers.

Mrs. Pearse, who, with a noble heroism, accompanied her husband to his post of duty, and entered upon the acquisition of the language with great assiduity and success, while drawing to herself the hearts of many of her own sex, was arrested in her labours by alarming illness, resulting in death, scarcely more than seven months after her arrival in the country.

Besides these bereavements, the Christians had been affected by the evident instability of the existing government, and the danger of violent interruption to the peace of the community. But, notwithstanding these and other disturbing elements, the confidence of the believers in the foundations of their faith, and the assurance of their hopes of salvation through Jesus Christ, were still strengthened.

On the whole the year had been a great gain to the mission. Its numbers had been increased by the arrival of three additional missionaries, with their wives. The printing-press had been employed and the medical branch of the mission had been extended, adding to the benefits previously conferred on the people. Three new places of worship had been opened, chiefly by the efforts of the people themselves, and larger and better places had been built for two of the most important congregations in the city. New congregations had been gathered and churches formed in three of these buildings, and they had largely increased in the others. There was also reason to believe that the attention given to the Christian communities in the surrounding villages had been the means of increasing to an equal extent the Christians in those localities.

The daily conduct and social life of the Christians had in no respect deteriorated, but in some instances had greatly improved. Marriage, according to the divine law and Christ's own teaching, had been more extensively recognised as the true foundation of domestic happiness and social progress,—a covenant entered into by the appointment of God, and in dependence on His blessing. And thus, without neglecting those observances which the laws of the country rendered necessary to secure its legal recognition, the marriage contract had been solemnly and publicly entered into in the house of God, with the assistance of the minister of the congregation; in this way a registry of marriages had begun to be kept. Parties of different ranks of society, from those connected with the highest families down to the Christian slaves, had thus, before their respective friends and fellow-Christians, solemnly entered into this sacred engagement.*

The spiritual work of the mission had been truly cheering. There were now seven congregations in the capital itself, and about seven thousand Christians, of whom six thousand attended public worship every Lord's day. Connected with these avowed Christians there were, in the several churches in the city, one thousand four hundred communicants; in addition to which some of the churches received two hundred during the following year. The Christian churches in the villages around had also received, in equal measure, the Divine blessing. No aspect which the Martyr Church of Madagascar has presented, augurs more hopefully for its stability and progress than this proof of the steady increase of its numbers, and of the consolidation of its institutions.

A number of the Christians worshipping at Amba-

* Nothing has received more careful attention from the native churches than their regulations for preventing divorce from frivolous causes, and for guarding the security of the marriage covenant. At the half-yearly meeting of the Congregational Union of Imerina, the representatives from the seven city churches, and of the separate churches in the province, in June, 1869, a regulation on this subject, adopted at the previous meeting of the Union, was brought up for confirmation. An officer of the government, a member of one of the churches, who was present as a representative, stated "that the Prime Minister had authorized him to say that he entirely approved of their proceedings on this subject, for it was good, and interfered with no law of the land."—*Teny Soa (Good Words), July,* 1869.

tonakanga belonged to the village of Lazaina, about nine miles to the north of the capital. This village was the birthplace and the residence of Ranivo, who occupied a noble and conspicuous position at the trial and execution of the martyrs cast over the precipice in 1849. I had twice travelled from the coast to the capital with the nearest relative of this distinguished woman, and had long desired to visit her family in their ancient home, as well as to become acquainted with the Christians of the place. At length I arranged to spend Sunday with them, and reached the village on the afternoon of Saturday.

Some of the scenery near Lazaina is extremely rich, with a considerable extent of ground under cultivation. Outside the walls I found fewer vestiges of former greatness than at Imerinamandrosa, but better houses within, and apparently a more active and enterprising population. I was struck with the large number of children; I counted a hundred and sixty from the window, before I had been an hour in the house, all of a suitable age for receiving instruction. I found two hundred Christians belonging to the village, and a nice new chapel, in a central spot, in course of erection; and although it was on public ground belonging to the village, the head men of the place had readily consented to this occupation of the spot for a building devoted to Christian worship.

It was truly delightful to see the kind and neighbourly feeling with which the inhabitants, Christian and heathen, seemed to dwell in peace and good-will

House used for Christian Worship.   VILLAGE OF LAZAINA.   New Chapel, in course of erection.

had passed during the time of "darkness" or persecution.

The house in which Ranivo was born was nearly opposite my lodgings, and I was informed that in the one adjoining, several members of her family still resided. Some of these had been among my earliest visitors, and had formed part of the congregation to which I had preached in the early part of the day. I was pleased with this simple and affectionate party; indeed, the whole of my intercourse with them left an impression on my mind which is gratefully retained.

On the following morning Mr. George Cousins came from the capital, and arrived at the centre of the village in his chair, or palanquin, just as I was taking a photograph of the house in which we had held our worship on the previous day, and not far from the new chapel in course of erection. I requested him, while I did so, to remain a moment in the middle of the road, and in front of the house on the pavement, in the verandah of which a large number of Christians were assembled. I left Lazaina soon after, but had the pleasure of visiting it again, and of assisting at the opening of the new chapel before my final departure from Madagascar.

After the death of Radama, the Malagasy government sent an embassy to England to propose a revision of the treaty concluded with the late king. In due time the ambassadors returned with the draft from Earl Russell, and in the month of June the treaty was officially presented to the Malagasy government. It was subsequently signed in presence of the queen by the principal officers of the government at the royal palace. This treaty secured to Englishmen liberty to travel and reside in all parts of Madagascar, excepting three cities, of which Ambohimanga was one. By the third article, the treaty also secured to British subjects liberty to exercise and teach the Christian religion, and to erect suitable places of worship; these to be recognised as belonging to the Queen of Madagascar, as is the case with all other property in the country.

In reference to the agreement respecting the churches belonging to the queen as a trustee for their legitimate appropriation, the following document, executed immediately afterwards, signed by the officers who had attached their signatures to the treaty, and attested by the signature and seal of the British consul, was furnished by the government:—

"In accordance with the meaning of Article III. of the English treaty (with the Malagasy), the churches to be built by the London Missionary Society at Faravohitra, Ambatonakanga, Ampamarimana, Ambohipotsy, and Fiadana, shall be put aside by the sovereign of Madagascar for the teaching and worship of those missionaries, and for the Malagasy who unite in the same worship with them, and for their successors for ever. And the sovereign shall set apart and protect (those churches), and not permit them to be used for worship by persons who do not unite with them, and whose worship is not the same as the worship of those who built them."

No title in Madagascar is more valid than that by which the Memorial Churches are secured.

The most welcome part of the communication, to the Christians, was the statement, in the letter which accompanied the treaty, that Queen Victoria requested, as an expression of friendship to herself (or words to that effect), that Queen Rasoherina would not allow the Malagasy Christians to be persecuted on account of their religion.

The following are the words by which, in the treaty, Queen Rasoherina responded to the generous and humane solicitation of the Queen of England:—

"Her Majesty the Queen of Madagascar, from her friendship for her Britannic Majesty, promises to grant full religious liberty to all her subjects, and not to persecute or molest any subject or native of Madagascar on account of their embracing or exercising the Christian religion."

When I read these paragraphs I thanked God that He had disposed our gracious Queen to make this request, and had inclined the Queen of Madagascar to agree to it so promptly and fully. It is only just to say that this engagement was faithfully kept. Often in our places of worship on the Sunday, when I have heard the native ministers pray for their own sovereign, I have been gratified to hear them, at the same time, implore the divine blessing on Queen Victoria.

The frequent rumours of anticipated change, to which allusion has been made, interfered with the progress of the first memorial church, which Mr.

Sibree was erecting; but the greatest hindrance had arisen from want of lime, which was not abundant, and was, besides, a government monopoly. It therefore became necessary to take further measures for securing an adequate supply; and Mr. Cameron having obtained the consent of the government, I accompanied him to Antsirabe and other places, thirty or forty miles west of the capital, in search of limestone for building the church.

During the first ten miles of this journey we crossed a number of rivers descending from the lofty Ankaratra, and spanned by stone bridges erected by the late king, the last of which, over the river Andromba, appeared the best constructed and least damaged of any we had seen. We then continued our route over a tract of country of richer soil, better watered, and more generally cultivated than that to the north; the population was also less scattered and the villages larger. I was glad to find that Mr. Toy, with his accustomed energy and zeal, had visited several of the most important of these, and preached to the people, sending them also on Sundays native preachers from his own congregation at Ambohipotsy.

The sun was setting when we entered the broad, extensive, and park-like valley of "The Silkworm Trees," and we were glad to rest for the night. Failing in the morning to find a sufficient quantity of what we were in search of, we proceeded in a northerly direction to Madera, which we reached at noon; here we found limestone sufficient for our purpose. We agreed with

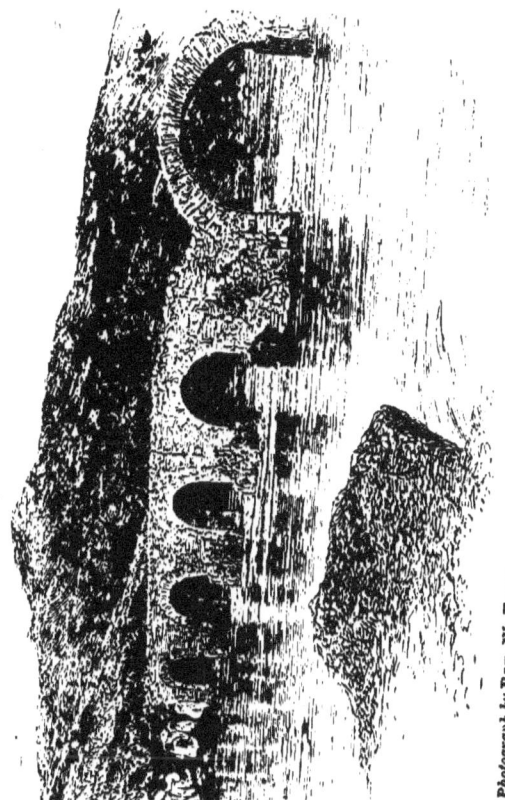

BRIDGE OVER THE ANDROMBA.
Built by Radama II.

From Photograph by Rev. W. Ellis.

the people to prepare and convey it to the capital, and fixed a day on which they should come to have the contract confirmed by the government. Leaving early the next morning, we prevailed upon our bearers, by the promise of a little extra pay, to endeavour to reach the capital that night, as the next day was Sunday. Stopping at Andromba for refreshment and a short rest, we arrived at home a little before midnight, relieved from all anxiety about the means of completing the memorial churches.

On the first Sunday in July, I administered the ordinance of the Lord's Supper at Ambatonakanga for the last time; and at a subsequent meeting took leave of the church and congregation, commending them to the care and the blessing of the Great Head of the Church. I was deeply affected by the evidences of their kindness and Christian feeling on that occasion. Mr. George Cousins, who had for nearly twelve months been associated with me in the pastoral duties there, and who had entered with ability and energy upon the great work before him, afforded me every encouragement in relation to the care of the flock over which he was now to become the English pastor. With him was to be associated Ratsiliangia and the young preachers whom Mr. Cousins was training for their work.

The native pastor, who was one of the first converts baptized in the church in 1831, I found acting as minister of the people when I arrived. The church then consisted of seventy-six members. When I left, without reckoning fifty or more who had been sent to help in the formation of other churches, they amounted to two hundred and seventy-nine.

After receiving many farewell letters, and some welcome tokens of good-will, I went to take leave of the queen, who expressed her regret at my departure. The prime minister, of whom I had also taken leave, sent me a letter expressive of the queen's satisfaction with my proceedings. I received my passport on the following Monday, and on the same day met Mr. Pool, who had a very short time before reached the capital to assist in the building of the memorial churches.

When I left the capital on the 18th of July, the Christians met me on the road at the foot of the hill on which the city stands. I addressed a few words of encouragement to them as they stood around me, and then my native co-pastor affectionately bade me farewell on behalf of the church and people. There were present a number of the widows and orphans of the martyrs; and Ratsiliangia asked me to accept from the church a silk lamba for my wife. I gratefully received their present, and, taking leave of them and the missionary brethren, pursued my way.

On reaching Tamatave on the tenth day after my departure from the capital, I preached to the Hova congregation on the Sunday, and was pleased with what I saw there of the progress of the Church of England missionaries. I sailed on the 3rd of August, and having received from friends in Mauritius their wonted hospitality, proceeded to England, where I arrived in safety on the 14th of October, 1865.

The review of the mission at the close of the year

exhibited marked and cheering progress. The new hospital had been finished, and proved a source of more extended benefit to the people. A new substantial chapel had been built at Analakely, where the labours of Mr. Pearse, as well as among the villages to the north, appeared to be followed by increasingly satisfactory results. A church had been organized among the people worshipping in the temporary building on the edge of the precipice, and the male and female scholars were being carefully taught by Mr. and Mrs. Briggs.

Mr. William Cousins, returning from England with Mrs. Cousins, had not only received a joyous welcome, but had found, under the care of Andriambelo and his native assistants, an augmented church, comprising nearly six hundred members, and a prosperous congregation. The large supply of Malagasy Bibles, which had been received from the British and Foreign Bible Society, with smaller books, had supplied the long and deeply felt wants of a large portion of the Christian community; while, besides the advantages of the mission press, Mr. Parrett rendered valuable aid in the Sunday schools and Bible classes.

Mr. George Cousins had enlarged his temporary chapel, still too small, and rejoiced with Mrs. Cousins in the progress of the scholars in both schools. He also met with much encouragement in the extension of the gospel among the villages to the north, where eight of the most important places were connected with his city church. When he visited Ambohimanga, the officers appointed by the queen to guard that sacred city and its idols from the intrusion of Christians and foreigners, were amongst his most attentive hearers. The village stations under the care of the other missionaries had also increased and were prosperous. When I left in July, there were one thousand five hundred communicants in connection with seven of the churches in the city, and by the close of the year their numbers had greatly increased; the influence of the Christians was also recognised in every section of the general community, and Mr. Toy stated that all the churches were crowded every Lord's day.

The following year, 1866, opened with still more promising indications. In April, Mr. Toy received into fellowship with his church a hundred and forty-five; thus increasing the number of communicants in the church under his care to five hundred. Two months later, those under the care of Mr. W. E. Cousins exceeded six hundred. The statistics of the mission in June, 1866, gave a total of seventy-nine city and village churches, under ninety-five native and European pastors, with a total of 4,374 communicants, and nearly 900 children in the mission schools.

The year 1867 opened with the most important and joyous event which had yet marked the progress of the Madagascar mission—the opening at Ambatonakanga, for the worship of the true God, of the first of the memorial churches given by England to Madagascar. Its foundation had been laid with prayer, its top-stone had been brought forth with ascriptions of praise to Him by whose guardian care the sacred edifice had been completed.*

The opening day partook of the character of a national festival. Christians from the surrounding country, as well as from every part of the capital, in their holiday attire, gathered in the early morning in the surrounding space. Even the heathen gazed with wonder at the structure, and felt that the Christian worship was something deemed to be of far greater importance, and to be offered under circumstances vastly more impressive, than had ever been conceived of by the votaries of the idols.

The queen sent in state seven of the highest Christian officers of the government, to testify her approval of the building with which the city was beautified, as well as of the sacred use to which it was to be dedicated.

The building was constructed to hold 1,200, but more than 1,500 had forced themselves within the walls before the services commenced, and more than a thousand, it was calculated, remained outside during the whole of the service. After the singing,

---

* When the top-stone with the vane was fixed on the pinnacle of the spire, Rainimahazo, the chief mason, proposed to Mr. Sibree, and Mr. Cousins the minister of the church, who, with the workmen, were sitting on the scaffolding around the top of the spire, that they should then and there offer thanks to the Lord, who had enabled them to complete the building without accident or injury to any one engaged in the work. All took off their hats while this devoted man, who was a deacon of the church, offered their united thanksgiving to God, who had thus far prospered the work of their hands.

Ratsiliangia, the native pastor, read the Scriptures. Mr. G. Cousins, the English minister of the church, then read a statement of the steps by which the object of their generous friends in England had been so far realized, thus binding the Christians of Madagascar in stronger ties of grateful affection to their earliest friends beyond the sea. Mr. Toy explained the principles and order of the Christian Church. Sermons were preached by one of the ministers of the church at Andohalo, and by Mr. W. Cousins. The dedicatory prayer was offered by Mr. Briggs. Native ministers also offered prayer between the sermons. At the close, Mr. Jukes pronounced the benediction, and the assembly dispersed.

As soon as the congregation had left the church, those who had been waiting outside entered, and filled a large portion of the building, in which they waited until the afternoon to attend the second service, when native and English ministers again took part in the proceedings, as in the morning.

A full account of these proceedings, including the statements and sermons, was printed at the mission press and given to the people, as a memorial of the consecration to the service of God of the first Martyrs' Memorial Church in Madagascar.

The mission had been strengthened by the arrival of Mr. Jukes, appointed to the long vacant station at Ankadibevava. Writing of the united missionary prayer meeting, which he first attended at Mr. Toy's church, at Ambohipotsy, Mr. Jukes observes,—
"Although the service was announced to commence

at nine o'clock, there were crowds in and around the building long before that hour. Mr. Toy told me that the keys were fetched from his house as early as six, to open the doors to the people, who were at that time waiting for admission. When I went, a few minutes before nine, the church was densely filled, and large numbers were standing round the windows and doors, because there was not room for them inside. I should think there were at least 1,600 persons present, all of whom appeared to manifest great interest in the service. It really did my heart good, and caused me to praise God for His goodness, as I sat there, remembering that I was in a heathen land, and looked down upon that vast concourse of people, assembled together the first thing on a Monday morning to hold a missionary meeting."*

The increased attention paid to the training of young men, to take part in the great work of extending the gospel among their countrymen, was increasing the efficiency of that important agency. Mr. Hartley had added a class of this kind to those already under the training of the earlier missionaries, and was greatly encouraged by the industry and progress of his pupils.

The year was not, however, without its trials. In some neighbourhoods the small-pox, which was regarded by the natives with absolute terror, made its appearance, though in a mild form. This, of course, kept some from the public services; but a

* The meetings at this season of the year are held in the morning, as heavy rains often fall later in the day.

far more widely spread uneasiness among the Christians arose from an order of the queen, issued at the instigation of the priests, that all swine should be removed to a still greater distance from the capital, because it was pretended that the presence of these animals was offensive to the idols. It was not that the people cared much about being refused permission to keep them; but that in the reign of the late queen, when the government had been anxious to propitiate the idols, and to afflict the Christians, the removal of all swine to a greater distance from the capital had always preceded measures of severity and repression against the Christians. The only accompaniment of the banishment of the offensive animals on this occasion was an increased disregard of the Sabbath privileges of the Christians, by the fixing of public government transactions, dancing, and other amusements for that day; these prevented a large number of officers and soldiers from attending public worship with their families, while small congregations were sometimes entirely deprived of their preachers.

Whatever the object of the government may have been—and possibly these orders were given with a view to prevent the priests attempting greater mischief—no other public proceeding troubled the Christians. They bore this patiently, for God was accompanying the extension of the preaching of His truth, with deep impressions upon the minds and the hearts of His people, especially among the younger members of the highest families of the country;

increasing numbers of whom preferred the worship of God to the pageants and amusements of the court, having themselves become earnest and sincere disciples of Christ.

While the gospel, by the zealous efforts of the young Christians sent forth by the missionaries, was introduced to a greater number of villages, and was attended with a larger measure of blessing to those into which it had already been sent, no special services were appointed, nor any extraordinary means employed, beyond the diligent, prayerful teaching and preaching of the great truths of salvation, and the urging of them on the attention of the Bible classes. More than one of the missionaries, in referring to the increase about this time, observed, "We can only account for it as the work of God."

The good effect of the opening of the memorial church in the beginning of the year, which, in the opinion of some, produced considerable impression on the minds of the heathen, especially in connection with the public approval which the queen had distinctly expressed regarding it, was still further increased in that locality, when a substantial school, built on the west side of the church, and capable of receiving a hundred and fifty scholars, was shortly afterwards opened. This school had been erected and the fittings supplied by the generous aid of the Society of Friends in England, who, since the reopening of the country to missionary efforts, had very liberally contributed towards the promotion of education amongst the people, in connection with the operations of the London Missionary Society.

Not satisfied with simply aiding others in providing buildings and materials, the minds of Friends in America, as well as in England, were influenced in favour of rendering more decided and valuable help in missionary work than their Society had hitherto given; and, early in 1867, Mr. and Mrs. Street, American Friends, came over to England, in the hope that some way might be opened for their proceeding to Madagascar. Joseph S. Sewell, who had had considerable experience in education among Friends, was also preparing to enter upon the same work. Towards the end of May, soon after the opening of the school at Ambatonakanga, these Christian helpers, sent out by the Society of Friends, reached the capital, and commenced assisting in the school.

These brethren were welcomed with affection and pleasure by the missionaries, who felt themselves strengthened in that important department which, by the death of Mr. Stagg, had been left most deficient. By friendly arrangement they have been able, with God's blessing, to carry forward in harmony, and with mutual kindness, the great and important objects in which they are unitedly engaged.

Although but recently a resident in the country, Joseph Sewell, in writing home, bore testimony to the earnestness of the people in listening to the words of instruction. On one occasion he stated, " I was particularly interested when one of my young missionary friends read from the Bible the ten commandments. Some of the congregation were so intent that they stood with their mouths and eyes wide open. My heart quite ached in its longings to sound the glad tidings upon the heathen ear. My friend, the missionary, had been preceded by a native minister, a young man of twenty-seven or eight years of age. He and his wife were people of rank, but had been disowned by their family and friends for their love to the Saviour, and were reduced to comparative poverty. They now live in a small mud house at the foot of Ampamarinana, from whose lofty precipice the martyrs were thrown; and he tells me that he was an eye-witness of some of those scenes."

Native-built chapels at Imahamasina, Amboniloha, and other places, were opened in this year. Mr. Pool was proceeding, as rapidly as the aid available would allow, with the erection of the Memorial Church at Ambohipotsy, and before the close of the year, Mr. Cameron had laid the foundation of the Children's Memorial Church at Faravohitra.

But the great event of the year, or of the reign, was the royal progress of the queen to the eastern coast, attended by her chosen bodyguard, and, it was said, by 6,000 troops, besides their officers and camp followers. Her Majesty required the attendance of the representatives of subject races in the west and the south, as well as of civilians and others from Imerina, amounting to 12,000 or 15,000.

Whether the object was to impress the tribes of the eastern provinces with the greatness and power of the sovereign, to secure homage and tribute, or merely to see the ocean and seek renovation of health, does not seem to have been very clearly known; but the providing of tents and equipments, to say nothing of provisions, occupied the people of the capital for nearly three months, before the vast multitude commenced what was truly a formidable journey for so large a host, with such a commissariat as they were able to provide, and over such a country as they would have to traverse.

All classes, from the officers and members of the court to the bearers or slaves, included a large number of Christians; and three of the missionaries, anxious for their spiritual welfare, offered to accompany them, one at a time. But the government preferred that they should remain at the capital. The Christians were not insensible to the loss they would sustain by the absence of their teachers, nor to the dangers arising from the associations and irregularities of life to which such an expedition would expose them; and for a week before the time fixed for their departure, prayer meetings were held in the churches to which they belonged. These meetings were all well attended, and on the last Sunday before they departed, a united prayer meeting of all the churches was held at Ambatonakanga, to commend their brethren to the divine care, and to ask that they might not only be preserved from evil themselves, but be made a blessing to the heathen amongst whom they were about to sojourn.

The queen and her court set out on the 20th of June, a considerable number of her party having gone forward in advance some days before. Her Majesty travelled in considerable state, the royal tent being pitched every night, and surrounded by a *rova* or palisade, which was fixed whenever the queen halted. Her own immediate attendants, including the diviners who directed the movements of the camp, were within this portable inclosure, the whole being under the especial protection of the idols and their priests or keepers.

The queen, it was said, did not travel on the Sunday, but whenever the camp halted for any considerable time, as well as on the Sundays, the Christians gathered together and held their meetings for worship, generally in the open air. These meetings, from the first, appear to have been attended by large numbers of the travellers who, at home, had never entered any place of worship. Men of rank and position in the palace or the army, not before recognised as regular preachers, on these occasions sometimes astonished their fellow-Christians by the boldness, earnestness, and feeling with which they recommended the Lord Jesus Christ as the Saviour of all who believed in His name. Nor was this the only gratifying circumstance connected with this remarkable journey.

The gathering together of the Christians, their preaching and praying, but especially their singing, drew around them, at every place where they halted, numbers of their heathen countrymen, who, on these occasions, heard for the first time the great truths of salvation. The longer they remained at any place, the larger grew the numbers that attended these religious meetings; while the attendance, the interest, and the inquiries awakened among the heathen, encouraged the Christians to greater watchfulness and prayer, at the same time that it increased their earnestness in setting forth before the heathen the love and grace of the divine Saviour, and the blessedness of those who believe in Him.

After an absence of between three and four months, the queen returned, halting at Ambohipo, within about five miles of Antananarivo, until the diviners should declare the favourable day for entering the capital.

On the 6th of October, the queen, as directed by the priests and diviners, entered Antananarivo. It was Sunday—the first Sunday of the month—and in the afternoon, when the excitement and commotion attendant on the event had subsided, all the churches and chapels in the capital were thronged to overflowing by the rejoicing worshippers. During the following week, a united meeting for thanksgiving to God, for the protection and safe return of those who had been away, was largely attended. A feeling of deep gratitude prevailed among the assembly. Many of the Christians had gone forth, if not weeping, yet under apprehension of sickness or other trials which might await them; but they had "returned rejoicing, bringing their sheaves with them."

The journey to the coast, as was to be expected, had proved unfavourable to some of the Christians, some of whom had relapsed; but the instances in which the integrity of the Christian character was not maintained were few, while many returned more earnest in promoting their own spiritual improvement, as well as more zealous in their endeavours to bring others to Christ. Those who had been first brought to attend the worship of God in the camp, continued regularly to attend the meetings of the Christians in their places of worship in the city and suburbs. The native preachers became more zealous and faithful, and the entire families of those who had associated with the Christians on the journey, afterwards became worshippers, and in due time many were baptized and united in the fellowship of the church.

Another remarkable feature in the awakening at this time was the enlarged interest, increased attendance, and spiritually beneficial effects connected with the Bible instruction. The aged, adults, and youth of both sexes were regular, earnest, and deeply attentive learners in these classes. Sometimes the chapels were the only places large enough to contain the numbers who came to hear and to learn. God mercifully raised up and brought to the aid of the missionaries additional native helpers, or they would have been unable to lead the people onward in the path of life. As it was, their strength was taxed to its utmost limit, and they were often obliged to relax for a season, to enable them to continue their arduous but delightful work.

In this, as in previous seasons of remarkable revival of religious earnestness amongst the people, there were no additional services and no new methods of procedure introduced; all was effected by increased concern in the minds of the people, and by the enlarged experience of the influence of the Holy Spirit on their hearts. The several pastors of the churches had devoted a longer time than heretofore to the preparation and admission of members to their fellowship, yet the increase is described, even in regard to accession to their numbers, as greater than ever known since the establishment of the mission; for, at the close of the year, there were twenty-one thousand native adherents to the Christians, and five thousand communicants.

CHAPTER XIV.

Illness of the queen—Failure of the conspiracy to change the dynasty—Death of the queen—Proclamation of her successor—Trial and punishment of the conspirators—Ranavalona's refusal to acknowledge the priests, idols, and diviners—Edicts respecting the Sabbath—Christian worship within the precincts of the palace—General religious awakening among the people—Missionary visit to Fianarantsoa—Buildings of stone and bricks authorized in the capital—Multitudes assembled at the coronation—The crown and the Bible—Speech of the queen—Declaration of religious liberty—Influence of the coronation—Opening of the second memorial church—Presence of the queen and court—Review of the year—Baptism of the queen and prime minister—Religious services within the palace—The queen and prime minister partake of the Lord's Supper—Training of a native ministry—Mr. Sewell's testimony—Spread of the gospel in Betsileo—Foundation stone of the Chapel Royal—Fifty years of missionary labour in Madagascar—Their glorious results—Madagascar in 1869—Inadequacy of the present missionary agencies—Appeal for help.

THUS far the course of Christianity in Madagascar had been one continued unfolding of the divine care and blessing. The instrumentality employed had been weak and imperfect, as all human agency in such a work must necessarily be, but the evidence of the divine efficiency attending it was thereby rendered more unmistakable and strong.

The progress of Christianity in that country has

2 B

been, from the beginning, remarkably instructive; but the events which have marked its course during the last two years have been, perhaps, unsurpassed by any that have recently occurred among other portions of mankind. It is as if the Most High had been repeating, among a small and isolated portion of our race, for the encouragement of His Church in the present day, the process by which Christianity achieved its earlier triumphs, and by which all nations shall see His great salvation.

The opening of the year 1868 was accompanied by increased desire on the part of the people after acquaintance with the Holy Scriptures, especially their practical teaching. Classes for reading and explaining the word of God were multiplied; and these were attended by numbers so large as to require the meetings to be held in the places of worship. Some of the missionaries held several of these during the week, and found them attractive and valuable aids to the services of the Lord's day, in building up the faith and Christian character of their people. These services continued to be well attended, and the missionaries were continually cheered by additions from among the heathen. Messrs. Toy and Pearse, who, at this time, paid a visit to Vonizongo, met with eight hundred Christians and two hundred communicants.

The queen, whose health had been failing ever since her visit to Andevorando, went, early in the year, to Ambohimanga, the favourite resort, as well as the sanatorium of the royal family. But the change of air and the charms of scenery, as well as the trusted influence of the idols, all failed to restore her wasted strength, or renew her waning life.

Rumours began to circulate in the capital of a vacant throne, and certain partisans of the late prime minister, and opponents to his successor, formed a plan for seizing and binding, or slaying, the officers in charge of the city; their object being to take possession of the palace, and to change the dynasty, by proclaiming a young man of their own party king of Madagascar; and they only waited for the queen's death to execute their project.

In the meantime the prime minister sent and issued a proclamation against circulating unfounded reports, and ordered all his officers to remain in their houses, or at their posts with their men. The queen was now rapidly sinking. The officers endeavoured to persuade her to return, but, as the idol had promised her recovery, she refused to make the attempt. The prime minister then requested the chief of the priests to induce the idol to recommend her Majesty to return. The veteran hierarch is reported to have replied that he could not force god. The minister replied that was true, but, perhaps, he might influence his keepers. The priests afterwards brought the idol Kelimalaza to the queen, and said the oracle declared that her Majesty must go to Antananarivo; but the queen doubted their word, asking if they had really received such inspiration; and although they answered that they really had, she still refused to return.

About this time a rumour reached the conspirators that the queen had actually expired, and they began to execute their purpose by attacking the officers and entering the palace; but the prime minister, having intelligence of their proceedings, sent troops, with orders to seize their leaders.

The queen being informed of this movement, sent a message that all the men in Antananarivo who were loyal to her, should repair to the spot where she was; and that night there was scarcely a man left in the capital except the conspirators. Ill as she was, her Majesty was brought out on a couch under the verandah of the house, and was cheered by the loyalty and devotion so promptly tendered by her subjects.

The leading conspirators had been already captured. The former minister, who at their call had nearly reached the city, hastened back when he heard of their seizure, but was overtaken by four hundred men sent after him, and brought to the city a prisoner. The queen was conveyed to the capital, and died at the palace on the 1st of April. On the following morning, her younger sister Romomo (also called Ramorabe, on account of her gentle disposition) was proclaimed queen.

The tomb of Rasoherina was built in the palace yard, next to that of Radama I. Mr. Cameron had been requested to prepare the plan and construct the tomb, and when all was completed, the funeral ceremonies were observed with much pomp and splendour.

Rasoherina was a just and considerate ruler, and shared, though perhaps in a less degree, that aversion to the shedding of blood which characterized her husband Radama. The eighteen victims who were put to death on account of the reports that Radama was still alive, were the only judicial deaths inflicted during her reign, which was marked by many instances of personal kindness; especially so was the liberating, at her own expense, of the women and children brought as captives from the west to be sold as slaves. These unoffending victims of war the queen set free, and sent home to their native country. Her promise, when she came to the throne, to protect the Christians was faithfully kept to the end of her life. Her confidence in the idols would seem to have been shaken, by her conduct after the last pretended communication from them; and some incidents during her last illness seem also to indicate that she was not ignorant of the value of prayer to Jesus Christ. The prime minister, in a letter which I received from him shortly after her death, spoke of her as having prayed to God before she died.

Ranavalona, the name adopted by the newly proclaimed sovereign, sent word to the missionaries, on the morning on which she became queen, that their privileges would be preserved; and the prime minister, in a letter to them, gave his assurance that the change which had taken place would not affect any of the advantages enjoyed by the missionaries or the Christians.

An examination of the conspirators had taken place before the death of the late queen, and so soon as the ceremonies connected with her funeral had terminated, their trial commenced at Analakely, the spot where, in the reign of the first Ranavalona, so many of the Christians had been sentenced to die—some sent to the flames, others to the precipice—for their faithful testimony to the goodness and love of their God and Saviour. The trial of the conspirators appears to have been fairly conducted; but their forcible seizure of the queen's officers, and their entrance to the palace, left no doubt of their intention to prevent the next in succession from becoming sovereign, and to place on the throne a young noble descended, on his mother's side, from the family of the first Radama.

At the close of the trial the evidence was laid before the queen, who summoned a kabary of the heads of the people of Imerina. Having had the evidence presented before them, together with the laws of the kingdom in reference to rebellion, she asked their advice as to the punishment which should be inflicted. The head men of two royal villages counselled that the conspirators should be put to death. The assembly was then dismissed until the following day, when additional representatives of the people were present, and the same opinion was expressed.

It ought to be mentioned, that before this trial the queen had stated to the officers her wish that no one should be put to death in consequence of anything connected with her having become queen. After the opinions of the representatives had been given, the prime minister proposed that the conspirators should be put in irons, and imprisoned for life. But the prison in which it was at first proposed to confine them would have rendered their sentence little better than being buried alive; and in consequence of the representations of the missionaries, and other foreigners, their circumstances were greatly ameliorated.

Sixteen of the prisoners were condemned to perpetual confinement, including some men of rank, and a number of those who had been chiefly instrumental in causing the death of Radama; but what was most distressing to the missionaries and the churches was that some of the conspirators were Christians, and men of influence in the churches. The movement itself was entirely one of party, and had no connection whatever with Christianity or heathenism, as such. Both heathens and Christians were found among the loyal and devoted, as well as amongst those who had attempted to destroy the existing government. It may be stated also, that during the present year rumours existed of disaffection towards the government, and although the parties suspected entirely cleared themselves, the prisoners in confinement near the capital, and who had the privilege of receiving attention from their friends, were separated, and sent as prisoners to distant parts of the country.

Decisive evidence of the principles and purposes of the new sovereign was soon given. On the morning after the funeral of the late queen, the priests of the idols came, as priests or keepers, to offer their hasina, or acknowledgment of her sovereignty, to the new queen. She declined, however, to receive it, and informed them that she could not recognise them as priests, but only as subjects. The idol of Rasoherina was also removed from the palace. The astrologers, or manipulators of the sikidy, and the diviners were also informed that the queen could only regard them as subjects, as she did not recognise their pursuits.

After the termination of the national mourning, when the people returned to their ordinary employments, the queen issued an order that all government work should cease during the Lord's day. About the same time the prime minister sent for some of the native preachers, and had the Scriptures read and prayer offered within the court of the palace. A proclamation was some months afterwards issued closing all Sunday markets. Weekly markets are held throughout Madagascar in different towns and villages, on different days, and the people whose markets had been held on the Sunday were directed to choose some other day.

On resuming the work connected with the mission, after the national mourning, Mr. Pool urged forward with constant attention and diligence the memorial church at Ambohipotsy; and Mr. Cameron's work at the children's church at Faravohitra was earnestly resumed; also a building for a school, in which might be gathered for public worship on the Sunday the inhabitants of the neighbourhood who would use the memorial church when finished.

Whether the minds of the people had been impressed by the decease of the late queen, at an age when she might have been expected, according to the ordinary course of nature, to reign many years, does not appear. Or whether a sense of the uncertainties of life, produced by the imminent peril and hopeless suffering of the conspirators, some of whom were young men, and most of them only in the prime of life, had in any measure excited reflection, and aided in producing the religious awakening which appeared in renewed vigour after the close of the national mourning, is not stated, and perhaps was not known; but at the time now under review, all the places of worship were crowded. The movement in favour of Christianity became general and more strongly marked than it had ever appeared before. Respectable families came in company to attend the public Sunday services. Officers came, attended by their subordinates. The most influential portions of society, as well as the more numerous members of the servile class, appeared to be simultaneously drawn to the house of God on the Lord's day, and at other seasons of public worship. The existing places of worship were enlarged, but the attendance was still in excess of the accommodation at every place; while additional meetings for reading and explaining the Holy Scriptures attracted increasing numbers, and appeared to arouse more earnest attention among all classes.

Sensible of the dangers to which such a state of feeling exposed the people, the missionaries held special meetings for prayer and conference amongst themselves, and arranged to devote greater attention and a longer period to grounding their catechumens in the great foundation truths of Christianity, before they administered baptism or received them to the fellowship of the church. This earnest religious concern among the people was not confined to the city or the villages of the province. The same attention to the claims of the word of God, and the welfare of the soul, appeared to be manifest in remote provinces, as well as in Imerina; messengers and letters relating to this subject came from Betsileo, with its hundreds of thousands of inhabitants, two hundred and fifty or three hundred miles from the city, a race more closely allied with the Hovas than any other in the country.

The government, which had heretofore been unwilling that missionaries should visit the Betsileo, more enlightened now themselves, encouraged the communication of the gospel to these people; and, early in July, Messrs. Toy and Jukes spent about two months in visiting that country. They found, at the chief place occupied by the Hovas, chapels built, congregations gathered, and churches formed. They proceeded to other places at different distances, and found villages, each containing some thousand inhabitants, willing to receive Christian teaching, and others already meeting for worship on the Sabbath day; few of them retaining any very firm hold on their idolatries, and many ready to listen to the Christian teachers. At the end of August the two missionaries returned, filled with thankfulness and joy at having beheld the wide surface of fallow ground apparently broken up, and ready to receive the precious seed of that divine truth which bears fruit unto holiness in the present world, and eternal life in that which is to come.

The great national transaction equivalent to coronation in other countries, but here called the showing or presenting of the sovereign, took place on the 3rd of September, 1868. The large parade ground at Imahamasina was covered with encampments of strangers from a distance, and with representatives of the subject races. On the day of the coronation, Andohalo was thronged from an early hour.

When, at the appointed time, the queen, preceded by a hundred ladies of rank, who walked before her palanquin, advanced across the plain, ascended the richly decorated platform, and appeared before her people, she was enthusiastically cheered. Then, surrounded by the high officers of her court and kingdom, she took her seat beneath the canopy, on the front of which was inscribed in shining letters the Malagasy words signifying "*Glory be to God;*" on the other sides, "*Good-will among men,*" "*On earth peace,*" and "*God shall be with us.*" On one hand of her Majesty stood a small table with the crown, on the other a small table bearing the handsome Bible sent to her predecessor by the British and Foreign Bible Society.

In the truly appropriate and excellent speech which the queen delivered to the representatives of the nation, there was a frank avowal of her confidence in them, and her assurance of their loyalty to herself; she made a slight reference to her ancestors, as the source whence she had derived her position and her kingdom, but no allusion whatever to the idols. There was reference to the laws, which were declared to be, not the expression of the ruler's will, but of the united will of sovereign and people, for the well-being of the country. There was an appeal to the officers of government, the nobles, judges and higher ranks, as leaders of the people, to teach them wisdom, adding, "It rests with you to make them wise or to make them foolish;" and warning all, that "If any, relying on good service formerly rendered, or trusting to my compassion, shall do evil to my country and kingdom, I condemn them to death." Respecting the praying,* the queen said, "It is not enforced, and it is not forbidden, for God made you." When the representatives of the assembly had replied and tendered their hasina, the queen spoke thus:—"Since such is your answer, O chiefs, and ye under heaven (all people), I take courage, for I have father and I have mother; therefore *veloma!* may you live, ye under heaven: may God bless you."

* The term includes preaching as well as praying, viz., the whole of Christian worship.

In an account of the coronation which I received from one of the native pastors, he mentions four things as having deeply impressed him—the absence of idols and priests; the mottoes on the canopy; the Bible by the side of the queen (in the position in which at the coronation of her predecessor we had seen the idol); and the clear, distinct proclamation of religious liberty. Perhaps these were particulars of the great event which would most forcibly impress the Christians of all classes.

An event so unprecedented and so important as the public recognition of Christianity on such an occasion, by a sovereign who promised to become exceedingly popular, could not fail to have great influence with the people; and while the missionaries were gladdened by the fresh security given for the undisturbed prosecution of their sacred work, they were all profoundly impressed with the new and not less fearful dangers to which such high sanction of Christianity might expose the communities over which they had so sedulously watched. They had recourse to special prayer for divine guidance and protection, and for the more abundant influences of the Holy Spirit, that prosperity and patronage might not succeed, where persecution had failed, to weaken the love of Christ in the hearts, or destroy the beauty of holiness in the lives of the Christians. They also inculcated on their helpers in the work, and studiously exercised themselves, an increased prayerful watchfulness over their respective flocks.

Ambohimanga has already been mentioned as the favourite resort of royalty, and, according to the custom of her predecessors, Ranavalona, accompanied by her court, paid a visit to this celebrated place, which, having been the birthplace and the burial-place of distinguished rulers, as well as containing the shrine of one of the national idols, had been considered peculiarly sacred.

Accompanied by Andriambelo, and with Radama's approval, I had, with other Christians, visited this city. We had ascended the steep path at the eastern end of the mountain, and we had addressed the few Christians there on the Sabbath day. The king's recommendation had secured for us courtesy and hospitality; but our presence had been regarded, not by the queen, but by the priests, as an offence to the idols, and as the usual rains were late in descending, the priests declared that the idol was withholding the rain, that the crops would fail and famine and want ensue, because the white man and the praying had polluted the place. Hence, in the treaty with England concluded just before I left, it was stipulated that although Englishmen might enter, and Christians might be taught and exercise their religion in any place in Madagascar, no foreigner should enter, nor Christian worship be offered, in three sacred places, of which Ambohimanga was the first. A friendly chief gave the Christians ground for a chapel just outside the gate, and they worshipped there.

During the visit of the queen after her coronation,

Mr. G. Cousins spent a Sunday at Ambohimanga; the Christians there being connected with the church of which he is the pastor. He preached in the morning in the open air to two or three thousand persons, including the prime minister and several officers of the court, and in the evening to a still larger number; and this only three short years after Christian worship had been forbidden. Two good congregations now assemble there every Sunday, and the French treaty opens the place for the residence of foreigners.

Much zeal and earnestness existed at this time among the churches generally, of which the following extract of a letter from Mr. Jukes, minister of the large church on the east side of the capital, is evidence :—

"At Ankadibevava we have been greatly blessed. Our chapel, though enlarged, is crowded to excess; and last Sabbath at least two hundred persons went away, unable to gain admittance.

"At our last church meeting we admitted forty-five persons, who have had five months' instruction, to the full privilege of church membership ; but what is far more gratifying to me, than a mere increase of numbers, is a growth of spirituality—a striving after a higher and purer Christian life, and a fervent desire, which many of them manifest, that those who are still in the cruel bonds of sin may be brought to that glorious liberty wherewith Christ makes His people free.

"A few weeks ago, Raindratavy and several of the

preachers gathered round me after the Sabbath morning service, and said they would like to meet with me on a Monday morning, to plead for God's blessing on the preaching of the gospel in town and country. Of course I approved of this proposal, and preachers and deacons have since met with me at sunrise every Monday morning, to seek the Master's blessing on our previous day's labour. At first we met in my house, but that soon became too small, so that we hold our meetings in the chapel; and when I went at seven o'clock last Monday, through a drizzly cold morning, there were about two hundred persons present. At these meetings fervent prayers are offered for the outpouring of the Holy Ghost upon the Church and the world; and I feel assured that, in answer to such believing pleading, the blessing must come—and will come."

Towards the close of this eventful year, the attractive and beautiful church erected from a plan by Mr. Sibree, close to the spot where the first Christian martyr of Madagascar suffered, was so far completed as to admit of its being opened for public worship on the 17th of November, 1868. The dilapidated temporary building in which the Christians had worshipped, after being repeatedly enlarged, was taken down, and a number of tombs were removed which had stood on the high road from the city to the commanding promontory on which this church stands. The road was levelled to the site of the building, which affords perhaps the most commanding and extensive view in the whole city, of the east,

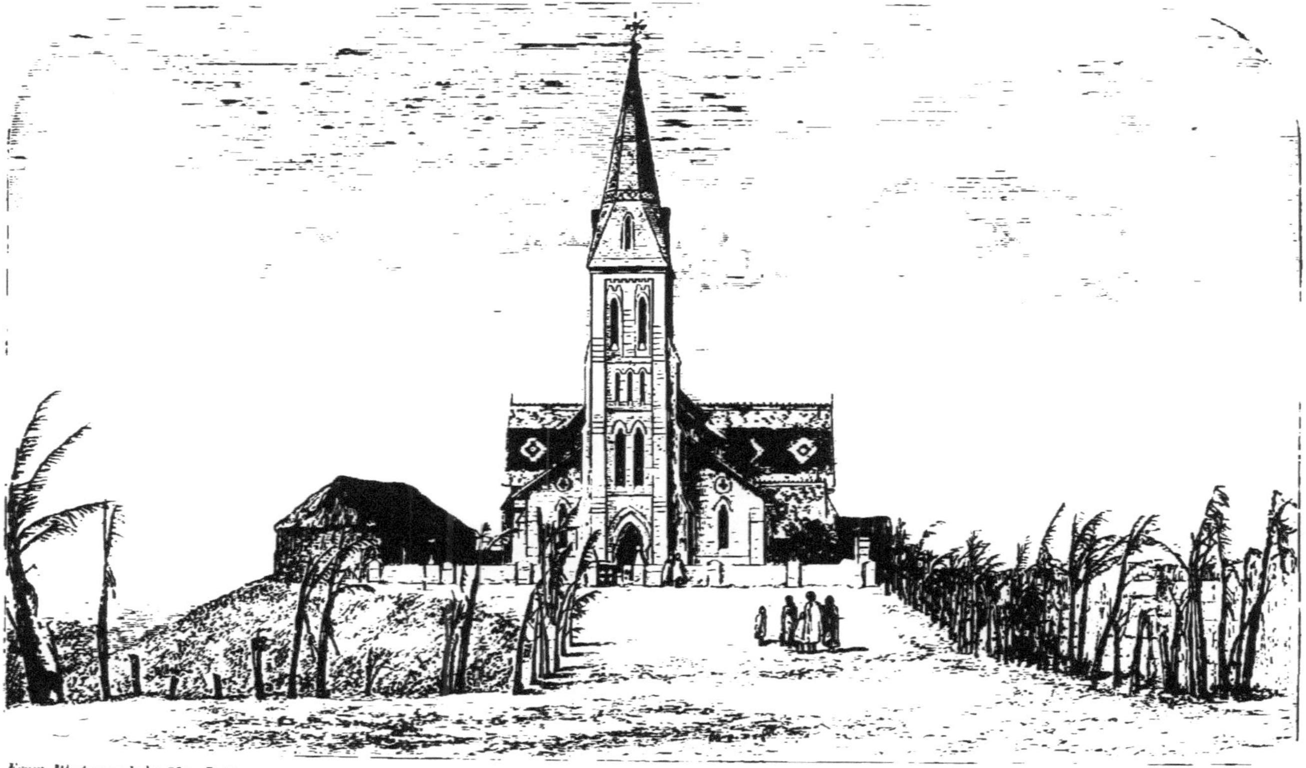

MARTYR MEMORIAL CHURCH, AMBOHIPOTSY.

From Photograph by Mr. J. Cameron.

west, and southern ranges of the country around. It will be the first object to strike the eye of the traveller in these directions. With the exception of Mr. Toy's small garden, all around this spot is arid and sterile. For the occasion of the opening of the church, the Christians therefore provided a number of green plantain trees, which were planted along the narrow neck of land leading to the end of the mountain. The foliage of these trees was fresh and green when planted, but the keen winds that sweep over the mountain soon reduced them to ribbons, and left the stems unsightly.

The queen, who seemed to share her people's joy, had intimated her intention of being present, with her court, on the public opening of the church. Some time after nine o'clock, on the day above specified, the missionaries awaited the arrival of the sovereign at the northern door of the building (as shown in the illustration), and accompanied her Majesty and the leading officers to the seat which Mr. Pool had specially provided for the queen. The singers also proceeded to their appointed place; after which the doors were opened, and the crowds who had been for hours outside soon filled every available space.

As soon as there was silence, and the national anthem (a prayer for the sovereign) had been sung, the prime minister, in the name of the people, paid the usual hasina to the queen. Then, turning to the people, he urged them to become Christians, by trusting in Christ and by accepting the Bible as the word or message of God to men. "By doing so," he said, "they were not worshipping the ancestors of the white people, but the God who created them all, and Christ who died to take away their guilt." He closed by exhorting the people to cleave to the religion of Jesus Christ.

Mr. Toy then stated the purpose for which the church had been built, and the arrangement made with the late queen for securing it in perpetuity to the London Missionary Society, and the Christians associated with it. Mr. Sewell read a portion of the Scriptures,* and the son of the prime minister's eldest sister offered prayer; after which Mr. Briggs read a paper on Church Principles. The native pastor of the church then preached from Psa. lxxii. 18; Mr. W. Cousins delivered an excellent and impressive discourse; and Mr. Street closed the service with prayer. The national anthem was again sung, and the people, after saluting the sovereign, left the place.

All present appear to have been astonished at the building, and gratified with the services by which it was dedicated to the worship of the living God. The impression left by the transactions of this happy day will be long retained, and it could not but be earnestly desired that they might prove of lasting spiritual benefit to many. There could not be many present who would remember the constancy and love to Christ with which Rasalama yielded up her

* The queen, seeing before the commencement of the service the old mission Bible lying on the pulpit, sent her own handsome copy, a present from the British and Foreign Bible Society, with a request that the ministers would use it on the occasion.

life on that very spot; but if there were any who had witnessed her last moments, how strange and full of wonder must their thoughts have been this day.

With grateful feelings the Christians had been accustomed to present themselves on the morning of Christmas day before their sovereign, to express their gratitude for their continued privileges. Most joyfully therefore did they on Christmas day this year present themselves with congratulations before their friendly queen, in larger numbers than the spacious court of the palace could contain. They were received with evident kindness and welcome, and they mingled with their grateful acknowledgments, thanksgiving and prayer to God.

The year, of which this was the last public act, had been, with one exception—that of the conspiracy —a year of active labour, as well as of unexampled success. New, large, and substantial churches had been completed, and dedicated to the service and worship of God. The gospel had been widely extended in the provinces, increased educational efforts had been made, and from the press, besides other publications, ten thousand native spelling-books had been disposed of, and an edition of five thousand more was in hand.

In addition to the attention required for these minor publications, literary work imperatively required, but for which it was scarcely possible to secure the requisite time, had been accomplished. The native periodical, *Teny Soa* (Good Words), had in its second year attained a higher character and a wider circulation, fostering among many a taste for reading. The extremely popular native hymn-book had been enlarged, revised, and forwarded to the Religious Tract Society; by whom a new edition has been printed, under the supervision of Mr. Hartley, now in England on account of the failure of his health. But more important still, the missionaries had completed the revision of the Malagasy New Testament; twenty thousand copies of which the British and Foreign Bible Society have printed, also under Mr. Hartley's superintendence.

This year also the missionaries had succeeded in concentrating and organizing their influence and energies for the consolidation of their own Christian institutions and privileges, as well as for extending the influence of the gospel, by the formation of the *Congregational Union* of the Malagasy Churches.

A large portion of the year, according to the testimony of the missionaries, had been distinguished by unusual earnestness, diligence, watchfulness, and prayer, or, as Mr. Jukes in one of his letters expresses it, "a striving after a higher spiritual life," as the fruit, we cannot but believe, of an enlarged outpouring of the Holy Spirit. The adherents to the Christians during the past year had exceeded all the previous years of the mission.

The statistics of the mission in December, 1868 were—

12 English agents, of which 8 were ordained ministers.

20 native pastors.

437 native preachers and teachers.
37,112 adherents to Christianity.
7,066 communicants.

Of these, 20,909 adherents, and 2,050 communicants, were added during the year.

One of the missionaries, in writing to me, stated that although these were the numbers reported, in his opinion 50,000 would not exceed the number actually associated with the Christians.

Marvellous as were the tokens of divine favour to the church of Madagascar during the year which had passed, richer blessings were in store for that which followed. The reading of the Scriptures and prayer with the prime minister, within the precincts of the palace, has already been noticed. After returning from her visit to Ambohimanga on the 1st of November, the queen sent for two of the native pastors to preach every Sunday morning and afternoon in the palace, where her Majesty and the prime minister, with many of the officers, the children of the nobles, and the attendants of the court were present at the preaching of the word of God.

At the annual festival of the Malagasy new year, which was held on the 21st of January, 1869, the Christians and the English were invited, with other guests, to the palace, where the feast, in former years, had been celebrated with idolatrous ceremonies. But on this occasion there was neither idol, priest, nor recognition of the gods of the ancestors. Instead of this, three of the preachers engaged in prayer, and, in her address on the occasion, the queen said, "This is what I have to say to you, my people. I have brought my kingdom to lean upon God (or I sustain my kingdom by leaning upon God), and I expect you, one and all, to be wise and just, and to walk in the ways of God."

Andriambelo and his companions had been engaged for some time in instructing the queen in the word of God. On the 21st of February, on the invitation of the queen, the high officers, the judges, the nobles, the head men of the people and preachers from each of the city churches, assembled in the large court in front of the palace. After singing, prayer and preaching, Andriambelo, according to previous arrangement, publicly baptized the queen and the prime minister. The people who were spectators were greatly surprised when they saw the queen, the prime minister, and all the Christians greatly moved and weeping. We cannot wonder, however, when we recollect how many edicts, sentencing to death all who called on the name of Jesus, had gone forth from that palace; perhaps carried into execution by some of those officers, or by the fathers or brothers of some gathered on this occasion to behold, in the broad light of day, and in the midst of the highest dignities of the nation, another Ranavalona, now filling the throne of Madagascar, publicly and for ever renouncing the idols and every form of heathenism, and openly, by this act, avowing her faith and associating herself with the disciples of the Lord Jesus Christ. Well might the Christians weep from sympathy, thankfulness and joy.

On the following day the queen gave a feast, in the same court of the palace, to the officers, the leaders or head men among the people, the preachers, and the soldiers. Addressing them on this joyous occasion, she thus expressed her own feelings :—"I rejoice in the blessing of God. I have called you to eat and to drink with me." On behalf of the guests, the prime minister replied, "Let our thanksgiving, O queen, be unto God, for we all rejoice in the approach you have made unto Him." Three of the native ministers engaged in prayer during the feast.

Andriambelo adds, "From this time the queen and the prime minister have been diligent, and have made good progress in the knowledge of the word of God. I am surprised at the readiness with which the queen acquired the instruction in the book of lessons, for persons desiring to be baptized or received to the Lord's Supper. The prime minister also took lessons with me, and I thanked God when I witnessed his progress, and commended him for his diligence. I told him that God had been merciful to him, in enlightening his mind to know these things."

In a letter which I have since received from Andriambelo, he speaks of his continued Sunday services in the palace, and of his pleasure in the diligence and attention of the queen and prime minister to his instructions, as well as in their understanding of the Scriptures. He then communicates the truly gratifying intelligence, that on the sixth of June, nearly four months after their baptism, they commemorated the death of Christ by partaking of the Lord's Supper, and have thus taken their places among those who declare to the world that they have given themselves to Christ their Lord, and build all their hopes of salvation and eternal life upon the great Sacrifice offered on the cross once for all.

From the windows of her palace, the queen may now see the dwelling of the man of God who nurtured the martyrs' faith, and died a martyr's death, and who, in his visits to her brother, Prince Ramonja, first implanted in her young mind the germs of that heavenly truth which yields the precious fruit we now behold. The prime minister appears to be equally earnest and sincere in the manifestation of the influence of the gospel on his own spirit, and the commendation of it to the people. He must sometimes look at the spot within the palace court in which he buried the martyr's gift, the Bible, which he has since so diligently learned to prize.

The missionaries regard the public avowal of the Christian faith, and participation in the ordinances of the church, by these high personages with grateful feelings. Speaking of their baptism and their partaking of the communion, Mr. Toy, in his letter on the subject, remarks:—"One thing is certain, the queen received the same course of instruction as that provided for other Christians, whatever may be their station in life, and none ever studied more earnestly, or manifested a more humble and becoming spirit. And the same must be said of the prime minister."

These encouraging movements were not confined to the palace or the city, but affected parties least likely to be brought under such influences. It seemed as if, simultaneously with the events above described, though without being immediately connected with them, interest and concern on the subject of personal religion were exercising the thoughts of men, and urging inquiries on the minds of many in the country around, as well as in more distant parts of the provinces.

Numbers of individuals were almost constantly resorting to the houses of the native Christians or teachers, to ask what they must do to be saved. These and others were thronging the Bible classes and the meetings, amongst them individuals the least likely to be seen there,—astrologers, diviners, and others—sometimes aged men, the greater portion of whose lives had been spent in the service of the idols, or in the cruel and superstitious customs of their country. One of the missionaries mentions that even the late queen's astrologer, or revealer of destiny, was a member of his class of candidates for baptism.

The strong and rapidly extending interest on the subject of personal religion, without either places to meet in, or suitably qualified teachers to instruct those anxious to be taught, led the missionaries to avail themselves of the services of young men, who, while truly devoted to the work might, in some instances, be less competent than they could have desired.

In one of their communications the missionaries state, as indicating the rapid increase of the adherents that one hundred congregations were looking to them for help to build either new or larger chapels; aid being only given towards providing what the natives themselves are unable to supply—such portions of the building as have to be bought; and they add that one-third of the buildings, for which aid was sought, would accommodate from 800 to 1,200 persons each.

The missionaries had endeavoured to instruct a few suitable young men in their churches to become native preachers; but the limited attention they were able to give to this important service, and the few they could even partially teach, were so utterly unequal to the wants of the country, that Mr. Toy and Mr. George Cousins, at the request of their brethren, undertook to commence the more effectual training of young men for the Christian ministry. They commenced, early in April, with thirty-four regular students, and any others already engaged in teaching were allowed to attend. The tutors have been encouraged by the attention and industry of their students. At the same time they find it quite impossible to continue this most necessary work, without transferring to other hands some of the duties which they now discharge.

The arrival of missionaries from the Society of Friends has already been noticed. A clear and valuable statement from Joseph S. Sewell, of the condition and prospects of the Friends' Foreign Mission in Madagascar, where he and Mr. and Mrs. Street have been successfully engaged for the last two years, has been recently published.* In advert-

* *Friends' Monthly Record*, October 15, 1869.

ing to this communication, it is satisfactory to state that Mr. Sewell and his companions were cordially welcomed by the missionaries of the London Society; that their co-operation, especially in the educational department, to which their attention is chiefly although not exclusively directed, has been most valuable, thorough, and harmonious. Their presence is a source of strength and encouragement; their removal would be a loss to both missionaries and people. Mr. Street has been chiefly engaged in visiting the villages, and has found a useful sphere in conducting Bible classes; while Mrs. Street, now ably assisted by Miss Gilpin, of the same society, has given her attention to the education and improvement of girls. These Friends have erected two substantial schools, one for boys, the other for girls, to be under their especial care.

"As to the great truths of the gospel," Mr. Sewell observes, "which we long to see laid hold of by the natives of Madagascar, we and the agents of the London Missionary Society are of one faith. And we are very desirous not to introduce among the Christians questions as to forms and ceremonies which, even regarded from our point of view, might have a tendency to unsettle their minds unprofitably, and distract their attention from what is of most importance, by leading them into nice inquiries as to the importance or otherwise of what we consider unessential."

Speaking of the capital, the chief seat of the mission, the same writer says, "There are few towns in England where the Sabbath is better observed, or where there is a better attendance at the places of worship; and since I came I have not, to my knowledge, seen more than two persons drunk. There are but few people seen about the streets during the hours of public worship, and there cannot be much fewer than 10,000 people who are in the habit of attending one or other of the thirteen Protestant places of worship, within the town and its suburbs, every Sabbath. About three or four hundred preachers are frequently engaged in preaching, either in the town or the surrounding villages; of whom about sixty or seventy go out every Sabbath day to assist the village congregations,—most of them walking five, six, or eight miles, and some much further."

After enumerating the defects amongst the preachers and the general body of the Christians, Mr. Sewell bears the following testimony to the great change now in progress among the people:— " My own firm conviction is, that with much that is unsatisfactory, there is a great work going on in this country, of which the Holy Spirit is the author, and that, with much that is merely outside profession, there is a large amount of genuine Christianity which is decidedly on the increase."

A glance at the introductory chapter of this volume, where the despotism of the religion and government of the country, together with the sanction, encouragement, and the reward, often, of immorality are noticed, will do much to account for the low standard of morality which Mr. Sewell with truthfulness and great candour reports, and which every Christian must deplore; while it will increase our thankfulness that so many have been raised from the mournful degradation in which all were originally held.

The narrative of the progress and triumph of the gospel in Madagascar would be incomplete without some further notice of the astonishing growth of Christianity in the Betsileo province, which has received only native culture and a brief visit from the English missionary. From this country, Mr. Jukes, one of the missionaries from Antananarivo, writes in August, 1869 :—" I am filled with wonder and gratitude at the showers of grace with which God is favouring His Church. Everywhere that I go, the cry is for instruction in divine things, and Christian congregations are being formed in every direction. The progress made in the Betsileo country is quite equal to, if it does not surpass, the progress in Imerina last year. Here, where I am staying, two days west of Fianarantsoa, there is a most interesting congregation, composed almost entirely of Betsileo, who come to chapel with no dress but a mat, and listen most attentively to the gospel.

"I find in preaching to these people, as I did in England, that nothing gains their attention and wins their hearts so much as the 'old, old,' but ever new 'story' of the Saviour's love. The people here are about to build a new chapel, capable of accommodating 1,000 hearers; but I think it will be too small for the crowds who flock to hear the gospel. From this village right onward to the west coast, congregations have been formed, and the Christians have begged me to visit them."

To this large province of the Betsileo, which has hitherto only received the culture of native Christians from Imerina, and occasional visits from the missionaries, an English missionary has now been sent out; and others are early expected to proceed to this truly inviting field.

In closing the narrative of the glorious progress of Christianity in Madagascar, it only remains to notice its last and greatest achievement, a truly national triumph, which will impart a character of dignity and permanence to the worship and service of the living God that will affect every town and village in the kingdom. The foundation stone of a stately Chapel Royal, to be built of granite, was publicly laid within the precincts of the national Palace at the capital, by the Queen of Madagascar, on the 20th of July, 1869. After Malagasy and English ministers had invoked the divine blessing on the work, and on the sovereign by whom it was undertaken, a regal document was read and deposited within the stone. This edict, printed copies of which were widely distributed, enacted that the building should neither be destroyed nor diverted to any other purpose than that for which it was built; and further declared that any successor of the present ruler or sovereign who should destroy that edifice, or appropriate it to any other use than that previously stated, should not be allowed to be sovereign of Madagascar for ever.

We have reached the fiftieth year since Christianity first entered the capital of Madagascar, and the results of its progress during the intervening years demand our unfeigned thankfulness to God. Multitudes of the people have renounced their household idols. The national idols have been removed from the palace, the priests no longer form part of the court, and the astrologers and the diviners are no longer recognised; some of these have since found a place in the missionaries' Bible class, at the Christians' prayer meeting, or among the numbers who have, by baptism, publicly renounced heathenism and avowed their faith in Christ. A royal sanctuary for the worship of the living God is in course of erection, within that place which was deemed so sacred to idolatry that the head of every one who crossed it was uncovered, and obeisance rendered to the tombs of the deified dead which it contained. Christianity, in the person of the queen, now sits enthroned in the royal palace, which resounds with the preaching of the everlasting gospel, and with Christian prayer and praise.

Every Christian household in the city has its family altar, and ten or twelve thousand of the citizens publicly worship their God and Saviour every Sabbath day. The towns and villages in the province share these privileges, which are extending to remote regions of the country, and the Christians are now supposed to number 60,000. Other results have followed. The standard of morals is surely though gradually rising. The laws are becoming less sanguinary, and greater care is taken in the appointment of those who administer them; a large portion of the judges at the present time being Christians.

The conflict was long and sanguinary before Christianity gained the citadel of the nation's idolatry. The battle has now been won; but it yet remains to secure the fruits of the victory which God, by His Spirit, has achieved. The agencies in the field are unequal to the demands made by the very success of the work. The missionaries cannot maintain their present position without help, and Christianity cannot remain where it is; it must advance in the direction in which its divine Author is encouraging His servants to proceed. To halt will be to court desertion, reaction, and loss. May the friends and supporters of that society which God has honoured, by employing it instrumentally to accomplish this great work, while rendering to Him all the praise, bear the mission in its present joyous but critical position upon their hearts in prayer, and encourage the London Missionary Society, by whom the mission was originated and is sustained, not only to preserve in the faith those already gathered unto Christ, but to send the gospel to the multitudes around,—many of whom are earnestly seeking and asking what they must do to be saved.

POSTSCRIPT.

Since the foregoing sheets were printed, and a few copies bound up, the most important intelligence which has yet been received from Madagascar has arrived,—the public burning of the national idols, and the satisfactory completion of arrangements for establishing and maintaining an extensive native agency in the central provinces. This information is, in part, contained in the following letter from the prime minister, and the remaining part in communications from the missionaries :—

TRANSLATION.

"ANTANANARIVO, *Sept. 8th*, 1869.

"To THE REV. WILLIAM ELLIS.

"DEAR FRIEND,

"I have received the letter which you wrote on the 14th of April last, telling me of your joy and praise to God when you heard how the queen loved the word of God, and proposed to walk in His ways; also to trust in the great Saviour, our Lord Jesus Christ.

"Yes, there was true reason for your rejoicing, for things greatly to gladden the heart indeed are these. We may indeed praise God, for it is as His Word, which says, 'The sovereign's heart is in the hand of the Lord; He turneth it whithersoever He will.' God has guided the heart of the queen to that which pleases Him, and caused her to understand that in which He delights; and now the queen has been baptized, and has partaken of the feast of the Lord.

"We are also building a beautiful stone house within the court of the palace, to be a house for the worship of God. The good friend, Mr. William Pool, made the *marky* (drawing or plan) of that good house. Joyous are the men in this good work; energetic are the Christians, because they see the worship of the sovereign; for those who believe in

Jesus Christ have no anxiety and no fear. Truly rejoicing is it to behold the deportment of the people at Antananarivo on the Sabbath day. Scarcely is any one to be seen in the streets until the close of the public worship, because the great majority of the people assemble in the houses of prayer. No public *work* is done on that joyful day.

" And this, my friend, is another fresh cause of rejoicing here. On the same day that I write this letter to you, the queen sent for the officers and the heads (of the people) to come within the court of the palace, and when they were assembled, the queen said,—'I shall not lean upon nor trust again in the idols, for they are blocks of wood; but upon God and Jesus Christ do I now lean or trust. And as for the idols (viz., the national idols), I shall burn them, or cause them to be burned; for they do no good whatever; they are all deceit and falsehood.'

" And when the people heard this they expressed their pleasure, and asked the queen if she would summon a kabary, or general assembly, to cause all the idols of the people to be burned.

" The queen answered, and said, 'That would please me. I have no desire that there should be idols any more in my kingdom. Nevertheless, I do not force, or compel you, my people.'

" Then agreed, or consented the people, there before the queen, to the burning of all the national idols in Madagascar; and the queen, consenting, rejoiced. And on the same day the queen sent officers to burn all the idols of the queen, which are called Rakelimalaza, Rafantaka, Ramanjakatsiroa, Ramahavaly, &c., &c. And they were all burned, and some of the people also burned theirs.

" And astonished to the utmost were the keepers of the idols when they saw the idols in the flames; for they had said that the idols were too sacred and powerful to be affected by the burning.

" That was a new thing here, therefore we sincerely thank God, for He has manifested His power here in Madagascar. And (we thank God also) because He has given to the queen a true heart to put away the root of belief in things that are nothing (have no existences).

"I rejoiced when I heard that you (the Christians in England) prayed unto God for me. For that I thank you, indeed, greatly. May the blessing of God be with you.

"I visit you, and your family, and my desire for you is that God may bless you.

"Saith your true friend,
"RAINILAIARIVONY,
"*Prime Minister.*"

A short time before the date of the above letter, the service of all the people was required by the government. On this occasion the keepers of Kelimalaza, one of the national idols, sent to the queen to say that as keepers of the idol they had hitherto been exempt from public service, and that though the queen did not use her idols, these idols were still in their keeping, and they petitioned that on that account they might not be required to do public work with the rest of the people. The queen replied that the idols had never been her idols, that her purpose was to trust in God and Jesus Christ, and to lead her kingdom to do the same; but not being quite certain as to the best way of disposing of the idols, the queen summoned the assembly mentioned in her minister's letter given above. One of the officers observed that the best course would be to burn them, and when this had been approved by the assembly, a number of officers were sent, on horseback,* to Ambohimanambola (the village having money), where the idol was kept, to destroy it.

* Horses were said to be very offensive to the idols, and one of the causes for which Dr. Lyall, the British Agent at the capital, was sent out of the country was the riding of his horse into or through a village where an idol was kept.

On arriving at the house where the idol was kept, they inquired of the keepers whether the idol belonged to them or to the queen. The keepers answered that it belonged to the queen. The officers then directed them to bring the queen's property out to them, and when the idol was brought, the keepers were desired to bring some fuel; but every one of them refusing to do this, the officers ordered their attendants to bring wood, which was, kindled, and, to the almost frantic terror of the keepers, the idol was soon consumed in the midst of the flames. Other parties were sent to the different sacred places where the rest of the national idols were kept, and all these, together with some of the people's idols, were also destroyed.

A number of the people expressed their fear that their rice crops would be no longer protected, and would probably be destroyed by hail, but those who had any misgivings about the result of the destruction of the idols were few in comparison with the great body of the people, who rejoiced that they had been committed to the flames.

Simultaneously with this action of the queen, the additions to the number of adherents to Christianity have been so vastly increased, that the churches have been unitedly organized for selecting from among themselves, sending out, superintending, and supporting a large number, probably between one and two hundred, additional preachers; and to encourage the churches and the missionaries in these movements for the evangelization of the country, the government will exempt from public service all who are approved and appointed to this work by the missionaries, and the churches to which they belong.

Personal service is required by the government from

all classes, and even Andriambelo and other native pastors have had to attend at fixed times, as government servants, at the houses of the chief officers. Carpenters, masons, and other skilled workmen were, however, occasionally released from government work when employed in furthering the objects of the mission, as in the building of the memorial churches. But no exemption so valuable as that which the queen has now given was ever before granted.

The queen and her ministry have also united with the Christians in their endeavours to send forth the additional native preachers now so urgently needed. Besides the applications sent to the missionaries, a number of people in the eastern part of the country—through which the late queen and her court travelled in 1867—wrote to the prime minister, asking for teachers. The minister invited the missionaries to a conference, at which it was agreed that the queen, the congregation connected with the palace, and the congregations in the capital, should unite and form a sort of Malagasy Home Missionary Society in furtherance of this object. It was at the same time arranged that the congregations in the city should select, appoint, and send out, as many suitably qualified men as were willing to undertake this service; and that the queen, the congregation connected with the palace, and the other city congregations, should collect or give money to sustain the men approved and sent out by the missionaries and the congregations.

In order to encourage and aid all, it was arranged that the gift of the queen, and the money raised by the congregation connected with the palace, should be divided amongst the congregations according to the number of teachers which they might respectively send out. The queen and the congregation connected with the palace did not send out any preachers, but only united in furnishing the means of support for those whom the other churches sent. A considerable number have already entered upon their work, having been commended to the care of the great Head of the Church by the missionaries and the churches to which they belonged.

The queen required that a list of the names of those who had been appointed should be sent to her before they entered upon their work, and when satisfied of the loyalty of these men, she exempted them from government service, and sent a messenger with them to show her approval of their object and to recommend attention to their teaching. The queen also sent, or gave, to each teacher a short, sensible, and earnest letter, exhorting them to fidelity by reminding them of the words of their divine Lord, and warning them against teaching error or encouraging lawless conduct.

The intimate relation that was formerly believed to exist between the rulers of the country and the objects of their idolatrous worship, might have been expected to induce a Christian ruler to think it right to use some degree of authority in connection with the movements of her Christian subjects; but, however individual members of the government may have shown a disposition to influence religious matters, no official act of the government has interfered with the free action of the Christians in their religious proceedings; and our hope and prayer is that the Lord Jesus may preserve unto them that Christian liberty wherewith He has made them free.

The following translation of a copy, in the native language, of one of the letters sent by the queen to the preachers, which I received by the last mail from Mr.

Cameron, will show her own view of their work, and the responsibilities associated with it :—

TRANSLATION.

"I, Ranavalona-Manjaka, Sovereign of Madagascar, have agreed that the men selected by the Church north of Andohalo should go to teach and preach the word of God, according to the command of Jesus Christ, which is written in xvi. chap. of Mark, and the 15th verse, saying, 'Go ye into all the world, and preach the gospel to all people.'

"I, Ranavalona Manjaka, Sovereign of Madagascar, and the congregation (assembling) within the enclosure of the palace, with the congregation to the north of Andohalo, have each one paid money to form a Malagasy Society for you to go to teach and preach the gospel of Jesus Christ; and on account of that, I, Ranavalona Manjaka, Queen of Madagascar, counsel and exhort you who go.

"I.—In reference to that for which you go. If you should not teach well the word of God, and seek to increase the kingdom of Jesus Christ, according to the word in the Holy Scriptures; but if that be changed, and especially if something different be taught, not according to the word of God, then remember the word of Jesus Christ which is written in Luke xvii. 2, 'It were better for him that a millstone were hanged about his neck, and he cast into the sea, than that he should offend one of these little ones.' Therefore walk well, conformably to that for which you are sent, lest should come the word of Jesus Christ which declares, 'Cast into outer darkness the unprofitable servant, to the weeping and gnashing of teeth!'

"II.—I also say unto you that if your teaching be not according to that which I have stated above, but if you make my people the means of getting money and property, especially if you lead them to do evil, to break the laws of my kingdom, shall I not treat you as guilty? for I shall not have (the people of) my kingdom taught as fools, for I have brought my kingdom to rest upon God.

"III.—Finally, 'Be diligent, and endure hardness, as good soldiers of Jesus Christ.'—2 Tim. ii. 3 ; 1 Peter, v. 2 : 'Feed the flock of God which is among you, taking the oversight thereof, not by constraint, but willingly ; not for filthy lucre, but of a ready mind.'

"May the blessing of God be with you, and render successful the good work in Jesus Christ for which the Church has selected you. And may Jehovah bless you, and keep you, and cause His face to shine upon you.

"Jehovah bless thee and keep thee.

"Jehovah make His face to shine upon thee, and be gracious unto thee.

"Jehovah lift up His countenance upon thee, and give thee peace.

"And may the grace of the Lord Jesus Christ, the love of God, and the fellowship of the Holy Spirit, be with you and all the people whom you teach. Amen."

"This is the true word in which Ranavalona Manjaka, the Queen of Madagascar, exhorts the men who go forth to teach, saith

"RAINILAIARIVONY,
"*Prime Minister.*

"Antananarivo,
"*November* 15, 1869."

www.ingramcontent.com/pod-product-compliance
Lightning Source LLC
Chambersburg PA
CBHW032138010526
44111CB00035B/611